JOHN ROGERS

THIS OTHER LONDON

ADVENTURES IN THE OVERLOOKED CITY

FOREWORD BY
RUSSELL BRAND

HarperCollins*Publishers*

HarperCollins*Publishers*
77–85 Fulham Palace Road,
Hammersmith, London W6 8JB

www.harpercollins.co.uk

First published by HarperCollins*Publishers* 2013

10 9 8 7 6 5 4 3 2 1

A catalogue record of this book is
available from the British Library

ISBN 978-0-00-749427-9

Printed and bound in Great Britain by
Clays Ltd, St Ives plc

MIX
Paper from
responsible sources
FSC C007454
www.fsc.org

3 4015 07146 8555

CONTENTS

For Heidi, Oliver and Joseph

FOREWORD BY
RUSSELL BRAND

John Rogers is an important person in my life. As well as being one of my best friends he serves as a navigational point in musings and conversations. Often when discussing the non-negotiable nature of sin my mates and I will say, 'Well what would John Rogers do?' As you will learn in these pages John lives in Leytonstone with his two sons and his wife, Heidi, and in spite of the inferred domesticity of that set-up he is a man who lives on society's margins. Not through occultism or deviance but through his astonishing ability to accumulate and more importantly relay extraordinary information. He is like Prospero crossed with Mr Chips.

I met John in London whilst participating in one of the many half-arsed sub-fringe sketch shows that go on in the capital. We were performing at Riverside Studios in Hammersmith where they used to make *TFI Friday*. It quickly became clear that the show we were involved in would yield very little and equally clear that John would become a friend for life. John is endowed with a gentle, humble, humorous wisdom, which is evident through-out these pages. You can learn from John on topics as diverse as Marxism, botany, football, punk, astronomy, gastronomy and love. However where John really comes to life is when perpendicular with his boots on. I mean when he's walking, we don't have a physical relationship.

Someone once described being in love as like finding a secluded ballroom in the house in which you'd always lived. To walk through London with John is like that. The city is suddenly alive with concealed plaques, submerged rivers and unnoticed gargoyles. John is like an alchemist, not only in that he is unkempt and dresses like a person who has fallen through the cracks, he also makes the mundane and unremarkable glow with newly imbued magic. We once walked through my hometown of Grays in Essex, past the ambulance station at the top of our street, and I instinctively jumped on the knee-high wall to stroll along it as I'd always done as a child. When I told John who was beside me, he said that we could consider memories of a place as objects: left strewn about until we return to collect them.

Once when I was staying on The Strand John, like the tangle-haired shrub shaman that he is, knew all manner of secret doors and passageways that lay unchecked on Fleet Street. We walked through an old, creaking oak door and were suddenly in the quads of Temple. John knew it was there and didn't care if we were allowed in. This, in fact, is where we saw Thatcher watering roses just months before her death. We went into Lincoln's Inn, which I never knew existed, and it was like falling down a time tunnel. Not least because a costume drama was being made. Past Aldwych John described two stone giants that adorned a church now used primarily for Romanians, telling me how 'Gog and Magog' were Britain's Romulus and Remus.

Sometimes I think he knows everything. Like most people who are truly wise he never makes other people feel small for not knowing something. John patiently smiles as I tell him all about stuff he knows much more about than me then nods and gently puts me straight. This charming and engaging didacticism is abundantly present in his first book. I am excited that through his writing a wider audience can now share in the joy of John Rogers. That now thousands will, as I have done, begin to understand the character of place, the relevance of history and, most importantly, that adventure is right outside your front door if you're prepared to take the first step. You, like me, could have no better guide than the man who has written this book.

INTRODUCTION

'Exploration begins at home'
Pathfinder, *Afoot Round London,* **1911**

Backpacking in Thailand in my early twenties I climbed down off an elephant in a small village in the mountains of the Golden Triangle. The streets of 1994 East London felt far away – I had broken free for new horizons. I entered a small wooden hut where a villager prepared freshly mashed opium poppy seeds in a long pipe. In Hackney such men were called drug dealers – here they were known as shamans. 'Across the rooftop of the world on an elephant', I wrote in my travel journal. The flight to Bangkok had been the first time I'd been on a plane; my previous travels hadn't extended beyond a coach trip to Barcelona. The top of this mountain was the edge of my known world – the real beginning of an adventure.

In the gloom of the hut was another group of travellers – fellow explorers and adventurers. I spoke to the pale, willowy girl sitting next to me, dressed in baggy tie-dye trousers, a large knot of 'holy string' on her wrist from a long pilgrimage around India. She told me stories about an ashram in the Himalayas and gave me the address of a man with an AK47 who could smuggle me across the border into Burma. A few more minutes' conversation revealed that this wise-woman of the road was an accountant on sabbatical who lived two doors down from my sister in Maidenhead. I had come 6,000 miles to a remote mountainous region to sit in a shack with a group of Home Counties drop-outs chatting about a new Wetherspoon's in the High Street.

Hostel dorms were full of wanderers who claimed to have 'discovered' beaches and villages merely because they weren't in the latest *Lonely Planet Guide*, ignoring the fact people were already living there. Seemingly there was nowhere left to 'discover', the whole world was very much *ON* the beaten track. I spent two years bunkered down on Bondi Beach but longed for windswept, collars-up London evenings, to be in this city indifferent to the whims of the individual, a slowly oscillating hum of existence, to feel millennia of history squelching beneath wet pavements. I also missed a decent pint of beer that wasn't served in a glass chilled to the point that it stuck to your lips.

Returning to London and eventually starting a family didn't mean settling down. I usually wear walking boots and carry a waterproof jacket just in case I spontaneously head off on a long schlep towards the horizon. I've remained on the move.

One Sunday winter evening I travelled five stops on the Central Line from Leytonstone to Liverpool Street to walk along the course of the buried River Walbrook. I didn't see a soul until I popped into Costcutter on Cannon Street to buy a miniature bottle of Jack Daniels to drink on the pebble beach of the Thames beside the railway bridge. The backpacker trail had been as congested as the rush-hour M25, whereas the pavements above a submerged watercourse running through the centre of one of the biggest cities in the world were deserted. If I'd taken an afternoon stroll in the Costwolds I'd have been tripping over ramblers at every field stile, but here I had the streets to myself, the only other people I saw were the snoozing security guards gazing into banks of CCTV monitors. This walk, inspired by an old photo I'd seen in a book bought in a junk shop of a set of wooden steps leading down from Dowgate Hill, had led me to a land twenty minutes away from my front room more mysterious than anything I'd encountered in Rajasthan or the Cameron Highlands.

Randomly flicking through the pages of an old *Atlas of Greater London* a new world revealed itself. The turn of a wad of custard yellow pages and there was Dartford Salt Marsh reached by following the Erith Rands past Anchor Bay to Crayford Ness. Skirt the edge of the Salt Marshes inland along the banks of the River Darent, down a footpath you find yourself at the Saxon Howbury Moat.

This atlas of the overlooked was richly marked with names written in italics that would be more at home on Tolkien's maps of Middle Earth in *The Lord of the Rings* than in the *Master Atlas of Greater London*. *Hundred Acre Bridge* should be leading you to a Hobbit hole in The Shire rather than to Mitcham Common and Croydon Cemetery. *Elthorne Heights* and *Pitshanger* sound like lands of Trolls and Orcs but where the greatest jeopardy would be presented by my complete inability to read a map or pack any sustenance beyond a tube of Murray Mints.

I set out to explore this 'other' London and pinned a One-Inch Ordnance Survey map of the city to the wall of my box room. It felt unnecessary to enforce a conceit onto my venture such as limiting myself to only following rivers, tube lines or major roads. I also didn't fancy the more esoteric approach of superimposing a chest X-ray over the map and walking around my rib-cage. I wanted to just plunge into the unknown – ten walks, or what now appeared as expeditions, each starting at a location reached as directly as possible with the fewest changes on public transport, then hoof it from there for around ten miles, although it'd be less about mileage and more about the *experience*. I'd aim to cover as much of the *terra incognita* on the map as possible, spanning the points of the compass and crossing the boundaries of London boroughs as I had done borders between countries.

It was essential to embark on this journey on foot. For me walking is freedom, it's a short-cut to adventure. There's no barrier between you and the world around you – no advertising for winter sun and cold remedies, no delayed tubes or buses terminating early 'to regulate the service'. Jungle trekking in Thailand and climbing active volcanoes in Sumatra were extensions of walking in the Chilterns with my dad as a kid, and wandering around Forest Gate and Hornsey as a student. Through walking you can experience a sense of dislocation where assumptions about your surroundings are forgotten and you start to become aware of the small details of the environment around you. At a certain point, as the knee joints start to groan, you can even enter a state of disembodied reverie, particularly with the aid of a can of Stella slurped down on the move.

When you walk you start to not only see the world around you in a new way but become immersed in it. No longer outside the spectacle of daily life gazing through a murky bus window or ducking the swinging satchel of a commuter on the tube, on foot you are *IN* London.

The explorations I'd carried out over previous years had taught me to expect the unknown, to never deny myself an unscheduled detour, and that even the most familiar streets held back precious secrets that were just a left-turn away. Most of all I knew that the more I gave in to the process of discovery the more I'd learn.

I'd initially been inspired to head off travelling round the world by reading the American Beat writers who gallivanted coast-to-coast across America looking for a mysterious thing called 'It'.

INTRODUCTION

After finally landing in Leytonstone I wondered if enlightenment was just as likely to be found on the far side of Wanstead Flats as at the end of Route 66.

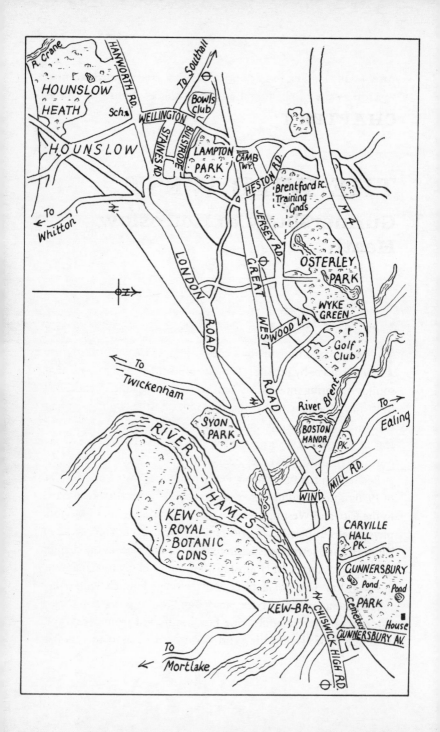

CHAPTER 1

THE WILD WEST
Gunnersbury to Hounslow Heath

I'd been coaxed into buying a copy of Walter George Bell's *Where London Sleeps* by the sheer banality of its title. Surely a book that sounds so boring must be brilliant, as if it were a kind of code. Bell must have thought that if the title reflected the sizzling content inside the cloth-bound cover then readers would shy away for fear of overload. I'd suspected that the real action was out in the dormitory suburbs and now here would be the written proof.

Bell recognized that lying latent beneath the newly built suburbs of 1920s outer London there was a history as rich as that celebrated in the City and Westminster. He writes of monasteries in Merton, physic wells in Barnet, a world-famous Victorian astrophysicist in Tulse Hill and Jewish mysticism in Mile End. But it was the chapter on the highwaymen of Hounslow that captured my imagination.

Hounslow was not a place that resonated much within my psyche. It was a series of back gardens and rooftops that you passed through on the Piccadilly Line heading to and from Heathrow. A sketch show I wrote for and performed in used to rehearse above a pub on the High Street. A gloomy bunch of struggling comics and actors gathered once a week, attempting to master the art of savage satire too early on a Sunday morning, hungover, with nostrils saturated in the odour of last night's stale beer and vomit. These were my only associations with Hounslow, but then I'd never been to the Heath.

You can pass through Hounslow today and not notice the Heath, reduced as it is to just over 200 acres, roughly a third of the size of the Square Mile of the City of London. But in the 17th century it was a vast and dangerous waste on the western edge of London spanning over 6,000 acres. 'Time was when the heath seemed illimitable, stretching north and south across the old Bath Road far out towards the horizon,' Bell tells us. To head west out of London towards Bath and Bristol meant a hazardous journey across this land that was so infested with highwaymen and footpads it was dubbed the most dangerous place in Britain. Compared with the level of crime in North Manchester, the current holder of that dubious honour, 17th- and 18th-century Hounslow Heath was more like Mogadishu.

On the rare occasions the highwaymen were apprehended a great show was made of their executions outside Newgate Prison, then their bodies were hung from gibbets that lined the Heath roads, 'gallows fruit that ripened along their sides', each rotting corpse marking your journey like zombie lampposts. Bell gives us a macabre vision of the scene that a Georgian traveller would have encountered: 'Not unseldom a wind blew over the heath, sharpening at times to a gale, and then these grisly phantoms would take unto themselves movement, though denied life, swaying to the creaking of chains in a dreadful death dance.'

How could I not follow in Bell's footsteps out to the badlands of the Wild West on Hounslow Heath?

*   *   *

Where London Sleeps was the inspiration, but short on the kind of detail I'd need for an exploration of the area. In my hunt for materials I found a battered old copy of *Highwayman's Heath* by Gordon S. Maxwell, published by the *Middlesex Chronicle* in 1935.

Discovering Maxwell's *The Fringe of London* (1925) had been an epiphany for me, realizing that there was some sort of heritage for this odd practice of wandering around neglected streets, following the city's moods, tracking myths and retracing old paths. It's somehow more acceptable to be engaged in an activity that pre-dates TV and jukeboxes. Just look at Morris dancing and basket weaving: nobody questions these, because your granny probably knew someone who did them (thankfully this doesn't apply to marrying your cousin or cooking Starling Pie).

I'd worked out the simplest route to get within reasonable walking distance of the Heath – to skirt North London on the Overground train from Stratford to Gunnersbury and hoof it from there. But the territory between Gunnersbury and Hounslow Heath was completely unknown to me, aside from journeys along the A4 in my sister's groaning white Vauxhall Cavalier as she ferried me back to polytechnic for the start of each term. So the 388 pages of *Highwayman's Heath* were the topographical mother lode.

In common with the celebrated Victorian explorers of the Amazon Basin and the Central African Highlands, the old topographers had more than a touch of the eccentric about them. In the preface Maxwell explains the origins of his book:

> One night I had a dream – a vision, if you will. I was on a vast heath stretching desolate and wild for miles. I was alone yet in the midst of a great company – of ghosts that moved as shadows around me. Not malevolent spectres, you understand, but vastly interesting, for in their dim outlines I recognized many famous in history, song and story.

3

This vision comes to him as he was sitting on Hounslow Heath one morning. He is approached by a group of maidens wearing white robes who tell him they are the 'Nine Muses'. They scatter jewelled beads across the Heath, hand Maxwell a magic cord and instruct him to travel about the Heath threading the beads together, and that is the contents of the book, like a Middlesex *Book of Mormon*.

Armed with these potent images of the ripening gallows fruit and the magic cord threaded with the beads of history, I left Leyton-stone one Saturday lunchtime. I'd put on a double pair of socks and strapped up my dodgy left knee, as Google Maps had informed me the route I'd plotted from Gunnersbury along the Great West Road, across Osterley Park, through Heston and down to Houns-low Heath would be around ten miles, and that was without the inevitable diversions and detours.

Since an arthroscopy I'd had performed on the knee in Homerton Hospital it had developed the annoying habit of ceasing to perform the basic function of a joint, bending, at almost bang on the eight-mile mark. It's as accurate as a pedometer. From that point I'm swinging a useless leg-shaped post as if I've suddenly received a grant from Monty Python's Ministry of Silly Walks. This affliction has struck me down all over the London region, from a slip road beside the M40 near Beaconsfield to late night at the wrong end of Lea Bridge Road as I attempted to make it back to my local in time for last orders. It's then that I reflect on Homerton Hospital's reputation as the best place to be treated for gunshot wounds this side of a military hospital in Afghanistan. The most minor keyhole surgery probably lacked a certain jeop-ardy for the surgeons there.

On the packed Overground train I cram in a few more pages from *Highwayman's Heath* and read about the old rural paths that led from Heston to Lampton, adding these to my itinerary. Arriving at Gunnersbury I start out in the direction of Gunnersbury Park, former home of mad King George III's aunt, Princess Amelia, and later the Rothschild clan. As a tourist exploring foreign cities I've sought out palaces and grand houses as a reflex first resort, so why not do the same in the London Borough of Hounslow?

The traffic on Gunnersbury Avenue is bumper-to-bumper heading southwards but northbound you could skip down the white lines in perfect safety. There are allotments along the roadside with ramshackle sheds made from foraged materials that look as if they are left over from the wartime Dig for Victory effort. The sign for a salsa bar props up one end of a planter sprouting triffid-like weeds.

I pass above the traffic on a footbridge and enter the gates of Gunnersbury Park. One possible derivation of the name 'Gunnersbury' is from Gunnhild or Gunyld's Manor, the niece of King Cnut. The Danes held lands in the area up to the time of the Battle of Brentford in 1016, when they were defeated by Edmund Ironside – how could he ever lose a battle with a name like that? Well, he did later on, and ended up having to divide his kingdom with the Danish.

From that point on the manor changed hands through various minor royals, merchants and bankers till it was finally handed back to the people in 1926, fittingly enough the year of the General Strike when the British establishment genuinely teetered on the brink of collapse. In the end it was the building of the Great West Road along the edge of the park that forced the aristocrats and bankers out of their city retreats, rather than a popular uprising.

Neville Chamberlain, then Minister for Health, presided over the grand public opening of the house and its grounds just a week after the strike had ended and Parliamentarians had returned to harrumphing at each other across the Westminster benches as if nothing had happened. There's twenty-eight seconds of silent Pathé newsreel that capture the dignitaries lined up on the veranda above a huge crowd – 'Another Lung for London' the title declares.

When he was Prime Minister, Chamberlain passed through Gunnersbury again, on a more historically resonant occasion. In 1938 he flew from Heston Aerodrome, just a couple of miles away, to appease Hitler in Munich. Chamberlain pictured on the runway at Heston waving the treaty he'd signed with the Führer to a triumphant crowd is one of the enduring images of the 20th century, and it took place in a field that I'll traverse later. As he made his way back into central London along the A4 did Chamberlain remember that May afternoon twelve years previously when he'd cut the ribbon at the house?

The exterior of the house now shows signs of neglect and decay. The white paint on the walls and wooden window frames is chipped and peeling. Buddleia sprouts from cracks in the foundations and crevices around the guttering and spills out of the chimney pots. Weeds flourish in a Grecian urn.

Gunnersbury Park House

Through grimy windows I can see sparse rooms furnished with trestle tables and moulded-plastic school chairs. What were the guest rooms of the Rothschild dynasty now host education workshops and talks by local community arts groups. On the veranda that boasted one of the finest views across the south of London out to the Surrey hills the only other person is a forlorn-looking bloke sucking on a can of lager where once royalty took tea. The intensity of the birdsong adds to the feeling of abandonment. I'm heartened by this first impression of Gunnersbury; I wasn't in the mood to pay my respects to the gentility of former times.

The house now hosts the Ealing and Hounslow municipal museum. I drift about half-looking at the exhibits but mostly enjoying the current incarnation of this grand country residence as a council utility with its scuffed skirting boards and fire exit signs. In a room with gold-leaf trim around the ceiling and lit by a crystal chandelier there is an exhibition of children's art mounted on free-standing boards that obscure the finery of the room. This could be the place where the antiquarian Horace Walpole was summoned to entertain Princess Amelia and commissioned to write verses for the Prince of Wales. There is little reverence for its former glories.

It's a brief glimpse of what Britain might have looked like if the more radical elements of the General Strike had been successful. We could be going to Buckingham Palace to make a housing benefit claim, or you might be residing in a council flat in the converted Windsor Castle.

The revolution has yet to come, of course; we're a nation still enthralled by monarchy, addicted to *Downton Abbey* and ruled by a government of privately educated millionaires. But there was something about this house that made me feel optimistic. Maybe it was the photocopied information sheets on sale in the gift shop for 20 pence each.

According to conspiracy theorists, this would have been the nerve centre of the shadowy Illuminati whom they believe were established by the Rothschild banking family to control the world. Being unimaginably rich and Jewish, the Rothschilds have been a magnet for conspiracy nuts. My favourite bonkers Rothschild conspiracy theory is that, not content with owning the Bank of England, between them Nathan Mayer Rothschild and his son Lionel fathered most of Queen Victoria's children. I'd have thought they'd have had their hands full containing the weeds in the huge garden.

Lionel might not have cuckolded Prince Albert, but Victoria's Prime Minister Benjamin Disraeli is believed to have asked him for a loan in the library of this house to buy shares in the Suez Canal. Disraeli had been the first Jewish MP, holding out for eleven years to take his seat in the House of Commons until the law had been changed to allow him to swear a modified non-Christian oath.

The history hits you from all sides, but ultimately it is people who create the narratives. It's the mundane day-to-day lives of the small army of domestic workers who churned the butter in the kitchens, lovingly tended the grounds and groomed the horses in the ruined stables propped up by scaffolding in a shady corner where I watched a robin redbreast sing from the aluminium security fencing.

The 1881 Census records thirty-three servants residing at Gunnersbury, including George Bundy the head coachman, his wife and three children; William Cole the coachman from my home town of High Wycombe; Fanny South the domestic servant; Elizabeth Kilby the kitchen maid; and Emily D'Aranda, one of three nurses. I wonder what memories they had of Gunnersbury Park.

The green space is huge, and littered with crumbling boathouses and stone follies. The remains of a Gothic building stand just over shoulder-high, ivy-draped with thick branches rising from the soil like the muscles of the Green Man himself, Pan reaching out to reclaim the structure for the earth and restore the natural order. Kids run around with ice cream-smeared faces. I hear the clatter of studs on a concrete path by the cricket pitch as a batsman makes his way from the squat pavilion out to the crease. You could easily spend the day here in what Maxwell calls 'London's Wonderland', but I need to push on to reach Hounslow Heath by sunset.

I emerge from Gunnersbury Park under the M4 flyover on the A4 Great West Road. Facing me are the Brompton Folding Bicycle Factory and the Sega Europe HQ. A huge image of Sonic the Hedgehog flies overhead like an avatar of the Sky God.

The Great West Road rises in central London and scoots along Fleet Street, following the path of the Roman road that headed west from Newgate bound for the health resort at Aquae Sulis (Bath). It's been suggested – in my imagination by a man with a beard wearing sandals – that this section of the road follows an ancient ley line and the Romans merely built along a pre-existing trackway. There could be something in this theory as the route takes you past the Neolithic sites of West Kennet Long Barrow and Silbury Hill, places that are over 5,000 years old. It's an interesting revision of the idea of the Romans as great innovators into a new role as conservationists.

The ancient trackways have been described as the 'green roads of England', but there's nothing green about this particular passage of the A4 built in the 1920s. The new Great West Road horrified Gordon S. Maxwell, 'This arterial horror sears the face of rural Middlesex,' he declaimed. I have a vision of him in tweeds standing by the roadside angrily waving his walking stick at the vehicles trundling past in a futile protest at the onward march of the motor age.

I'd read a letter in the *Hounslow, Heston and Whitton Chronicle* from a man who'd worked for the Sperry Gyroscope Company on the Great West Road, manufacturing 'highly secret components for the war effort'. Steel rings produced here ended up inside the Enigma code-breaking machines at Bletchley Park, ultimately hastening the end of the Second World War.

This part of the road was known as the Golden Mile due to the concentration of big-name manufacturers. There were Smith's crisps, Gillette razor blades, Beecham's pharmaceuticals, Firestone tyres, Maclean's toothpaste, Currys electrical goods and Coty cosmetics, illuminated by a 'kinetic sculpture' of a Lucozade bottle pouring neon orange liquid into a glass. It was like a Sunset Strip for factories.

This was the centre of a new 20th-century consumerism. British companies seizing the era of mass production and advertising, and American corporations branching into the European market spearheaded their campaigns from this stretch of tarmac through Brentford.

Art deco was the dominant architectural style that captured the mood of the moment, led by the practice of Wallis, Gilbert and Partners. Their crowning glory was the Hoover Building on the Western Avenue, now a branch of Tesco. They did for art deco in London what Banksy has done for graffiti. Commissioned to build factories they produced artworks that outlived the industries they were erected to house.

I now approached another of their signature constructions, Wallis House, originally built for Simmonds Aerocessories, which sits at the centre of what Barratt Homes are calling the Great West Quarter or GWQ. The new-build elements of the development look as though they've been more inspired by post-war East German social housing than the art deco masterpiece that looms over the grey blocks named after the factories of the

Golden Mile. Like much of East Germany, the place is deserted.

From the moment I gazed through the window of the Sales and Marketing Suite at the scale model of the 'premier development scheme in Brentford', I had a feeling that I wouldn't be welcome inside. I go in anyway and half-consider posing as a potential buyer, but my current look as an out-of-work Status Quo roadie gives the game away before I can even start my spiel.

'I'm writing a book …' I say, thinking this must convey some sort of respectability, but don't get much further.

There is light jazz playing softly and a clean-cut corporate vibe is sucking up the oxygen. The immaculately dressed young man behind the desk repeats the word 'book' like someone mis-pronouncing the name of the aforementioned King Cnut. He's on to me straight away and probably could have composed my previous paragraph for me in advance. I've got 'long-term renter and ex-squatter' written through me like a stick of rock and he probably works on commission.

We silently acknowledge the gulf between our worlds and attempt to make small talk. He tells me all the flats are sold, but not much else. I wish him well and skulk off back towards the Great West Road with the Barratt Homes flags fluttering in the pollution like the standards of a conquering army. I spot the first signs of civilian life, a child circling the empty car park on a scooter; it reminds me of images of Midwestern trailer parks, isolated and forgotten.

The large block next to the GWQ still awaits its Cinderella moment. The ivy has started to wind its way around the concrete and steel frame, the lower loading bay has flooded, possibly from the brook that gives Brook Lane running down one side its name. The New England Bar and Restaurant on the corner is boarded-up and fly-tipped. It reeks of the foul stench of decomposition.

A scene from an early Sid James Ealing Comedy, *The Rainbow Jacket*, was shot in this street. For the filming, a prop-built post-box was placed on the street corner. Some residents mistook this for the Royal Mail acknowledging the long walk to the main post office and dropped off their letters. But at the end of the day the celluloid letterbox was loaded into a van and driven away, with the mail dispatched at the post office.

I've been jungle trekking in Thailand and have explored the vast Niah Caves in Sarawak, but this walk along the A4 felt like the hardest slog yet. After sucking in car fumes for a couple of miles I crossed the River Brent and was sorely tempted to jump in. With my head starting to spin and the exhaust gases shimmering on the asphalt horizon, the scene started to resemble the classic Western movie moment when the cowboy is lost in the desert, vultures circling overhead, except in my case it's jumbo jets coming in to land at Heathrow.

Standing in the shadow of the boarded-up Gillette Building, which is preparing for a new life as a swanky hotel, I decide I can take no more of this road walking. I've tried to conjure up images of the Neolithic trackway, of Romans heading off on holiday, of stagecoaches and open fields, but all I see is a blur of high-performance automobiles. It's incredible that anything manages to live here, but where soil has blown into gaps in the concrete and tarmac a diverse ecology of roadside plants flourishes. The organisms we brand as weeds soak up the toxins of the man-made world, even managing to sprout the odd flower to lure in pollinating insects. People somehow inhabit proud inter-war villas lining the kerbside of the type that George Orwell described as 'rows and rows of prison cells', their net curtains stained carbon-monoxide grey.

This road has chalked up quite a death rate since it was opened, somewhere in excess of the Falklands War and the Afghanistan campaign combined – all in the pursuit of pushing London further westwards. Even in the 1940s the Assistant Commissioner of Scotland Yard, Mr H. Alker Tripp, described road death rates in London as having reached 'battle level' – and he said that during the Second World War.

Gordon S. Maxwell proposed his own radical solution – 'Hang a motorist for murder!' He justified this position by pointing out that within ten years of the opening of the new Great West Road, drivers had killed more people than the highwaymen had managed in over 200 years. At this stage I'm tempted to follow his line of reasoning. 'A gibbet, duly loaded, by the side of the Great West Road to-day would be more effective, I think, in stopping these murderers than some quite inadequate fine.' With the speeds of modern drivers they would barely register the dangling corpse of a White Van Man, or if they did it would cause another accident as they attempted to grab a picture of it on their iPhone.

Gillette Corner marks the end of the Golden Mile and I feel like I've paid due homage to the fading art deco neon strip – the lights on the four faces of the Gillette clock tower would struggle to raise even a blink in their current state. The main function of Sir Banister Fletcher's redbrick temple at present is to offer a meaningful challenge to intrepid urban explorers whilst a 'development solution' is sought.

I cross Syon Lane, a name so laden with various ancient meanings I should have known opportunity was approaching. In Sanskrit *syon* means 'followed by good luck', and the turning for Wood Lane that followed presented itself to me at the ideal time. Despite winding off away from Hounslow Heath it would take me towards the village of Wyke Green snugly submerged in suburbia.

Yards away from the A4 and the predominant sound is of birdsong, hedgerows bursting with anthems as if there were competing avian hordes of football fans in full voice. 'Sing us your best song,' the starlings taunt the thrushes, whilst the blackbirds know they've got it all sown up and launch into full-throttle renditions of the early-evening roosting chorus.

A group of teenage lads play in the nets of Wycombe House Cricket Club. I played on this ground once when I was their age, when coming out here from the Buckinghamshire village where I grew up felt like a voyage into the city. What was urban to me then now possesses all the charms of a rural retreat away from the 'blood and ugliness' of the Great West Road.

The sports ground sits on the site of the old manor house, which became part of a chain of private lunatic asylums spread across West London in the 19th century. Wyke House was at one point run by Reginald Hill, who pioneered the practice of non-restraint treatment of mental illness, the enlightened idea that the psychiatrically impaired didn't need to be chained to a wall. At his asylums the patients dined together and lived a relatively civilized existence in the fields of Hanwell, Brentford and Isleworth.

This was a time when 'trading in lunacy' was big business, a convenient way to dispense of a troublesome wife. You could buy a diagnosis of insanity for less than a divorce. The doctors were condemned as quacks and 'nostrum mongers'. The Irish novelist Rosina Bulwer Lytton was confined to Wyke House by her husband, the politician and novelist Edward Bulwer-Lytton, who is now best known through phrases he used that have become well-worn clichés. 'The great unwashed', 'the pen is mightier than the sword' and the classic opening line, 'It was a dark and stormy night,' all came from his feathered quill.

You can judge which was the greater crime, but his serial infidelity that led to their separation, then denying his wife access to their children and finally having her committed to an asylum because she heckled him at a political meeting don't look too good. Fortunately, a public outcry in support of Rosina, which even attracted the attention of Karl Marx, meant she was released from Wyke Green after a month.

It is Edward Bulwer-Lytton who appears to have been the one with the troubled mind, seeking cures for various maladies, taking on leeches and potions and hydropathic treatments. His influential novel *Zanoni* drew on the Rosicrucian quest for the Elixir of Life and centred round a theme of divine madness.

A later science fiction work, *Vril* or *The Coming Race*, published in 1871, describes a subterranean master-race that has access to a powerful source of universal energy known as vril. Occultists and conspiracists took Bulwer-Lytton's writings as fact and various secret societies claimed him as their own. There is a persistent belief that a Vril Society existed in pre-war Berlin, whose members included SS head Heinrich Himmler, Luftwaffe Commander-in-Chief Hermann Goering, and Party Chancellery head Martin Bormann. It's alleged that the Vril Society urged the Nazis to embark on a global quest for ancient artefacts such as the Ark of the Covenant, which it believed could contain the key to the source of vril, and that the Society helped to design the Luftwaffe's failed 'flying saucer' project under the guidance of extraterrestrials.

In the year that *The Coming Race* was published, Rosina authored *Where There's a Will There's a Way* and *Chumber Chase*. I've found it difficult to discover what they were about, probably because her writings didn't inspire a genocidal regime and end up as the subject of a documentary on the History Channel.

I sit and revive myself, absorbing the view westwards across farmland. With the early-evening sun on my face, the songbirds and the distant ring of leather on willow, it's almost a picture-postcard pastoral scene – wedged between a major death road and the M4 motorway. Maxwell cautioned that the bucolic nature of the area was under threat in the 1930s but perhaps the building of the roads has helped preserve it. Now you have an express route into the *'real'* countryside, why bother with Wyke Green?

The path across Wyke Green

Maxwell noted the flavour of 'bygone times' hereabouts and reported how a friend had told him that one of the last bare-knuckle prize-fights had taken place on the green where I was now recovering from being floored by the traffic. Bare-knuckle boxing must have survived in the area as I later read about ex-fighter turned pro-golfer 'Gypsy Joe' Smith from Wyke Green, who won the London Heavyweight Unlicensed Boxing Championship at Osterley. Wyke Green sits on the edge of Osterley Park.

The golf course where Joe learnt to play is home to a circular Neolithic earthwork, absorbed into the contours of the course. A miss-hit drive could end up back in the Bronze Age.

I now have just over an hour to reach Hounslow Heath if I want to explore it in the light. I follow the footpath that cuts through a field of young wheat. Legend has it that the wheat produced in this area was so fine it was used to bake Elizabeth I's bread.

Looking south from here the spire of a church pokes above the rooftops. Low-hanging horse chestnut trees are in full bloom. There are bluebells growing among the stinging nettles and the hawthorns are heavy with their May blossoms. In Celtic mythology hawthorn, also known as May Tree, is where the Little People hang out, waylaying unwary travellers. Maybe that explains my extended rest within the grove on Wyke Green. The workaday world of London life feels far away from here, faery magic temporarily transporting me to a different realm of time. A lad sprawled across the path supping a can of Tennent's Super and chatting loudly on his phone relocates me to the digital age and so I push on.

This now feels like a country walk. I skirt the edge of Osterley Park, which I had tentatively planned to visit. Osterley is maintained by the National Trust so I imagine that it has preserved its aristocratic trappings. The house earns its keep as a film location, convenient for London-based crews. It's starring as Batman's mansion, Wayne Manors, in *The Dark Knight Rises*, but has also passed for Buckingham Palace in *Young Victoria* and scored credits in *Horrible Histories* and *The Chuckle Brothers*.

The manor houses and mansions form a line through West London now marked by the major roads – Chiswick, Gunnersbury, Boston Manor, Syon Park, Osterley, Strawberry Hill. This part of West London seems to have had the same relationship to the *demi-monde* and fashionable society of the 18th and 19th centuries that Buckhurst Hill and Chigwell have with Premier League footballers and reality TV stars today. In two hundred years' time will people be visiting the Brentwood gaff of Amy Childs, looking at mock-ups of her signature vajazzles and fine collection of weaves hung out like American Indian scalps?

The last hangers-on from the world of powdered wigs and miserable marriages were swept away when the 'age of mobility' demanded better and faster roads to ease the city-centre congestion. Motorways were built to 'by-pass the by-passes', such as the Great West Road, in a grand vision of modern London outlined in *The County of London Plan*, written in 1943. The M4 careered through the grounds of Osterley Park, leaving it to serve up cream teas and play a supporting role as a backdrop in period dramas. There was a certain democratizing zeal to the early days of the road-building craze, however misguided we might view it now. It also bequeathed us the legacy of these peculiar lands trapped between highways and somehow suspended outside time. That might explain why so many episodes of *Doctor Who* were shot in the area.

I follow the path in a happy daze, guided by a tower block marking the location of Heston, into an overgrown meadow of cow parsley and blackberry bushes. A group of Asian kids, giddy on Lambrini, jump to their feet and brush themselves down as I approach. Grazing horses saunter over the uneven clods of grass. This is a rare slice of remote London.

The exit from the field is through a hole in a hedge that dumps me on an over-active B-road. Brushing hawthorn flowers from my hair, it's as if I've dropped in from another era rather than skipped across from Wyke Green. This farmer is clearly no friend of the Ramblers and I can't blame him – they don't so much walk as organize mobile conversations.

This is now the final approach into Hounslow Heath, across the terrain where Maxwell wrote of getting lost when the fields of Heston were built over in the inter-war years. He'd returned to the area to take a friend on a 'country stroll': 'When I knew this walk it was pleasant field-paths, shaded by noble elms, as rural a ramble as the heart could desire, but now it is all bricks and mortar and new roads all exactly alike.' I pick up one of Maxwell's field paths I'd read about on the train. It leads me behind gardens of smoky BBQs and backyard water-fights over the Great West Road into Lampton.

I'd heard of Heston because of its famous motorway service station that serves cracking 24-hour fry-ups. Lampton on the other hand was virgin ground, a medieval hamlet hanging on in the suburbs. Cutting across Lampton Park there is more cricket, but this time an informal occasion with only half the players wearing whites. I ask the lad at long-on who's playing and he tells me with a smile that it's just a 'friends' match'.

Charles Dickens was apparently very fond of Lampton and often visited Lampton Hall. There are certain associations that any self-respecting London suburb will try to claim – a pub where Dick Turpin hid out, any kind of link to Dickens and a brush with royalty. Hounslow ticks all these boxes convincingly with a great big fat marker pen. I don't doubt that Dickens sojourned in this park; I fancy loitering a while myself and sit down next to the path to admire a great chunk of sandstone.

Lampton Sarsen stone

I read the plaque beside the Sarsen stone as kids whizz past me on scooters. The gist is that the rock was formed from a bed of sand that lay beneath the sea covering this area around 50 million years ago. There's a number to get your head around – Dickens coming out here 130-odd years ago I can cope with, but 50 million years ago and Hounslow part of a great sea? The sandstone gradually worked its way nearer the surface to rest on the London Clay about half a million years ago before it was excavated from a gravel pit.

The land submerged in water, then large beasts roaming the wild forests are sobering thoughts when looking across at children playing, gaggles of gossiping teenage girls and lads passing a ball around. This world we hold so dear is transient and there will come a time when all that is left of Lampton is this lump of archaic sandstone, and possibly the plaque.

I pass through a tunnel beneath the Piccadilly Line and into a clichéd landscape of outer London suburbia. An old lady watches me from her chair in a glass porch. There are bricks stacked in the front garden of the house next door waiting to be transformed into an extension. Tomorrow the men will emerge to wash their cars on the drive. The planes bound for Heathrow almost skim the chimney tops on their descent.

Only now do I realize that I haven't stopped for food since the café in Gunnersbury Park and have run out of water. But as an experienced suburban survivor I know how to source provisions in this seemingly barren landscape. I nip into the corner shop and bag a samosa and a can of Stella Artois.

With provisions for the onward journey I turn into Staines Road. The evocative images painted so vividly by Walter George Bell in *Where London Sleeps* loom back into view. This was one of the principal old coaching roads and the Middlesex section of the Roman road Via Trinobantes (better known as Stane Street) that passed through Pontes (Staines) on its way to the great town of Calleva Atrebatum (Silchester in Hampshire). It is along the pavement here that the gibbets would have decorated the roadside with their putrid drooping cadavers of highwaymen and footpads.

A highway robbery was reported in the *Hounslow Chronicle* in 2011 when three masked men leapt from a car and snatched a backpack containing cash and jewellery from two men 'oriental in appearance'. Aside from the use of a dark green car as the getaway vehicle, this could have been a crime from a different age. Perhaps Claude Duval or Galloping Dick slipped through a tear in the space–time continuum and then landed back in the 18th century with a stash of worthless bank notes.

This robbery lacks the class of the crimes committed by Old Mob the Highwayman, who also appeared in a double act known as Hawkins and Simpson (I bet they argued over whose name came first). Once when Old Mob robbed a stagecoach on Hounslow Heath he consoled the victims with a 'story in verse', earning himself the moniker of 'the poetical highwayman'. He also held up the coach of the Duchess of Portsmouth, who stupidly used the 'Do you know who I am?' line. Old Mob treated this with the contempt that a bouncer on the door of Bungalow 8 shows to a Z-list celebrity trying to gain entry using the same refrain. He told her to pay up because he was the King of Hounslow Heath and needed money as much as the other king. He even had the front to rob the feared Judge Jeffreys, a man known as the 'hanging judge'. Jeffreys thought mentioning his name would earn him a pardon; instead it led to a very long lecture on morals and ethics from the pistol-toting Old Mob, rounded off by 'thundering a volley of foul oaths'. The judge duly delivered his purse.

The highwaymen were the heroes of their day. They occupied the position we now reserve for footballers and X-Factor winners. They stuck two fingers up at authority and conducted themselves with a swagger and style that even Mick Jagger would be hard pushed to match.

Look at the exploits of Sixteen-String Jack, the original 'dandy highwayman', who earned his nickname from wearing 'breeches with eight strings at each knee'. After being acquitted for a robbery on Hounslow Road early in his career, instead of keeping a low profile he headed straight to Bagnigge Wells near King's Cross, the trendiest nightspot in Regency London. He strolled in dressed in a 'scarlet coat, tambour waistcoat, white silk stockings, and a laced hat, and publicly declared himself to be "Sixteen-String Jack, the Highwayman"'.

Shortly before his final capture he attended a public execution at Tyburn. These were big occasions and positions at the front were at a premium, reserved for the most wealthy and famous. Jack pushed his way through the crowd and then entered the roped-off gallows area protected by the constables. He requested permission to stand upon the platform, observing to the assembled throng that 'perhaps it is proper that I should be a spectator on this occasion.'

However flamboyant his public image, he was ultimately sentenced to death for stealing the measly sum of one shilling and sixpence from Princess Amelia's doctor in Gunnersbury Park. The night before his execution he had a party with seven ladies in his cell and went to the scaffold in a 'new suit of pea-green cloth, a ruffled shirt, and his breeches were, on this occasion, adorned with the usual sixteen strings – *but this time they were of silver!*'

Just before the Heath there is a plaque commemorating the fact that this was the entrance to 'London Terminal Aerodrome Hounslow Heath', from where the first commercial flights in Britain took off in 1919. That year a challenge was laid down by the Australian government, offering a prize of A£10,000 to the first Australian to fly from Great Britain to Australia within a period of thirty days. What followed was something akin to an episode of *Dastardly and Muttley in Their Flying Machines* pursuing that pigeon.

Six aircraft took off from Hounslow Heath aiming to make the inaugural flight from Europe to Australia. The Sopwith Wallaby had a hell of a time, with the crew being imprisoned as Bolsheviks in Yugoslavia, suffering a cracked engine in Constantinople and finally crash-landing in Bali. The Alliance P.2 nose-dived into an orchard in Surbiton killing both crew-members. The Blackburn Kangaroo staggered its way across Europe before finally getting tangled in the fence of a mental hospital in Crete with the crew unhurt. The Martinsyde Type A crashed in the sea off Corfu. The Airco DH.9 did make it to Australia but took a monumental 206 days, picking up a consolation prize of A£1,000 and earning its captain the nickname of 'Battling Ray' Parer.

Only one aircraft successfully completed the challenge – a converted Vickers Vimy bomber captained by Ross Macpherson Smith. It travelled via fifteen locations before reaching Darwin in Australia's Northern Territory – a feat that will remain unequalled until Ryanair starts operating flights Down Under.

In 1920 London moved its airport to Croydon and the skies over the Heath remained peaceful for a few years, until a small airfield on the edge of the Hounslow by Heath Row was developed after the war to become one the busiest airports in the world. Passenger planes now buzzed down over the gorse bushes resplendent in bright yellow flowers at a rate of around one every ten minutes. I spot a Qantas jet arriving from Australia at the end of a flight of twenty-odd hours that the passengers will have found arduous. They should try travelling by Vickers Vimy next time.

Hounslow Heath matches the descriptions I'd read of an open scrubby land of low bushes and rough grasses. There are joggers and dog walkers, butterflies and moths flitting between the sand spurrey and brambles. What was dubbed 'bad land' by William Cobbett on his *Rural Rides* is now a treasured public open space.

This last remainder of lowland heath with its acid grasses and dwarf gorse is a vital habitat that maintains many plant and insect species rare in the London area. The bees, beetles, spiders, ring ouzels, red-backed shrikes and honey buzzards that make their homes here are a vital component of the world that also produced the Great West Quarter and the Sainsbury Local soon to open over the road.

Following the winding pathways just before sunset the smell of hawthorn is there again. I'd happily be accosted here by the faery folk. There is a lusty rendition of the evening nesting call from a gregarious portion of some of the 132 bird species that have been recorded amongst the bell heather, silver birch and pedunculate oak.

Two lovers canoodle on a bench; she brushes her hair over her face as I pass. A rabbit skips across the path in front of me. When my grandfather courted my nan he would catch rabbits for her by throwing his hat over them. That was the way to a country girl's heart in the inter-war years, at the time that Bell and Maxwell wrote the books that guided me out this way.

I rest on a bench perched upon a mound almost in line with the approach run into Heathrow. I take a late tea of Stella and samosa, and survey the heath from this raised aspect. I try to evoke images and moods of the past life of this landscape – attempt to tune into its stories. People have lived in Hounslow for millennia – it's an area of prehistoric settlement.

Hounslow Heath

Labourers working on the heath in 1864 uncovered a set of Iron Age figurines that gives us a glimpse into the world of the people who made their homes here. The 'Hounslow Hoard' consists of three small bronze boars, two other dog-like animals and a model wheel, possibly suggestive of some sort of solar cult.

The boar motif was popular in pre-Roman Britain, being found in tumuli around Colchester, on a shield in Lincolnshire and on numerous Celtic coins. One reading of the fascination with boars, according to Miranda Green, is that they represented 'strength, ferocity and invincibility in a war-orientated heroic society'. On the other hand they might have been made by a craftsman who just happened to like boars and the two other animals were his failed attempts at dogs. Until we discover the secret of time travel we'll never be completely sure.

An Iron Age village was excavated where the planes now skid across the airport tarmac of Runway One. A complex pattern of hut circles was unearthed alongside the remnants of a shrine or temple, implying that this might well have been the religious centre of the region. Where people came to worship in time immemorial, today they ascend into the sky.

The antiquarian William Stukeley believed that he had found a camp built by Julius Caesar on the heath during his campaign against the Britons. The gunpowder for one of the first cannon used in Europe, at Crécy in 1346, was made on Hounslow Heath, part of a military association that continues through medieval tournaments and pageants, the Civil War, RAF raids against First World War Zeppelins to the barracks that are still present. This is just a sample of the rich history associated with these 200 acres of scrubland.

As a map-illiterate walker, the fact that most tickled me was that it was across the heath that the base line for the first triangle of Britain's original Ordnance Survey map was laid in 1784. The basis for all our modern maps was created across Hounslow Heath, a place now largely overlooked and 'off-the-map'.

I continue my lap of the space in high spirits as I'd reached the end of the trek with my left knee still functioning. A ghostly, pale, gap-toothed lad approaches me from a stand of coppiced trees and asks for directions to the 'forty acres'. I tell him I haven't a clue but offer up my 1975 *Greater London Atlas* for reference. He takes a quick look, says thanks and heads off into the sunset. The Ordnance Survey had now become more of use to a pair of aimless wanderers than the military that General William Roy intended it for.

I think back to Maxwell's story of the Nine Muses and contrast it with the world around me. Perhaps Maxwell found some magic mushrooms that morning in the 'forty acres' where the pallid lad was heading. Instead of following him to find out I slope back to the Staines Road. I considered a pint in The Hussar to round off the trip but as I was trying to work out if it was full of lagered-up squaddies a No. 237 bus pulled up bound for Brentford. Riding a 21st-century stagecoach along the old coaching road is a far better way to depart the scene.

From the top deck full of Saturday-night people I look out for 'ripening gallows fruit' and 'dandy highwaymen'. But all I see are waddling girls with Tesco bags and boys in caps and hoodies bouncing along past 'For Sale' signs on new-build apartments. Whether they realize it or not, in their hands they hold Maxwell's magic cord that connects our universe of iPhones and Nando's to boar-worshippers and mad men in their flying machines and 'passes over the old-time Heath of Hounslow'.

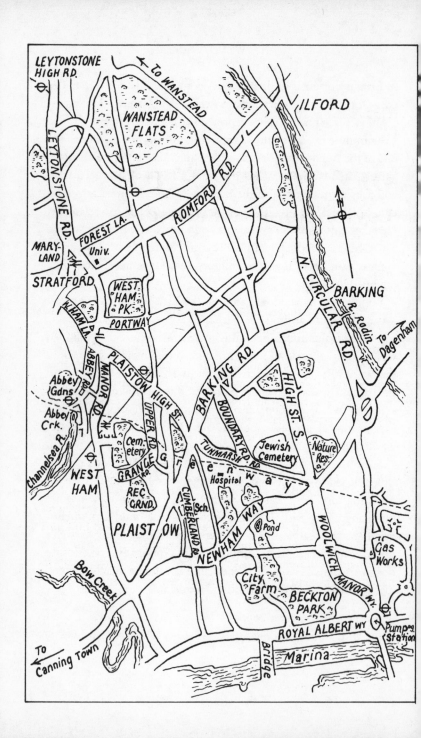

CHAPTER 2

OFF TO BEC PHU
Leytonstone to Beckton

When I first moved east to Leytonstone I orientated myself by studying its position on a large fold-out A–Z map that I bought from the cabbies' Knowledge Point on Penton Street. This map lived in my bag for about eight years until it finally fell apart into several strips. Leytonstone is just one fold away from the eastern edge of this black-cab driver's universe – getting a taxi beyond the Redbridge Roundabout is about as easy as persuading a medieval sailor to head west across the Atlantic. Looking south I traced a straight line through Stratford across Mill Meads to the point where the River Lea empties into the Thames at Leamouth. Between Leamouth and Barking Creek lies the ancient manor of Hamme.

To fully embed Leytonstone's alignment with the sacred Thames I'd have to walk the route, passing familiar territory at Stratford before lurching into the unknown lands along the Channelsea River and the Lower Lea Valley. As I researched the best path to take, my eyes kept being drawn along the embankment past the old Royal Docks to Beckton.

In my 1970s *Greater London Atlas* the East Ham Level is annotated with an outline diagram showing the Gas Works at Beckton and the beguilingly named Main Drainage Metropolis. A sewer city. This series of straight lines, circles and interconnecting threads resembles an X-ray image of a suspect package.

Beckton was lodged in a dusty corner of my brain as the unlikely location of Stanley Kubrick's Vietnam War movie *Full Metal Jacket*. This film was a pivotal point in my cinema-going life. Its release in 1987 coincided with the recent opening of a multiplex cinema just outside High Wycombe and the first of my friends to pass their driving test. After closing time at the local pub I blagged a lift to the Wycombe 6 alongside my mate Darren Smith, and whilst the rest of our troupe took in some Tom Cruise fluff, me and Darren enlisted for Kubrick's Vietnam nightmare.

We emerged from the cinema on to the M40 changed men – we'd never seen cinema like this before, we'd had an experience, felt like we'd been under fire ourselves. It took us a while to realize that the Tom Cruise mob had taken off and stranded us six miles from home at two in the morning. They clearly hadn't adopted the US Marine code of never leaving a fellow soldier behind. We walked home through the pitch black, short-cutting across fields in the rain, enthralled and troubled by what we'd seen.

The film had caught my eye after seeing a short item on TV about this mad American director who was transforming a disused gas works in East London into the killing fields of Vietnam. Thousands of palm trees had been imported and planted in the Thameside marshes to recreate the landscape of South East Asia at Beckton.

Kubrick famously refused to travel – he hadn't been back to America since the late 1960s – so the standard option of filming a Vietnam flick in the Philippines wasn't available. By a stroke of luck not only was Kubrick given permission to blow up the gasworks, but they 'uncannily resembled' the French industrial architecture of the Vietnamese city of Hue where the film was set.

The 'Vietnamization' of this windswept corner of East London would therefore not require such a great leap of the imagination as might be expected.

When the great director sent out his casting call and eager young American actors submitted their audition tapes they couldn't have dreamed that their prize would be to spend seventeen months marooned on an industrial wasteland, serving four months longer than an official war-time tour of duty. Kubrick commanded them, rolling around in the cold Thameside mud with percussive explosions knocking chucks off the crumbling buildings, each retake requiring a hiatus of three days as the walls were repaired for a repeat of the same attack. The longer his raw recruits bunked down in Beckton, the more they came to authentically behave like a unit of Marines in a hostile foreign field dreaming of home.

Over the years I'd picked up rumours that some of the palm trees had been left behind and were thriving in the polluted alluvial mud. I saw snaps people had taken of fragments of wall on which the set designers had scrawled Viet Cong graffiti. The gasworks also played the role of a totalitarian future London in the film version of George Orwell's 1984, the walls plastered in propaganda posters and the streets patrolled by jackbooted 'Thought Police'. I had to go to Beckton to see what I could find of Kubrick's Bec Phu, as it came to be known to the crew.

I set out on foot late morning one Friday in a fine mist of rain. The first section of my walk down through Leytonstone would be a preamble for a future detailed survey – eyeing up places en route that I'd later delve deeper into. Passing along the footbridge above the M11 link road I looked down to the Olympic Stadium by the Lea and to Canary Wharf in the distance – I knew that Beckton was on the far bank of the other creek. It was between those two tracts of water that I'd have to walk. I was consciously heading away from the Olympic jamboree taking place in the New Stratford that has been conjured up from the toxic earth on Stratford Marsh.

I pass the site of the childhood home of Alfred Hitchcock, a visionary director who made the reverse journey to Kubrick, heading west to Hollywood. When I've been out in Los Angeles on conscription writing trips, homesick for the streets of Leytonstone and daydreaming of a rainy night-time wander up to the Whipps Cross Roundabout and stopping for a pint in the Hitchcock Hotel, I've thought of Alf and wondered whether he ever pined for Leytonstone. Given the notorious anecdote of the young Hitch being sent to the police station over the road by his father with a note telling the officer to lock the boy in the cells for ten minutes, I'm not sure he had particularly happy memories of the place.

The excursion really starts as I enter Stratford. This stretch of the High Road is desperate, far enough off the beaten track to not have qualified for an Olympic makeover. If you peer along the streets of run-down terraced houses you can see the Olympic Village glistening on Angel Lane like a glorious Gulag. It seems to have been modelled on a despot's palace.

I'd toyed with taking the trail along Leyton High Road into Angel Lane, following a route I've walked periodically over the last six years as the Olympic development evolved. But I'm keen not to lapse into a splenetic rant against land-grabs and property developers, frothing at the mouth about the breaking up of one of Europe's oldest housing co-ops at Clays Lane, the horror of the state-subsidized shopping mall through which visitors to the Olympic Stadium have to pass – the way to the 100-metres final being via Zara, handy for a cheap Third World T-shirt but hardly the Wembley Way. Westfield Stratford City must be the only shopping mall in the world with its own running track, ideal if you've over indulged in the food court.

This description of the area in Dr Pagenstecher's *History of East and West Ham*, published in 1908, struck me: 'Turning down Angel Lane, you soon entered upon a country road, running between high banks topped with hedges. Now the fields are gone, and most of the land has gone into the hands of building societies or speculative builders.'

Dr Pagenstecher was passionate about what is today called Newham. He appeared to care deeply about the living conditions and opportunities for its mostly working-class inhabitants. I try to see through my cynicism to how he would have viewed what has happened in Stratford in recent years – progress for the local population and a chance for advancement, or a criminal waste of billions of pounds of investment that has by-passed the pockets of those who need it most. And this is me avoiding the venting of my ire.

In the end, I became resigned to what happened. My wife even bought tickets for the family to graze in the grounds around the stadium to soak up the atmosphere. I'd wandered around the Queen Elizabeth II Park site among the buddleia, Himalayan balsam, elderflower and fly-tipped fridges before the bulldozers crashed in and the security fences were erected. I also have to acknowledge I bought the boots I'm wearing from Westfield – I'm compromised from the ground up.

I need to change tack, and turn away from London 2012 across Maryland Point. Maryland really is named after its more famous North American cousin and seems to have benefited from the Games by obtaining a twisted silver clock tower, but not much else. On the other hand Maryland fell foul of a pre-Olympics brothel purge. Reading online message boards it appears that two massage parlours had been satisfying punters for a few years before the Met decided there was something untoward going on beneath the flannel-sized 'todger-towels' provided at the door. A *Daily Star* investigation proved that the moral crusade was unsuc'sex'ful. Stressed-out visitors to Stratford wouldn't have to look further afield in search of a happy ending after all.

Water Lane carries me past the Manby Arms pub with its huge garden. This is the first real hint of the rural hamlets that studded the marshes and the levels. There are multiple references to groves in the area – The Grove that sweeps from Maryland into Stratford Broadway, Manbey Grove where the pub sits, and across the Romford Road there's Barnard Grove – all of which lie around what is marked on old maps as Stratford Common. Add in the fact that they're in the proximity of Water Lane, a pagan past could be imagined for the site, with oak groves and springs having sacred, pre-Christian significance.

An official book celebrating fifty years of the Borough of West Ham in 1936 states: 'It is quite likely that the area was a centre of communal life of the (pre-Roman) period and that it saw Druid ceremonial at its best.' Not only do the authors claim the presence of Druids in West Ham but they've made a critical judgement about how their rituals squared up against Druids from other areas. Not content with having the best public baths in East London, the grandees of 1930s West Ham boasted that even their Druids were better going back to time immemorial. Try matching that in Tower Hamlets or Waltham Forest.

I'm a sucker for this stuff and will by-pass the other meaning of a grove as a tree-lined suburban street and the fact that, from what I've read, most of what we think we know of Druidry is an 18th-century invention rather than a tradition handed down through the mists of time. Drifting the workaday streets as I do you need to embrace the romantic whenever you get the chance – it can't be all Greggs the Bakers and tins of warm lager.

* * *

It's warm lager that comes to mind on Romford Road. Not because this is the old Roman road that crossed the marshes into Essex – I don't think lager had been invented at the time of Julius Caesar. The Romans brought hops to Britain as a vegetable rather than for brewing. The memory is of bad student parties in my first year in London when I moved to a terraced house in York Road just past the BP garage. I was a callow 18-year-old who had taken the BBC comedy programme *The Young Ones* as an instructional manual rather than a sitcom and was determined to 'live the dream' of pukey parties, farts, bad jokes and even worse music.

We did a fairly good job in our little three-bed terraced house with an outside toilet. The tone was set in the first week when one of my housemates took both his first taste of red wine and his inaugural spliff at the same time. Unable to negotiate the slide door to the toilet he projectile vomited over three days' worth of dirty dishes in the sink. We elected him as next on the washing-up rota as a consequence and carried on quaffing the £1.99 litre bottle of Valpolicella.

Another night in the first term, a visitor to our humble home, a public schoolboy who'd fallen through the educational cracks decided to urinate in an empty wine bottle rather than traipse into the garden to use the lavvy. We corked this fine vintage of Château Piss and popped it in the fridge. When our regular Friday-night group feed came round my female housemate rolled in three sheets to the wind, grabbed the chilled bladder juice from the fridge and poured herself a large glass. I swear I did attempt to warn her but she just assumed I was protecting my stash. Upon the first sip she spluttered the urine all over the food I'd just prepared, which our guests decided to eat anyway because everyone was so hungry and my baked bean and cheese-topped toasties were legendary. All the people in those gruesome anecdotes now have responsible jobs, mortgages and children – apart from me. I just have the children.

We felt that we'd so successfully distilled the essence of the Scumbag Polytechnic student lifestyle that, like an ambitious shopkeeper, we expanded the next year to a five-bed house on the other side of West Ham Park. The Spotted Dog pub on Upton Lane became our regular haunt. To us provincials this was a remnant of home, a country pub nestled among the East London grime. We didn't realize it at the time but the pub dates back at least to the 16th century. It was where the City merchants of the London Exchange conducted their business during the plague years of the 1660s. It was where we celebrated birthdays, exams, and Subbuteo victories.

Happy days. If nothing else my three years at Poly provided me with the cast-iron stomach that stood me in good stead on travels round India and South East Asia. This period also created a permanent connection to the area of London where I entered kidulthood.

In those two years traipsing along the Romford Road I have no memory of ever ducking down Vicarage Lane to West Ham Church. Shame then that I didn't take the trouble to study the 18th-century map of the area that shows the original name of Vicarage Lane as being Ass Lane. If that hadn't made us snigger, the *Victoria County History* records that, 'the cartographer may have been misled by a rustic informant: the form Jackass Lane, also recorded in the 18th century, seems more authentic.'

Jackass Lane brings me to an old Roman trackway, the 'Porta Via' or Portway, that linked West Ham to the Roman camp at Uphall Farm in Barking. Groups of 'rustic informants' are sunning themselves on the benches outside West Ham Church. The foundations of this church date back to the Saxon era, the main body being rebuilt by the Norman Baron William de Montfichet in the 1180s. When the eyes of the world fell on the running and jumping on Stratford Marshes I doubt many cast their gaze towards this building with a heritage older than Westminster Abbey. It sits beneath the shade of the lime, yew and oak trees – not a tourist in sight.

I go to take a rest inside and a group of builders on a lunch break wave me through. In 1844 a large, colourful mural was revealed that covered the interior of the church but for some reason was hastily hidden again beneath lime-wash. However, an anonymous pamphlet was published describing the mural as depicting 'the suburbs of Hell'. Parts of the mural were again revealed in 1865 during renovations, when it was examined 'under the superintendence of the Rev. R. N. Clutterbuck of Plaistow'. The lurid descriptions of the anonymous pamphlet were debunked before the mural was deemed unworthy of preservation, re-whitewashed and the plaster removed. It has a hint of intrigue almost worthy of a Dan Brown novel, in which no doubt connections would be made between the martyrs burnt at the stake on Stratford Green and the land owned by the Knights Templar around the River Lea nearby. In the Dan Brown version the forbidden mural in this backwater church would have contained the secret of some heresy. At some point a beautiful younger woman would have to be involved – she can play me as the bumbling amateur researcher with a dodgy left knee – and she discovers that the Olympic Stadium has been built to cover a hoard of Templar treasure that includes the Ark of the Covenant and the Holy Prepuce (Christ's foreskin). That might bring the tourists in.

Who the artist was, we'll never know. Was he a troublesome monk sent out from the nearby Langthorne Abbey to do good work in the community? Once confronted with a fresh white wall, a brush and paints, did he unleash the impulses repressed by ecclesiastical life? Was he some kind of Banksy character who wandered around East London daubing images of fornicating bishops on church walls. Somewhere within the West Ham mural was there a tag as identifiable as the signature on a Damien Hirst dot painting? 'The Final Doom of Mankind' that was painted here might have been as synonymous with this 15th-century painter as the Obama/Hope poster is with street artist Shepard Fairey. But then this was an era before artists had egos and dealers. When the mural was painted there would have been no Victorian squeamishness over images of cavorting naked sinners. Vivid, racy murals probably put bums on church seats in those days.

All the time that I'm studying Dr Pagenstecher's account of the church's history my ears are tuning in to the builders' lunchtime banter. The tranquillity of this rare pastoral East London scene is being disrupted by one of the workmen who'd let me into the church giving his mates a detailed blow-by-blow account of a fight he'd had. The image he paints of his rumble would be a true vision of hell if it were rendered as a fresco on the whitewashed walls.

As I make for the door, trying my hardest not to attract the attention of 'Bonecrusher', I spot one of the last surviving relics of the great Stratford Langthorne Abbey that is the next stop on my Kubrick schlep. High on the wall of the north tower is a stone tablet carved with a sequence of human skulls dug up in the garden of the Adam and Eve pub. 'Bonecrusher' comments to his mates as I take a photo, but they quickly lose interest and return to tales of bust-ups in Barking boozers.

As far as I know, the tablet is all that remains of the great abbey built by Montfichet in 1135 by the banks of the Channelsea River. The Abbey of Stratford Langthorne put the area on the map in the Middle Ages in the way that Westfield Stratford City is aiming to do today. The building of the Eurostar terminal, Stratford International, continues the historic symmetry, as continental visitors would sail up the Lea and disembark at Queen Matilda's bridge by the 'Street-at-the-Ford'. The area's French connection was sufficiently well known for Chaucer to make a sneering reference to the locals' attempts to converse with the tourists in their mother tongue, referring to 'French after the scole of Stratford-atte-Bowe'.

Stone tablet in West Ham Church

Heading down Abbey Road you'd need an active imagination to guess this was the way to a scheduled ancient monument. Where pilgrims trod a path through the marshes the route now reads like a history of 20th-century social housing, from its most enlightened pre-war phase, built by the London County Council, to the high-rise blocks being given a facelift. Straight ahead stand the Towers of Mammon at Canary Wharf and to the north you can just see the top of Anish Kapoor's sculpture in the Olympic Park, which is about as close as most people from the area managed to get.

Turning into Bakers Row a hint of rurality reappears as poppies poke through the metal railings of Abbey Gardens. A sign invites you 'to grow your things here'. The Cistercian monks of the abbey were known for their green fingers. The name 'Langthorne' was taken from the hedges of 'long thorns' that surrounded their gardens on this site. The present-day Abbey Gardens carry on the work of the monks, encouraging local people to use the 'open-access harvest garden' to grow fruit, vegetables and herbs in rows of raised beds.

Just inside the gate are the brick and flint foundations of a small building or room that would have been part of the medieval abbey. Around it grow lavender, wild geraniums, cabbages, lettuce and spring onions. An old signal box finds new life as a tool shed and a wind turbine provides whatever power is needed. I think the monks would approve.

The remains of Stratford Langthorne Abbey

Before the Cistercians and their impressive abbey, old Hamme was divided into two manors. There is a map of the area at 'Ye thyme of Edward ye Confessor'. I'd guess from the spelling that the map was Victorian; those 'Ye's' speak of a longing to connect with a halcyon past. It shows the Manor of Alestan with his eight hides of arable and sixty acres of meadow in West Ham. On the other side of Ham Creek is the Manor of Leured with only one hide of arable and fifty acres of meadow. There is also a parcel of land for Edwin the Free Priest, who sounds too much like a Monty Python character. Out here in the marshes, unshackled from the Church hierarchy, he probably ran around naked with a beard down to his knees. What comes to mind is the scene in *Life of Brian* when Brian accidentally jumps on a hermit's foot, making him break his vow of silence as he exclaims in pain. Although back in the 11th century it's unlikely Edwin would have been disturbed by anyone, let alone a reluctant messiah.

There is an even earlier record that Offa, the 8th-century King of the East Saxons, gave two hides of land in East Ham to the Monastery of St Peter in Westminster. The men of Westminster have again got their beady eyes on the region but they aren't thinking in terms of hides but office blocks and riverside housing developments.

When Ken Livingstone was campaigning in Leyton in 2011 during the mayoral elections he spoke of the real legacy of the Olympic Games being the 'vast potential' of the land 'from the Olympic Park south to the River Thames ... between Stratford and the Excel Centre a vast amount of brownfield site ... we've got enough land there for 40,000 homes and 50,000 jobs.'

Not-so-Red Ken was referring to the Manor of Alestan, which in Alestan's time was valued by how many hogs could be supported by feeding on the acorns and beech masts of the woodland.

When this area is being sold off to the corporations of the 'dynamic' economies in China, Brazil and India, they will be talking in hundreds of millions of pounds rather than the hundred swine that could be sustained by whatever fell from the trees. The ancient rites of 'pannage' will be omitted from the prospectus sent out boasting of West Ham's 'development potential'.

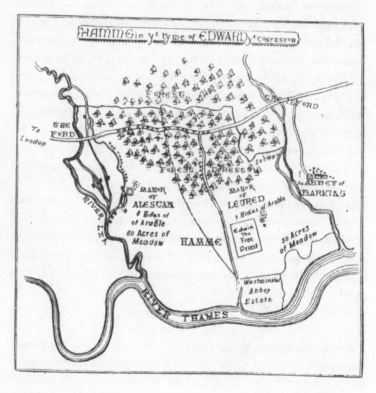

Old Hamme, from *The History of East and West Ham* by Dr Pagenstecher, 1908

*   *   *

Passing over the bridge at Abbey Road the pavement is streaming with men departing Friday prayers from Canning Road mosque, heading for the Docklands Light Railway like a procession of pilgrims. The traffic is intense for such a quiet backwater, and this is before the proposed 'Mega Mosque' has been built. The plans for the 9,500-capacity religious centre are being opposed by a Mega-Mosque No Thanks campaign group among fears that it will turn West Ham into an 'Islamic ghetto'. I've seen a few mosques before but not even the mighty Jama Masjid at Fatehpur Sikri in India calls itself a Mega Mosque. I have to take a look where this potential new landmark will emerge.

Given that the group behind the scheme have been accused of being 'extreme and isolationist' I don't fancy my chances of getting very far. But in fact I am able to amble through the open gates into the grounds unopposed. At present the Mega Mosque is no more than a series of portacabins laid out among the long grass. I try to cross the overgrown meadow to access the banks of the Channelsea River but find the way blocked by an aluminium fence. I seem to be free to wander the site at will. A man in Islamic dress emerges from the kitchens, passes me by with a slight smirk and goes about his business. There could almost be a heritage argument for building a religious centre near the site of Langthorne Abbey; the Cistercian monks could possibly have been described as 'extreme and isolationist'.

From the mosque I step up onto the Greenway – a path built on top of the Northern Outfall Sewage Pipe that cuts a straight line across the levels to Beckton. This is the most direct route for the unadventurous. It forms a kind of ramblers' highway above the rooftops, screening out the realities of metropolitan life with a surface optimized for soft-soled dog walkers and commuting cyclists. To confirm this jaundiced assessment my way is soon blocked by a party of about thirty ramblers being led by an enthusiastic guide pointing out the landmarks (I attempt to hear if she included the Mega Mosque). A cyclist in a hurry approaches and it takes the guide too long for the cyclist's liking to manoeuvre this bloated python of a walking party to one side.

Despite the pedestrian traffic jams the Greenway is a great vantage point from which to take in the course of Alfred the Great's Channelsea River. It's believed that the ingenious Alfred cut a series of channels to drain water from the River Lea, stranding a hostile Viking fleet that had moored further along the valley. The skeleton of a Viking longboat was excavated on Tottenham Marshes, lending weight to the story.

It's funny the way history accords these great accolades to a few individuals. It's unlikely that Alfred mastered such a feat of civil engineering whilst supposedly single-handedly rewriting the laws of England. According to his chronicler, a pithy Welsh monk called Asser, he had a raging libido and a terrible case of haemorrhoids. It's more likely that an unnamed group of people put their heads together and devised the scheme to create the Channelsea River, and Alfred approved the idea whilst some unfortunate maiden applied a balm to his throbbing piles.

It had been my original intention to paddle my way down the river to the mouth of Bow Creek, then head overland with the 7kg dingy on my back. I'd walked around this section of the riverbank back in November when the water was high. Looking across the muddy banks sprouting phalanxes of swaying reeds the age of Alfred, Alestan and the Vikings didn't seem so distant.

The current state of the dried-up July watercourse clogged with dumped car tyres would have left me as marooned as the marauding Danes. Some plans work far better in the imagination.

*   *   *

I've been on the move now for three hours and still have some distance to go on my loopy route to Bec Phu. I want to follow the journey the monks of Stratford Abbey took after the Dissolution of the Monasteries in the 16th century when they retired to a mansion in Plaistow. This would have been a traumatic event for the monks, kicked out of their home by Henry VIII once he assumed the role as Supreme Head of the Church in England after his split from Rome. Although there's nothing to suggest the monks of Stratford were wholly guilty of the crimes levelled at monasteries and abbeys – of exploiting dubious religious relics for financial gain and of growing rich, fat and lazy thanks to donations from pious simpletons – they had built up a substantial annual income that Henry wanted to get his lecherous mitts on. But to some extent theirs was a walk of shame from the wealth of their abbey to the relative modesty of the Plaistow retreat. As I'm wondering how far from the spiritual path the mucky monks of Stratford had strayed, I see another mob of recreational walkers and descend from the Greenway straight to the door of a café.

At this stage any café would do and I don't pay much attention as I enter. Inside, the walls are coated in a tiled layer of Polaroids that the owner tells me are of 'friends, enemies and events'. Standing before them is a mannequin dressed as an American Indian squaw but he says, 'She needs a change, really, for the summer.' This is more than a café; it's a project. The menu holders on the tables contain books, enticing you as much to read a few pages of Paulo Coelho as order a slice of cake with your cappuccino.

I take the chance to survey my options; I've already by-passed Abbey Mills – the pumping house and surviving Templar mills now converted into a busy film and TV studio. Where Joseph Bazalgette engineered the sewage system that sits beneath the Greenway, his great-great grandson returned to stage the original series of the reality TV behemoth *Big Brother* at what is now called

3 Mills Studios. I've heard it remarked that where one Bazalgette pumped the shit out of London, his descendant devised a way to pump it all back in. But whereas the sewage system still remains a vital part of our daily lives, *Big Brother* has faded into irrelevance. Abbey Mills is now better known for its association with the strange animated creations of Goth prince Tim Burton.

Ploughing onwards to Plaistow I pass East London Cemetery after stopping to note down the Bronzed Age tanning salon by the gates. Maybe people become conscious of their pallor when visiting dead relatives. I'd planned to pay homage to Dr Pagenstecher, who was buried in the cemetery in 1926. People leave strange mementos on the graves of the famous but I think my perambulation through the Hammes is tribute enough to this Prussian immigrant who formed a deep attachment to the area.

I soon realize that the chances of finding the plot of Dr Pagenstecher are remote – the cemetery is a vast necropolis of headstones dedicated to Mum, Dad, and Granddad. There's a large marble dartboard for BILLY and fresh flowers in West Ham colours. The notorious East End singer and actress Queenie Watts lies resting here somewhere as well. She starred in one of the great London films, *Sparrers Can't Sing*, filmed around Limehouse and Stratford, reprising the role she played in real life as the landlady and lounge-bar *chanteuse* of the Iron Bridge Tavern in East India Dock Road. She also appeared in *Alfie*, providing the soundtrack for Michael Caine's pub brawl. But I start to feel as if I'm intruding with this tombstone tourism and move on.

I've never been sure how to pronounce Plaistow – whether to give it a flat 'a' or to round it into a provincial, potentially poncey-sounding 'ar'. I'll go with whatever Ian Dury spits out in his bawdy ballad 'Plaistow Patricia'. Dury opts for the rounded 'ar' but growls through it with such venom that even Johnny Rotten would have told him to tone it down a bit.

The approach into Plaistow via Upper Road hints at the well-to-do rural past when this was a prosperous village favoured by City merchants and Old Money. Pagenstecher noted how in 1768 only four people in Plaistow were eligible to vote and they had to walk to Chelmsford to cast their ballot. In 1841 the population was eerily recorded as being 1,841. The building of the Victoria and Albert Royal Docks saw the population surge to over 150,000 by the early 1900s. The grazing meadows of the Plaistow Levels that produced the infamous monster ox on Tun Marsh, weighing in at 263 stone and sold at Leadenhall Market in 1720 for a hundred guineas, sprouted rows of terraced houses. Pagenstecher wrote that it was 'the most remarkable transformation from a rural to an urban community ... without parallel in the United Kingdom'.

I'm partly following the footsteps of Thomas Burke in his 1921 book *The Outer Circle: Rambles in Remote London*. Burke was an early champion of overlooked London. Eighty-something years before Iain Sinclair mapped the city's outer rim with his celebrated epic millennial yomp round the M25 in *London Orbital*, Burke was chronicling the changing face of what it is now fashionable to call 'edgelands'. He saw wonder in the new suburbs where the cement was still fresh on the redbrick villas. He was the original poet of the new commuter class, clerks and salary men, their aspirational wives and burping children, and was Edwardian London's psychogeographer.

Burke was scathing about places he disliked – Ilford gets a real pasting in *The Outer Circle*. Moving round into the High Street it speaks volumes of how badly the area must have suffered in the Blitz that Burke wrote glowingly of the 'Plastovians' and their neighbourhood. Any notion of Plaistow as a quaint village in the marshes fades away with the grubby Costcutter hugging the corner. It's a landscape of uninspired post-war blocks. Although there is still a buzz around the place, it has a feel of grim determination rather than the people 'full of beans' whom Burke described.

There is a poignant record of the bomb damage inflicted on Plaistow on the night of 19 March 1941. The Metropolitan Police kept detailed inventories of the losses of each night's raid, often short entries of a few sentences. But the roll call of destroyed properties and fatalities this time runs to over two pages. It was the worst night of bombing London had seen since the Battle of Britain. This is a sample, neatly typed out with administrative simplicity:

1 HE. Bomb at Rivett Street. 50 houses demolished. Tidal Basin Railway Station, 2 P.H.'s, and 20 houses damaged.

It records how 'about 1,500 Incendiary bombs fell on the section'. A convent and a furniture depository were logged amongst the buildings 'completely destroyed', along with Leyes Road School and numerous other houses and pubs.

If March 1941 wasn't bad enough, later in the war German V-1 flying bombs and V-2 rockets fell from the sky. One ward alone lost 85 per cent of its houses. It's a miracle anything pre-war is left standing. It's too easy at times when bemoaning the state of certain parts of London to forget that only sixty years ago some of them were still lying under piles of Blitz rubble. Consequently, I don't look too hard for the fragment of the mansion where the Langthorne monks retired, which was supposedly in the back garden of a Methodist chapel opposite the Black Lion pub.

I've been carrying my rain jacket most of the way and haven't needed it since Leytonstone. It's got hotter as the walk has progressed and my feet are starting to ache. I feel the heat coming off a No. 69 bus stuck in traffic. I'd seen that bus many times lumbering through Leyton and always wondered where it went. Now I know – it goes to Beckton. I could have just got a No. 69 straight to Kubrickland rather than hoofing it all this way. But where is the adventure in that?

Into Balaam Street, which, despite its Anglicized pronunciation of *Bale-ham*, is a reference to a character with occult powers written about in the Jewish Torah's Book of Numbers. Dan Brown would be having kittens by now – the martyrs burnt on Stratford Green, the destroyed mural in West Ham Church, monks driven from their monastery on Templar land, Christ's foreskin buried beneath the Olympic Stadium that I made up, and now a character from an ancient Hebrew text open to multiple interpretations. Even I'm intrigued.

It seems Balaam was a Gentile prophet from Babylon who rode a speaking ass. We are now far beyond the Pythonesque world of Edwin the Free Priest. From what I can glean, when urged by the hostile King Moab to predict the doom of the Israelites, Balaam instead sung the praises of the wandering Jews in search of the Promised Land. However much pressure Moab put him under, Balaam continued to produce prophecies of a glorious future for Israel. But after that heroic moment he introduced prostitutes and bacon sandwiches into the Israelite community, causing God to inflict a terrible plague upon them that killed 24,000 people, including Balaam himself. What this has to do with Plaistow I have no idea but rather than showing the way to the Promised Land, Balaam Street leads to the Barking Road. And you don't need a Princeton-educated semiologist to work out where the Barking Road takes you.

Another nod to Eastern influences is the 'Byzantine-style' Memorial Community Church just past Michelle's American Nails and Tooth Diamonds. It rises from the levels on the Barking Road, a majestic, cathedral-like structure built in 1921 to commemorate the dead of the First World War. The names of the fallen soldiers are cast into the bells that ring out from the east tower.

The building of the Barking Road in 1807 effectively killed off the marsh men who earned their living as cordwainers, potato growers and graziers. The road brought city clerks and dock workers. In 1963 it carried the Beatles to chaotic gigs at the Granada Cinema, East Ham. On the second occasion, their manager Brian Epstein told them the news that their forthcoming single 'I Want to Hold Your Hand' had sold over a million advance copies. Hanging around backstage pre-show, munching takeaways that had to be delivered by the police, this could have been the moment the mop-topped Scousers realized that they were seriously big news.

The Granada Cinema survives as a Gala Bingo Hall and I consider popping in to try my luck and see if I can access that hysterical moment in pop history. Perhaps there'll be an old dear crossing off numbers who was there at the gig that night. With the first twinges of pain in my left knee it could prove a detour too far, so I stay on track.

I do however allow myself to wander into Cumberland Road where the Duke of Cumberland lived. One of the dukes of Cumberland had the cheerful nickname of the 'Butcher of Culloden', which I don't think was meant ironically. He makes a peculiar appearance in the local version of a mummers folk play particular to the village where I grew up. The play was common all over the country and had a set of stock characters, but for some odd reason in the version played out in Wooburn Green, Bold Slasher or Saladin was replaced by the Duke of Cumberland. There lies a genuine historical conundrum and however much I allow myself to drift on flights of fancy I don't really expect to find the answer along this neat row of terraced houses.

I chat to a local resident walking his dog and mention the bomb damage the area suffered during the war. He cheerily tells me the roof of his house was blown straight up into the air and landed back firmly in place. He also tells me that this land was originally covered in market gardens.

I'm drawn across the road to a bright-red tin hut with emerald-green trim around the roof, doors and windows. Above the entrance it reads 'Gospel Printing Mission' on a small, black plaque. It looks curiously out of place. The man tells me that he's never seen anybody go in or out of the building. When I check online I discover that the mission was led here from its previous home in Barkingside after receiving word from God obtained through 'urgent prayer'.

The printing presses inside this tin shack send out Christian literature worldwide in several languages. The clatter of the Rota-print press must echo around the metallic structure, making a hell of a din. I didn't find a clue to the Butcher of Culloden question, but here was a parallel between Balaam acting directly on the word of God and the Gospel Printing Mission being instructed by the Lord to set up a publishing operation in an old shed off the Barking Road not far from Balaam Street. As God directed Balaam from the Plains of Midian to the eastern shore of the Dead Sea, he guided the GPM to Plaistow – no less epic a journey in its own way.

If God were speaking to me now he would probably tell me to get a bloody move on. The sultry weather has clearly befuddled my brain. I urge myself onwards by paraphrasing the Beastie Boys, singing to myself 'No Beer till Beckton' to the tune of their rap-rock smash 'No Sleep till Brooklyn'. It's probably not a deity feeding me this line but perhaps the spirit of recently deceased Beastie Boy Adam Yauch.

Tunmarsh Lane sets me on a direct track across the marshes to Beckton, except that here the wetlands have been tamed by housing. I almost instantly break my Beastie Boys pledge and suck down a can of Stella as a medical precaution against a seizure of the left knee. A good friend familiar with the workings of painkillers informs me that where codeine caused me anxiety and nightmares, my metabolism clearly responds well to beer-based palliatives. In an ideal world this would be a few pints of real ale supped in a comfortable pub. When I'm on the hoof I need something a bit more direct.

The Bobby Moore Stand of West Ham United's Boleyn Ground at Upton Park is visible above the rooftops. Legend has it that the ill-fated wife of Henry VIII resided in a castle here that survived into the 20th century. With West Ham soon to relocate to the Olympic Stadium, that element of their mythology will be left behind. The Hammers carry forth the memory of the dockyards in their nicknames – when the 35,000-strong Upton Park crowd bellow out 'Come On You Irons' they sing back into being Thameside Ironworks FC, which the club first played as when set up by the owner and the foreman of Thameside Ironworks and Shipbuilding Co. in 1895. They changed their name to West Ham in 1900 and then promptly moved their ground from Plaistow to a corner of East Ham.

There is an intense sense of belonging around Upton Park on match days. Football thrives on its tribalism, but as the claret and blue hordes filter along Green Street it has more the air of a regional clan gathering, an extended family of tens of thousands assembled for a folk moot.

This communality is also evident in the civic pride of the old municipal publications. I'm reminded of this as I pass the New City Elementary School in Tunmarsh Lane, built in 1897. When not boasting about the quality of West Ham's Druid ceremonies in times gone past, *Fifty Years a Borough* (1936) shows us photos of the 'latest motor ambulance', pupils sitting down to lunch at the open-air day school, the first electricity dynamos at Canning Town, the Turbo Alternator at the West Ham Generating Station, and children being met by their parents as they are discharged from Plaistow Fever Hospital. The first paragraph on local history states, 'Local history is the cradle of true patriotism, and local patriotism is the best stimulant to efficiency and progress.' Ramsay MacDonald, the first Labour Prime Minister, writes in the introduction that 'the New Society of social and moral responsibility combined with the new ideals of communal ideas is moving in the Borough.' It's stirring stuff.

It feels appropriate now to take advantage of another civic utility and jump back aboard the Greenway. The straight path that I was so scornful of earlier now opens up like a songline leading directly to the centre of my destination. The can of Stella Artois becomes my ayahuasca, a potent tribal brew that opens up channels of enlightenment. Amazonian Indians drink this hallucinogenic draught as part of a shamanistic initiation ceremony. Through the ritualistic imbibing of Belgian lager I see the Greenway as a ley line marked out in turds that takes me to the locked gate of the ancient East Ham Church.

This small flint and stone building dates from the early 12th century and claims to be the oldest church in London still in regular use. The site dates back much further, though. During the laying of the sewage pipes in 1863, Roman funeral remains, including two complete skeletons, were excavated in the churchyard. Of more relevance to me is the burial place of the antiquarian William Stukeley, laid to rest here in 1765. Through his celebrated accounts of Stonehenge, Avebury and 'the Curiosities of Great Britain', Stukeley is responsible for making a link between the Neolithic stone monuments of Britain and the Druidic religion. Aside from being a Freemason (do I even need to make the Dan Brown reference? – the church is also called St Mary Magdalene), he referred to himself as a Druid.

When I come over all pagan, as when speculating on a Druidic past for the Groves of Stratford, it is largely down to Stukeley's revival of the indigenous religion of Britain. There are now thought to be at least as many pagans in the UK as Jews and Sikhs. Upwards of 30,000 descend on Stonehenge to celebrate the summer solstice each year. The man buried somewhere in the churchyard beyond the bolted iron gate is in no small way responsible for this.

As I pass under the A13, Billy Bragg's 'Trunk Road to the Sea', Beckton is now firmly in my sights. I stop for a rest in the pub tacked on to the end of a Premier Inn. The place is buzzing with Friday-evening drinkers and diners. A lady sitting behind me says to her husband in a tone of complaint, 'I'm a lady who likes quality.' This must have been in reply to him bemoaning why they couldn't have saved a few quid and stayed at a Travelodge instead.

When I order my second pint (and get overly excited about the fact they sell Worcester Sauce crisps), I mention *Full Metal Jacket* to the young lad pulling my ale. 'Great movie,' he says. I tell him it was filmed at Beckton Gasworks and he does a comedy double-take. His eavesdropping colleague nearly drops the two glasses of rosé he's handing to a punter. I explain how the place was condemned and Kubrick was permitted to blow it up, and throw in that there would have been helicopter gunships fizzing over the roof of the pub during filming. The rest of the thirsty crowd at the bar don't seem as interested in this nugget of cinematic history as they are in placing their order, so I leave them with that vignette and return to the important task of lubricating my knee joint.

Heading back out into the bright early-evening sun I look for the grimy 'marginal' rows of workers' cottages that Kubrick's scriptwriter, Michael Herr, noted on their drives to set each day. According to Herr, Kubrick compared the proximity of the cottages to the gasworks to the Hollywood studio system keeping labour close at hand and dependent. This indicates how much Kubrick had fallen out of love with Hollywood – that he came to compare his lot in glamorous Los Angeles to that of a poorly paid London industrial-plant worker.

A generic modern housing estate has spawned upon this area once noted for its large population of sailors. Press gangs were common here in the 18th century, as were smugglers who sailed up Barking Creek with their contraband before stealing across the wetlands.

The environment may have been tamed but it still presents an uncanny landscape. To stand on the Sir Steve Redgrave Bridge with passenger jets parting your hair as they come in to land on the runway of City Airport is one of the most surreal experiences I've had in twenty years of travelling. When I made my way up the steps of the great temple complex of Borobudur in Java, one of many candidates for the Eighth Wonder of the World, I was a person who had just seen too many temples. My flabber had been gasted. That was until I sloped along this section of the Woolwich Manor Way.

Watching the jets take off from the tarmac, surrounded by water, into the dark clouds hanging low over Canary Wharf, then looking back to the hexagonal concrete pumping station sitting on a traffic island like a stranded UFO, I found myself in a state of incomprehension. To add to the craziness, DLR trains glide through the air along a concrete rail doing a waltz around the flying saucer. What was this place?

For the duration of the Olympics it was home to the US Olympic Team, who had shunned the official Olympic Village in Angel Lane due to fears over security. The danger here is not terrorism, but sensory overload.

The bridge leads to the Woolwich Ferry across the Thames. It's a journey I need to take at some point – south across the river. I'll return here later in my quest, but for now I need to find a corner of East London that is forever Vietnam.

Atlantis Avenue leads me from the UFO pumping station into Armada Way and on to the set of *Full Metal Jacket*. Fittingly, the Beckton-shot part of the film opens to a soundtrack of Nancy Sinatra's 'These Boots Were Made for Walking'. It's an expansive landscape of long, swaying grasses adorned with pylons. There's not a soul around – the remote London of Thomas Burke who passed through here in 1921, walking from Barking to Cyprus.

It's such a barren stretch of road that at first I forget to look for visual references to the film. But then the sequences in which red flares drift through the brush become recognizable. The chainlink fencing around the energy plant recalls the perimeter fence of the landing strip as a Westland helicopter, repainted US Marine green, comes in to land. I see the formation of M41 tanks and Marines working their way across the misty East Ham Level as they come under fire from the old gasworks buildings.

Armada Way snakes through to the Gallions Reach shopping complex that appears more stranded than Kubrick's unit of shell-shocked recruits with their 'thousand-yard stares'. From comparing various old A–Zs and my *Greater London Atlas*, this stands over the site of the buildings that feature in the film.

Beckton

Shoppers depart this retail outpost down a road that strongly resembles the highway flanked by ditches along which Vietnamese evacuees flee from the battle scene. Army trucks lumbered where delivery lorries today bring supplies to the consumer garrison.

The squad at the heart of the film gets lost near Tesco and comes under fire from a sniper that I'd place somewhere between

WH Smith and Sports Direct. As Matthew Modine's troops snaked around the back of the Hue/Beckton building harbouring the markswoman, I slide round the back of Tesco and rest on the grass beneath the pylons, where rabbits frolic in the evening sun.

The only physical remains of the gas plant are the gasometers, which naturally don't feature in the movie Beckton. I concede that it was fanciful to entertain the notion that I might find a brick fragment, discarded ordnance or even a thriving imported palm tree.

I go to head off towards the River Roding but am scythed down as if a Viet Cong sniper had been left behind to continue the fight. My left knee cramps up and I stagger into the fence around the sewage works. There's no point radioing for a chopper to airlift me out; I'll have to haul this useless lump of flesh clear of the war zone via the service road.

Maybe it was the heightening of my senses caused by the jolt of pain but I'm drawn to a high grass bank on Royal Docks Road. It catches the amber early-summer-evening sunlight on the tall stalks of cow parsley. In one last effort I clamber over into a secluded, overgrown enclosure. It's littered with odd dumped garments – single abandoned shoes are always more disturbing to find than a pair. Poking through the weeds are broken lumps of brick and concrete sporting blotches of orange lichen. Huge lengths of pipe lie beneath ferns and brambles. Are these the ruins of Kubrick's Bec Phu?

Full Metal Jacket ends at a similar time of day, what cinematographers know as the 'golden hour'. The Marines make their way across this same rough ground of Thameside Marshes drained by the Romans. Matthew Modine's character Joker narrates the closing lines: 'We hump down to the Perfume River to set down for the night.'

It had been my intention to set down for the night by the River Roding but I'd never make it. Instead of humping 'down to the Perfume River', I hobble to the Docklands Light Railway and home to Leytonstone.

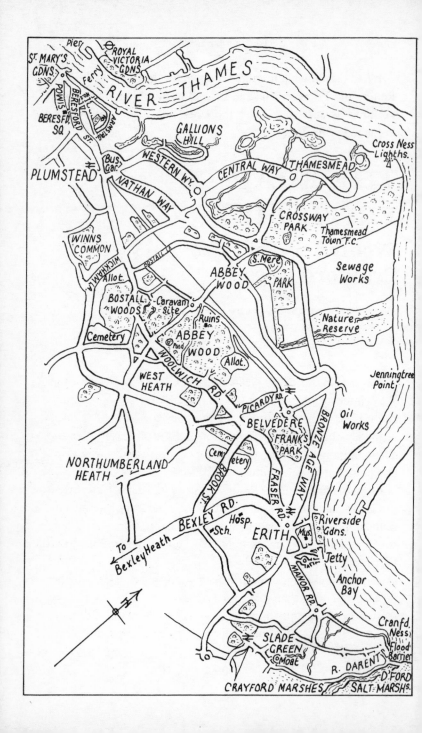

CHAPTER 3

THE ROAD TO
ERITH PIER
Woolwich Ferry to
Crayford Ness

On evenings between walks I decamp to my local pub with a clutch of old walking guides, odd municipal publications and various maps I pick up in charity shops and on eBay. It's here in the Heathcote Arms, slurping down pints of cheap bitter and decorating my belly with a sprinkling of cheese and onion crisps, that plans are made for future expeditions.

I scan the tables in *The Royal Commission on Local Government in Greater London 1957–60* as if they hold secrets of the magnitude supposedly encoded in the Mayan Long Calendar. I pore over the columns of Metropolitan Boroughs, Urban and Rural Districts and Parishes. A globule of Marston's Pale Ale falls on the acreage of Heston and Isleworth. In my reverie I consider whether this is a sign other than that I need a shave.

There must be something in these figures: Acreage, Est. Population June 1959, Rateable Value on 1st April 1960, Estimated

Product of £1 rate per head of population – it's a kind of Domesday Book for London. The report tells us that this 'sea of figures, statistics and administrative detail' is to be given great attention as 'the ways and means are of the utmost importance' and should be ignored 'at our peril'. I'd better get my head around it if I'm to gain any understanding of Greater London at all.

One August evening I was sitting there, staring at an Ordnance Survey map, searching for the high ridge of hills that I'd seen from the Greenway on the walk out to Beckton. My guess that it was Abbey Woods was not far off; it had most likely been the edge of Plumstead Common and Bostall Woods.

Scanning across the map I started to tentatively plot a journey beyond those hills that would take me down to the Thames at Erith. My finger slid further east across the map to the Dartford Salt Marshes. The more I looked at the blank area on the map criss-crossed with thin blue lines of streams and drainage ditches, the more it formed in my mind as somewhere exotic and remote.

The *Greater London Atlas* showed a wide red line marking the border of Greater London cutting right across the marshes – the south-eastern frontier of the city. I had no other tangible reason to place Dartford Salt Marshes on my itinerary, it was just a feature on a map and I can't really read maps – they're fairly useless to me as wayfinding aids but I derive so much pleasure from just looking at them, reading them as a pictorial document, a codification of the landscape. Experience has taught me that the reality on the ground is significantly different from the cartographic expression of a place – if that could be captured in a document it would rival the mad living texts of the library at Hogwarts. I felt compelled to go out there.

When I was having my mind blown on the Sir Steve Redgrave Bridge, I'd promised that I'd return to ride the Woolwich Ferry south – this would be the ideal departure point. Working out the route through Abbey Woods with its ruined Lesnes Abbey and around the shoreline at Erith to Crayford Ness took me over the 12-mile point where my post-operative left knee hands in its resignation. I started to experience what I've heard Iain Sinclair call 'range anxiety' – more commonly felt by drivers of electric cars who fear their batteries won't take them to their destination.

The path I plotted took me across commons, through ancient woodland and finally to a windswept tract of marshes on the edge of an industrial zone. It looked so remote on the map, I started to think that I'd be starved of human interaction – even of the few words shared with shopkeepers as I purchased my beer and samosas. I'd just have my own voice for company for at least eight solid hours. It reminded me of the difficulties I experienced travelling alone in Borneo enveloped in the rainforest. In the context of my current odyssey, this walk to the Dartford Salt Marshes had become the equivalent of the journey I took up the Rejang River to stay in an Iban longhouse. It was these fears that spurred me on and made this walk irresistible – this was the kind of challenge I had been after. How many strolls in the city can induce a fear of headhunters and hillbilly hijacks?

In preparation I started reading Henry David Thoreau's *Walden*, a classic of the wilderness-living genre that gave rise to legions of soft-skinned city types heading into the woods to live in a shack by the labour of their own hands. The possibility that it might in some way have inspired Hugh Fearnley-Whittingstall's *River Cottage* TV series of rustic food porn would surely have Thoreau thrashing around in his grave.

I started to find Thoreau too pious and picked up Carlos Castaneda's *The Teachings of Don Juan – A Yaqui Way of*

Knowledge in the Oxfam bookshop on Kentish Town High Road. It's the kind of book you expect to find in the fag end of Camden – no doubt originally purchased in the early 1970s when Castaneda's tales of ancient Mexican Indian wisdom gained by getting whacked on hallucinogenic plants was all the rage. I imagined it at the centre of a weekly discussion group held in a basement flat in Patshull Road, hosted by a sociology teacher at the Polytechnic of North London, where they experimented with jimson weed purchased from a roadside shaman outside the Camden Roundhouse.

My friend and fellow-traveller Nick Papadimitriou, a man steeped in both plant lore and roadside shamanism, once told me that thorn apple plants found on the Thames marshes contain a powerful hallucinogenic toxin in their spiky pods. The eastern flood plains would be the ideal place for an urban mystic to dwell.

In an attempt to engage with a more local form of ancient wisdom I picked up a copy of *The 21 Lessons of Merlin – A Study in Druid Magic and Lore* by Douglas Monroe. I learnt the Rite of Three Rays to potentially perform in Abbey Woods, where the godfather of modern Druidry, William Stukeley, had led the initial excavations of Lesnes Abbey. After passing Stukeley's grave at East Ham I felt that perhaps I owed him some sort of tangible tribute.

Just the thought of doing this walk was becoming a mind-altering experience. I needed to get out there on the road to Erith Pier before I stopped existing as a viable human being and fully transformed into the living cliché of a man not coping with entering his forties. My long, straggly hair was bad enough; if I started talking about tripping and mysticism a vortex could appear at any moment and I would disappear completely into my own rectum.

I left home uncharacteristically early, keen to give myself time to explore Woolwich before pushing on into the wilderness. My nine-year-old son was still slumbering in the top bunk whilst my seven-year-old was immersed in an alternative reality via the Xbox. He barely registers my final preparations as I give him a kiss on the head and he mows down several onrushing zombies with a machine gun.

It took a mere fifteen minutes on the DLR from Stratford to retrace the walk I'd done down to North Woolwich. It's a surreal journey, floating through the air past the giant golden syrup tin of the Tate & Lyle factory at Silvertown, gliding past the moth-balled Pleasure Garden that didn't even make it through the first Olympic fortnight to the Paralympics before it went into admin-istration, and then past cable cars drifting over industrial land between the Millennium Dome and the Excel Centre. The thirty seconds of video that captured this on my compact camera would need a soundtrack borrowed from a dodgy 1980s sci-fi TV series, or the sound of the wind that I once recorded blowing down the neck of a milk bottle on the beach near Tilbury Power Station.

North Woolwich is a windswept relic, left behind by the big-money redevelopments that have swallowed up the surrounding docks. Heavy trucks thunder through, heading for the free ferry service that I'll travel on as a foot passenger. The only other pedes-trians lining up to make the journey are a family. The young boys are excited, asking their mum and gran how long they'll have to wait. All the old accounts I've read of the Woolwich Ferry report that the boats played host to scores of local lads who spent their summer days and weekends travelling back and forth, enjoying the free ride and the passing slideshow of river traffic. The only other moving vessel I see today is the ferry service heading in the opposite direction.

Woolwich Ferry crossing

I could have walked across the river via the Woolwich foot tunnel, or just stayed on the DLR one stop to the Arsenal, but I wanted to make more of my first crossing of the river on these journeys – to savour the passing of the water. The sun reflected off the river as it sloshed against the iron hull. There are coils of rope on deck and other nautical paraphernalia associated with longer boat journeys than this four-minute crossing. There's the smell of diesel, the clanking of metal chains, the view of the pier from the waterline. It's an antiquated experience of what was once the beating heart of London – its river and the docks. It was said that more wealth passed through the docks at Woolwich than anywhere else in the world. Henry VIII chose Woolwich as the site of his royal shipyard, transforming the quiet fishing village that dated back at least as far as Roman times into a maritime stronghold. Henry's colossal *Henry Grace à Dieu* was built at Woolwich and launched in October 1514.

Woolwich was at the heart of England's seafaring empire. The ships of Drake slid into the waters down the slipway here, later followed by Charles I's mighty *Golden Devil*. Elizabethan explorer Sir Martin Frobisher's vessel that set out in search of the Northwest Passage also originated at Woolwich. Frobisher's failure to find the elusive route through to Asia might have had something to do with the fact that the celebrated occultist John Dee had a hand in drawing up the maps for the voyage. I'm glad I ditched the mystics for my inland journey and stuck with the more grounded Ordnance Survey and the Geographers' A–Z Map Company. I can't imagine too many chickens were slaughtered and entrails studied in the drawing up of the O/S Explorer 162 map.

The landing at Woolwich is inauspicious – the gangplank leads straight to a traffic-choked roundabout where you can literally taste the pollution. It feels like there are large, black chunks of carbon monoxide kicked up off the road into my mouth. The art deco splendour of the old Odeon Cinema, designed by the great picture-palace architect and Leytonstone lad George Coles, lends some faded glamour, but not as much as when its graceful curves were highlighted in bright-red neon at night. It feels a long way from the 'fashionable resort' noted in an early 19th-century guidebook.

Thomas Burke was a fan of Woolwich. It was his words that gave me encouragement. In *The Outer Circle* (1921) he wrote:

It does not attract at first sight. One could not love it for itself alone. It possesses no external beauties, no excellencies of line or feature, is tricked in no fair clothing. To love Woolwich one must love one's kind; one must hold an instinct for humanity in its most crude expression – soldiers, sailors, policemen, costers.

*   *   *

I tried to think of this walking down Powis Street processing my reactions. The phrase that particularly struck was 'To love Woolwich one must love one's kind', because initially the High Street seemed to be a bastion of white working-class London. Aside from six months in New Cross Gate, I've spent the rest of my twenty-plus years in London in more cosmopolitan districts north of the river. Although both white and from a working-class background, I felt like an intruder, a foreigner, as if I were noticeably different to the locals. Truth is, until I get a haircut and shave I'm going to stick out in most places beyond a ZZ Top gig.

My 'instinct for humanity' guides me to strike up conversation with a policewoman in Greggs the Bakers. As she loads up with filled baguettes and hot jumbo sausage rolls I enquire about Mortgramit Square. I'd passed the entrance on the way along Powis Street and it seemed as if it were a descent into another world – dark and mysterious. As I took photos, two ashen-faced men with baseball caps pulled down tight over their foreheads slunk off the street and into the square as if they had business to attend to.

At first she wasn't sure where I was talking about, and whilst thinking about it ordered a couple of iced ring doughnuts. Then her colleague said, 'Oh yeah, it's going to be a Morrisons.' 'No, a TK Maxx, I think,' she corrected him and that was it, not the notorious Dickensian crime pit I'd imagined, but the latest retail opportunity on Woolwich's long-established premier shopping street.

I take my Greggs booty and perch on a bench at the end of Beresford Square, which Burke considered to be the centre of Woolwich life. Today it's fairly sedate – there are a few market stalls, bunting laced between the lampposts fluttering in the wind blowing in off the river, most likely placed there to welcome Olympic visitors making their way from the DLR to the shooting at the Royal Artillery Barracks.

Woolwich has the feel of a Medway Town – a Kentish riverside settlement that in reality it was for most of its history. Our contemporary London has swallowed whole chunks of the surrounding counties of Middlesex, Surrey, Essex, Hertfordshire and Kent. With the archaeological evidence of early settlements around Woolwich, the town could lay claim to a heritage older than Roman London. There was perhaps a Woolwich before there was a London, just as there was a Barking and a Brentford before a brick had been laid in the London Wall.

The Royal Arsenal is a further barrier between the Kentish tribes and another London that sits behind the huge cast-iron gates. Aside from being Britain's largest armaments factory, workers from the Arsenal formed one of London's top-flight football clubs, Woolwich Arsenal, now based over in Islington. In the Georgian era the Arsenal sat at the centre of a powerful military complex, with the Woolwich Docks, the Royal Military Academy and the Royal Artillery all clustered around the town.

So strategically important was Woolwich to Britain's defences that it was one of the marked 'vulnerable points' on a secret map prepared by the Ordnance Survey at the time of the General Strike in 1926. These were the places that would be most at risk at a time of civil disturbance. An article in the *London Topographical Record* points out that when a public version of the map was published in 1933, 'all the detail of the land adjoining Royal Arsenal at Woolwich was omitted.'

A novel from 1871, *The Battle of Dorking*, imagines a German invasion of Britain in which the capture of Woolwich is a pivotal event. The London Topographical Record article explains how the German military used a version of the O/S maps for their bombardment of London during the Second World War, filling in the blank spaces around Woolwich and the artillery ranges on

Plumstead Marshes. On the 1960s One-Inch Map that is pinned to my wall at home, the site of the Arsenal is again bleached out into a long, white, formless void as far as Cross Ness Point. The existence of the munitions works and testing ranges, unavoidable on the ground, is again deleted from the cartographic record.

During the riots of August 2011 it took just a relatively small crowd of civilians to capture Woolwich town centre as they over-ran a flimsy vanguard of riot police, not with state-of-the-art weaponry, but by hurling bins, bottles and traffic cones. Wool-wich was annexed not by the Germans but by the local malcon-tents. Whilst elsewhere in London that night, camera crews and media outlets almost equalled rioters in number, down in Wool-wich the primary record of the events was taken by a couple of startled onlookers filming with a consumer device from a rooftop. On the YouTube footage you can hear their commentary: 'Holy fucking Christ, are you kidding me? ... They need back-up,' they say as the crowd advance upon the retreating coppers.

The Arsenal may have played its own small part in that out-break of civil insurrection. The munitions factory and the docks, in the words of the developer, have been 'tastefully' converted into a 'riverside development spanning 76 acres'. The site built by convict labourers imprisoned on hellish prison hulks moored on the river now offers up one-bed flats for sale from £180,000. The smallest apartments are let for upwards of £775 per month. It's a world away from the forlorn people I saw trudging along Powis Street.

Royal Arsenal Residential suggests its inhabitants hop aboard a special Thames Clipper service from a private jetty to London Bridge, avoiding any contact with the natives. With its own transport links and shops it becomes a colony of city workers, holding on to the Woolwich Reach with a large iron gate to keep the South London hordes at bay.

I saunter through the gate unopposed. The Greenwich Heritage Centre has an exhibition dedicated to Eltham boy Bob Hope – 'England was the scene of my greatest performance … I was born here.' A tank from the Royal Artillery Museum is parked on the gravel path, its barrel pointed ominously in the direction of Wellington Street where the rioters put the Great Harry pub to the torch. It is eerily quiet, like a large-scale version of the model village at Bekonscot where I went for my very first school trip in the summer of 1976.

I could spend hours exploring Woolwich; Thomas Burke would probably grab a pub lunch and then an afternoon movie before getting the ferry back across the river. But I'm not quite louche enough for that. I'm also not in the mood for a heritage trip to the Royal Artillery Barracks and the Woolwich Rotunda. This is a break for the border. I'm striking out for the wilderness and the 'promising uplands' that rise above the Thanet Sands.

Moving up along Plumstead Road my momentum is broken by the covered market. There's been a market on the site since the 1600s – the poor forgotten cousin of the more famous Covent Garden. Thursday is early closing, which probably accounts for the lack of activity. It must be a hard life grinding a living out of the stalls here. The Gurkha Café has a few punters supping tea on its outside tables. I do circuits, soaking in the atmosphere: the narrow ways between units, the coloured lettering all around, pulsing reggae music bouncing back off the glass ceiling. There are echoes of Grand Central Market in Los Angeles that provided the inspiration for scenes in Ridley Scott's sci-fi classic *Blade Runner*. A mash-up of ethnic influences coming together into a hybrid street culture, a Himalayan-Afro-Caribbean-Indian-Jutish cocktail.

I was zooming in with my pocket camera on a flashing neon 'Jesus Is Lord' window sign when a lady suddenly emerged from inside the shop to confront me. 'What you taking a photo of?' she challenges.

'Your sign – it's interesting.'

'It's for sale if you're so interested.' A fair point.

I explained the walk and how lugging a flashing multicoloured messiah sign round Crayford Ness might not be such a great idea. I would cease to be a topographical rambler and become a neon evangelical come to convert the heathen marsh people. Instead, she unpacked various brightly dyed African suits for me to try on. 'Well, not really my style.' I gesture to my dark-navy garb. 'Bit bright for me. But I'll tell everyone what a great shop you have,' I say as I back out of her emporium, and she grumpily packs the clothes away.

The Woolwich section of Plumstead Road is a strip of paint-peeled shop fronts offering a smorgasbord of phone cards. Hidden behind torn fly-posters for R&B acts and chipboard-covered windows is a slowly crumbling Georgian house. Perhaps it isn't Georgian, I'm no Nikolaus Pevsner, a man who spent his life logging the architecture of England county by county, town by town, but it's old. Buddleia sprouts from the roof and the side wall. A plastic bread crate is propped up beneath the parlour window as if fresh from that morning's delivery. There's an ornate lintel above the front door with an intricately carved woman's head. The dereliction casts a serene expression across her face.

It's rare to see a house with this heritage in London being left to rot in plain view of the voracious development at the Royal Arsenal over the road. Two miles further east in Greenwich, a restored house like this would fetch a tidy sum the fat side of half a million. Here it represents a prime poster spot.

Crumbling house on Plumstead Road

The military and royal connections of Woolwich brought many worthies to the area. General Gordon of Khartoum lived in the town, as did the Cavalier poet Richard Lovelace, whilst Samuel Pepys saw out the Great Plague here. Perhaps this house suffered the fate of being the home of someone who failed to carve their name in the history books. The face above the door and detail around the windows seem to be inviting investigation, teasing the passer-by with the narratives contained inside.

An email to the Greenwich Heritage Centre elicited the facts that the 1871 Census recorded engineering surveyor John McDougall, his wife Christiana and their eight children living in the house. Eleanor Kemp and her husband, Frederick Isaac Kemp, lived in the house with their two children at the time of the 1891 Census and were still there twenty years later in 1911. The heritage officer points out that the 1901 Census and the street directory also show 'Harry Mortimer Wise, surgeon and medical officer for the Plumstead and District Woolwich Union' living in the house with his wife Flora and a servant.

It was a busy family home with the ebb and flow of marriages, first steps, celebrations, arguments, illnesses, quiet Sunday afternoons and departures. It survived the continuous bombing of the Royal Arsenal throughout the Second World War and the regeneration schemes that followed. Now it stands quietly by, waiting to see what will happen next.

Further along I pass the brilliantly named Plumstead Radical Club painted yellow with its moniker daubed in firebrand red. I can imagine a line of Plumstead Radical Club merchandise, mugs, T-shirts and enamel badges that would do a great trade amongst the hipsters of Brooklyn and Dalston. It was suggested to me by a South London friend that the club was far from radical but he didn't illuminate further.

This is also the entrance to the southern section of the Greenway, the analogue of the raised footpath that I skipped on and off between Stratford and Beckton. Here the terminus of the Southern Outfall Sewer is the mighty Cross Ness Point Sewage Works.

I walked out to Cross Ness one year a few days before Christmas with Nick Papadimitriou. Nick studies sewers with the intensity with which theologians pore over the Old Testament. He reveres the grand sewage treatment works as if they were cathedrals of a lost religion. In Nick's faith system of 'Deep Topography', the Mogden Purification Works on the fringe of West London is Stonehenge.

The night before that walk I perused satellite images of the Cross Ness works on Google Maps. A perfect geometric mat of cylinders sits inside neat squares, with a green-baize border nestled snugly against the southern bank of the Thames at Cross Ness Point. Grass it over and the indentations in the ground would be as mysterious as the Peruvian Nazca Lines.

That was when I had my first sighting of Bostall Woods lining a high, dark ridge above the Plumstead Marshes. It was the monks of Lesnes Abbey just beyond that ridge who first drained the marshes and fought a constant battle against the flood tides of the Thames.

It was a fight they eventually lost in the 1500s when large swathes of Plumstead and Erith were consumed by water. They wallowed under this vast lake until an industrious Italian refugee gained permission from Elizabeth I to drain the land. Giacomo Aconcio managed to drain 600 acres before his death. It remains an inhospitable landscape. The waters returned in 1953 and again submerged the area.

The raised concrete walkways of the Thamesmead Estate that Stanley Kubrick exploited to chilling effect in his cult movie *A Clockwork Orange* were inspired by a desire to protect the living areas from the threat of flood. The architecture of the estate was not so much a recipe for social disintegration as a result of forward thinking. When interviewed about the film by the *New York Times* in 1972, Kubrick talked of how he found London 'in the best sense, the way New York must have been in about 1910', rather than mention the dystopian brutalism that provided such perfect locations for *A Clockwork Orange*.

Jonathan Harvey's teenage gay love story *Beautiful Thing* at least attempted to give the area a new, more benign narrative. But it's the poster image of Malcolm McDowell and his bowler-hatted gang of 'droogs' marching beside the Thamesmead lake that has stuck in popular consciousness.

Thamesmead takes you by surprise from the raised embankment of the path. It's as if a fistful of towers from the Barbican have been picked up and dropped on a conveniently empty patch of land, like a giant has put them down there whilst shuffling around the other city-centre blocks and forgotten to put them back. It appears as a kind of Brutalism-on-Thames, the grey of the concrete perfectly camouflaged against a leaden sky.

That December walk with Nick now feels distant in the mid-August heat. I make my way up Plumstead High Street as it forms a gentle incline following the course of a submerged river, leading into the uplands upon which spread Plumstead Common, Woolwich Common, Bostall Heath, Blackheath and Greenwich Park, forming a seven-mile-long body of heath and woodland. It's a grand geographical formation of open land some 200 feet above the level of the Thames, which can be seen from the northern heights of Highgate and Hampstead on a clear day.

As I lumber on up towards Bostall Woods with dark clouds moving in overhead I see it as one of the natural wonders of London. I catch my breath at a bus stop next to a woman actually using it as a bus stop, and survey the view westwards across Greenwich and the Isle of Dogs to the skyscrapers of the City of London and beyond. The council blocks that skirt the southern edge of the woods must have some of the finest views in London. As the bus approaches, windows dotted with the dark silhouettes of its passengers, you wonder at how different their impression of the city must be with this vista a feature of their daily commute.

Gordon S. Maxwell dedicated a chapter to Lesnes Abbey and the Abbey Woods in his 1927 book *Just Beyond London*. Apparently the ruins should be pronounced 'Le-Nay' Abbey, but that just sounds too French for South London. His vision of this area as 'romantic lands' stands up today even in the exhaust cloud of a No. 99 bus. Maxwell wrote lovingly of the tram journey that he took along the same route up Bostall Hill. It was perhaps Maxwell's description of the 1,000-acre woodland that had prepared me for a wilderness experience on this trek. So I found myself entering the dense Abbey Woods with a tinge of apprehension. I have clearly been a city dweller for too long.

The sound of children playing wafted through the trees, an echo of my own childhood spent building camps in the woods just off the A40. It's not a sound normally associated with South London. A group of boys pass pushing their bikes, with rucksacks of provisions and carrying fishing rods. The scene was more Enid Blyton than Henry David Thoreau, or indeed tabloid scare stories of gangs and feral rioters.

I was attempting to access the woodland spirits and reawaken my pagan instincts when I found myself back on the A206 Woolwich to Erith road buzzing with afternoon traffic. This is not the place to perform the Rite of Three Rays.

Plunging back into the undergrowth I came across the Belvedere Private Clinic discreetly nestled amongst the trees. The clinic not only claims to be 'One of the UK's leading providers of breast surgery for women' but also offers the same service to men. It's perfectly located to frustrate the efforts of telephoto -lens-touting paparazzi hunting for that priceless snap of a post-boob job Z-list celebrity. If a surgeon were to be wandering the grounds taking a fag break between shoving in silicon implants or sucking out unwanted moobs, I could always grab him for a quick second opinion on my liability of a left knee. However, it doesn't look like the kind of place that welcomes loiterers so I push on.

Maxwell tells us that the wood is just a fragment of the great forest of Kent. The stands of hornbeam that line the banks give a sense of scale belying the 217 acres that survive. It starts to rain, the drops sounding out a gentle tapping on the leaf canopy as

I by-pass the chalk pits and fossil beds where you are welcome to dig down into the Eocene epoch in search of prehistoric sharks' teeth.

Maxwell also wrote of a series of deep shafts in the West Wood descending 60 feet to a series of small rooms furnished with wooden furniture and earthenware pottery. He speculated that they are Dene or Dane Holes cut to provide a hiding place from marauding Vikings.

The ruins of Lesnes Abbey emerge through the trees, announced by a further sun shower. A gardener, unperturbed by the rain, strims the grass between the stone foundations. Two children clamber along the top of what remains of the outer wall of the great hall. Beyond them poke the high-rise concrete towers of Thamesmead Estate.

The word 'monk' derives from the Greek *monos* or *monachos* meaning 'solitary' or 'alone'. When Lesnes was established in 1178 it would have provided a secluded location for the few initiates to get in touch with their higher being after they had moved up here from the Augustinian priory in Aldgate.

The abbey had been dedicated to that 'turbulent priest' Thomas à Becket, despite the fact that, or possibly because, he had previously excommunicated its founder, the Norman regent Richard de Lucy. As Archbishop of Canterbury, Becket went on an excommunication binge to the extent that when Henry II muttered words to the effect that Becket had become a pain in the arse and he'd be better off without him, there was a queue of disgruntled, godless Norman knights around Canterbury Cathedral ready to lop the archbishop's head off. The year after his murder the pope made Becket a saint and, as a supporter of the murderous king, de Lucy was required to make amends.

The ruins of Lesnes Abbey

The records show that Lesnes was in a constant state of disrepair and financial disarray. When the Bishop of Rochester visited in 1349 the fabric of the building was 'so destroyed through lack of care that it could not be repaired during the present century or even before the day of judgment'.

Those kids aren't actually allowed to clamber on the walls, but given that they are still standing over 650 years after the Bishop of Rochester's visit it can't do much harm.

Not long after Henry VIII dissolved the monasteries Lesnes was being plundered for its stone. By the 17th century Britain was littered with the ruins of abandoned religious buildings in the way that the fringes of our towns and cities today are adorned with derelict factories. The antiquarian John Weaver toured these sites, recording the 'ancient funeral monuments' and 'their

Founders, and what eminent Persons haue beene in the same interred'. He surveyed Lesnes Abbey in 1631 and noted, 'What numbers of Citizens and others at this very time, go to Lesnes Abbey in Kent, to see some few coffins there lately found in her ruines, wherein are the remaines of such as haue beene there anciently interred.'

Farm labourers digging in the grounds had unearthed a lead-lined coffin:

> the full proportion of a man, in his coate armour cut all in freestone; his sword hanging at his side by a broad belt, vpon which the Flower de luce was engrauen in many places ... the remaines of an ashie drie carkasse, lay enwrapped, whole and vndisioynted, and vpon the head, some haire, or a simile quiddam of haire appeared.

It feels oddly serene to wander over that same ground amongst the footprint of the abbey. I enter the chapter house where de Lucy was buried and try to imagine it with all the monks of the abbey sitting on the stone benches laid into the walls as they gathered to discuss monastic business. There would have been some odd characters shacked up out here in the woods, spending their days gardening and painstakingly copying out vellum-bound manuscripts by hand. What would the monks have made of the Kindle? They'd probably have written it off as a passing fad and gone back to their quills. In the small information centre there is a yellowed display card mentioning the excavations performed by William Stukeley in 1753. He drew floor-plans of the buildings, identifying the uses of the various rooms. He may be better known for leading the Druid revival but his work also included the diligent logging of the relics of antiquity. My desire to pay a Druidic tribute to Stukeley has diminished in the face of the reality of the journey; the solitude high on this plateau that brought the monks here has been slowly eroded as the city has sprawled. I'm sure Stukeley would be satisfied that his labours have resulted in the care with which the site is now tended, and even that it forms an impromptu playground.

From a bench on a raised bank above the ruins I look out to the Essex Hills through my binoculars and also spy the top of a large, white cruise liner docked at Tilbury, slightly obscured by the domed roofs and wind turbines at Cross Ness. The river gracefully curves around the Erith Rands to Crayford Ness and the confluence of the Thames and the Dartford Creek – my destination. That feels a long way from this vantage point. I munch the remainder of a muesli bar that has been pulverized at the bottom of my bag, making it look like something that came out of de Lucy's coffin, and head back up through Abbey Woods.

I manage to miss the tumulus lurking beneath the boughs, a funeral monument so old it makes the abbey seem as modern as Thamesmead. Before I'm able to start jotting down an itinerary of woodland plants a Tudorbethan estate appears at the end of the footpath. The woods are an illusion, the forest of Kent has been felled and it's the land of the suburban semi that now holds sway – that's where the path leads.

Traffic thunders along the Woolwich Road. The Eardley Arms looks inviting on one level, but the salmon-pink-necked fellas in sports casuals swilling down pints in the car park next to the shellfish stall are off-putting. The Belvedere Wet Play in the park opposite is more appealing but there may be some sort of law against a 41-year-old man without his children frolicking in the kids' fountains.

Belvedere – *belle vedere* – my Italian is primitive at best but that translates roughly as 'beautiful view' – presents a vista stretching out across South London. It feels self-contained, a precious secret hiding behind Abbey Woods, desperate to avoid being nominated for one of those property columns aimed at bargain hunters and speculators. The boys clambering across the flat roof of the library sub-branch are doing their bit to keep the Guardianistas at bay. An old man chips golf balls across the climbing frames just to make sure.

With such a tantalizing view opened up there are so many distractions – Nuxley Road heading into Bexley, Lessness Heath a rising bank of heathland – but the push is for Erith.

From the top of Erith Road a panorama presents itself, deserving of the most lush velvet curtains to frame it – a sweep eastwards over Erith to Dartford and the Queen Elizabeth II Bridge, across marshlands and out to sea. There are few places in London where you can inhale the breeze and invoke waves splashing against your face. From the crest of Erith Road in Belvedere the sea feels very much a possibility.

Dropping down the steep tertiary escarpment into Erith you're presented with a cross-section of the geology of the eastern end of the Thames Valley. In 1907 Mrs Arthur G. Bell wrote that in Erith 'the whole life-story of the valley of the Thames can be read backwards.' The road into what Bell described as a 'picturesque settlement' is carved through the layers of rock, soil and gravels where the Thanet Sands meet chalk beds. Alluvial deposits from the Thames sit in layers with pebble and clay. London has been so extensively built upon in the last 150 years that it's easy to lose touch with the very ground beneath our feet. Entering Erith it's unavoidable.

The name 'Erith' apparently means 'ancient haven'. An arcane trackway leads into the town centre, indicating that it was a place of prehistoric settlement. The A2016 road from Plumstead to Erith goes by the romantic name of the Bronze Age Way. An archaeo-logical report from 2007 found evidence of extensive flint work-ing in the area dating from the Mesolithic period. Earlier excavations found grave goods buried by Bronze Age Beaker People – named after their love of drinking beer from distinctive crafted beakers.

The mud flats along the riverbank at low tide have the look of a primordial landscape. A sign warns of the dangers of drowning in the boggy ground. Long, wooden slipways reach out over the allu-vial sludge into the river. The only others taking in the fresh air on the esplanade appear to be direct descendants of the Beaker People, except that they've traded in their clay vessels for alumi-nium cans of super-strength lager. Maybe that's a sign of prog-ress. Bexley Borough Council's idea of progress is the arrival of Morrisons supermarket, boasting on its website that the store draws in people from 'as far away as Maidstone'.

You wouldn't think this was the same place that witnessed two of the most significant moments in the quest for liberty in Eng-land. It was at Erith that the rebellious barons met representatives of King John in the parish church to discuss the terms of Magna Carta in 1215. And one of the inciting incidents of the Peasants' Revolt of 1381 occurred at Erith when Abel Ker led a mob up the hill to Lesnes Abbey, ransacked the buildings and forced the abbot to swear an oath of allegiance.

Erith's transition to a superstore annexe is so complete that the Erith Riverside marked on maps is in fact the name of a shopping centre – without water in sight. In search of the Thameside resort town of the past I end up in a tangle of retail plazas, arterial roads and service lanes. I'd set my destination in Erith as the pier but weighed down by hunger, a creeping fatigue and disorientation I slope into McDonald's for a debrief.

I've seen all the horror videos about the food dished up beneath the Golden Arches, but I'm not here for nutrition. Fast-food outlets are the capitalist equivalent of the Soviet workers' canteen: everything is standardized, utilitarian, affordable – all are welcome. They're great places to press the pause button and take stock – and the tables are usually big enough to spread out a map and sheaves of notes. You can also mutter to yourself without anybody minding.

The lad who takes my order looks like a giant Oompa Loompa with tufts of ginger hair sprouting from beneath his uniform hat. He could easily get cast in an American indie movie set in a 'nowhere town', playing the very role he's filling in real life in Erith. My request as to what exactly an M burger is flummoxes him. He stumbles for an answer.

'It's a … well, a … I don't know how to say it.'

'Is it a burger? Chicken perhaps?'

'Yes, that's it.' He seems relieved that I cracked it. 'Would you like a large?'

'Why not … take that Morgan Spurlock!' This attempt to lighten the mood fails. Perhaps there aren't WANTED posters of the *Super Size Me* director pinned to the noticeboards of every MaccyD's after all.

I take a table by the window near a smartly dressed, canoodling couple. Scrutinizing the maps the right way up it becomes apparent that the road to Erith Pier is just outside the window beyond the glass. I slurp down my fizzy drink, slide the debris of the M meal into the bin, and fret about my carbon footprint and the legacy of the Peasants' Revolt.

Morrisons supermarket and car park (for all those eager consumers drawn in from Maidstone) occupy the site of a Victorian pleasure gardens and hotel. With daily steamers stopping at the grand pier the town enjoyed an all-too-brief status as a chic tourist magnet. The pier that I promenade along may only be a 1950s replacement but it feels like a sojourn from the city that I've left behind.

The camera I've mounted on a compact tripod to film the passing barges must give me an air of authority, as an old lady riding a mobility scooter draws up next to me beside the bench and asks if I know anything about the two large blue and white boats moored alongside the pier. 'I see their lights from my window at night and wondered what they were doing. One has blue lights and the other red, I wonder what the difference is.' She lives by the waterfront and tells me it's such a peaceful area: 'Never heard so much as an argument,' she says, 'wonderful place for children.' Once it's clear that I know nothing about the boats she trundles off.

Intrigued, I lean over the railing to see the Dutch crew of one of the boats having a beer on deck. They tell me that they're collecting sand excavated from the building of the new 'supersewer' at Beckton and ferrying it downriver. They're fed up with the ever-changing schedule, days then nights, then back on days. They're keen to return to Holland but find themselves marooned at Erith Pier awaiting instructions. They join the ranks of people throughout history stranded in the Thames downriver – convicts, sailors, fever sufferers, now Dutch cargo vessels. I wish them well and head for the last stretch of this expedition – the south-eastern frontier at Crayford Ness.

The road out of Erith along Manor Way is dominated by scrapyards and recycling centres. The array of brightly coloured mismatched signage creates a shanty town DIY Piccadilly Circus. 'Pulp Friction', 'Hel's Kitchen', 'Abbey Car Breakers', 'No scrap will be accepted by any person on foot'. From munitions works and prison ships at Woolwich, to sewage works at Cross Ness, through the dumping grounds of Erith and isolation hospitals on the Salt Marshes to the Littlebrook Power Station at Dartford, the unpleasant but necessary elements of the urban infrastructure are shunted downriver. This is the London not so much forgotten as taken for granted, the guilty secret.

The stretch of the Thames from Erith town to Crayford Ness is known as Erith Rands. Nestled in Anchor Bay is the Erith Yacht Club with the tinkling of wires on the boats being carried on the breeze that whips over the long grasses.

Erith Saltings and Anchor Bay

A gravel path cuts across the salt marshes. A heritage plaque informs us that this 'last significant piece of Salt Marsh along the inner Thames Estuary' is now being threatened by rising sea levels. The dark, fossilized trunks of a Neolithic forest, 5,000 years old, poke up through the muddy bank. For over 2,000 years a dense woodland of ash, oak, alder and elm grew along the Thames foreshore till the waters gradually eroded it away.

Looking inland across Crayford Marshes, horses graze amongst the ruins of Second World War anti-aircraft batteries and pill-boxes. They are strange 20th-century cousins of the derelict Abbey of Lesnes on the other side of the escarpment.

There is a familiarity now to solitude in these remote reaches of the city at the final stages of a walk at sunset. The path seems to stretch into nothingness, delivering the wilderness experience I'd sought when first plotting a route across the map in the pub. The workaday world feels far away and London is behind me, beyond the dangerous waters of the headlands at Cross Ness and Tripcock Ness.

The confluence of the Dartford Creek and the Thames forms the boundary of Greater London in my 1970s atlas of the city. At low tide it's little more than a boggy ditch. During the spring tides large barges ferried goods along the creek to the wharfs at Dartford. Today the huge flood barrier standing sentinel over the river looks like a dramatic over-reaction, although the recent £5 million investment is evidence that the threat of flooding remains.

The creek effectively marks both the symbolic and literal end of the journey. This point of conclusion is always a slightly odd experience and makes sense of the cliché that it's the journey that matters not the arrival. Across the creek sit the Dartford Salt Marshes, where the Vickers Vimy that flew from Hounslow Heath to Australia would have been test flown from the Vickers airfields laid out on the rugged grassland. There's the constant crack of

the shotguns of Dartford Clay Pigeon Club near the site of the
Astra Fireworks Factory that provided the pyrotechnics for the
Royal wedding of Charles and Diana. This point is so far from
human habitation that at the end of the 19th century floating
smallpox hospitals were moored here. It feels not just like the
outer reaches of the city but of the earth, with the Queen Elizabeth II Bridge acting as a tether to the rest of the world. The only
sensible thing to do now is to head inland in search of transport
back to the 'other' world.

Howbury Moat

The path that hugs the creek before making a split for Slade
Green is cosseted by steep hedgerows vibrating with birdsong.
A break in this mellifluous green tunnel reveals Howbury Moat,
the remains of a stone manor house originally dating from

around the year 900 surrounded by a wide, green tract of water. It's a place frozen in time, oblivious of the rooftops of the low-rise housing estate bumping up against its 16th-century tithe barn. The writer Roger Deakin started his epic open-water swim across Britain in a moat like this. I play the image in my mind of a wild-haired, middle-aged man 'breast-stroking' his way through the algae. I have a momentary temptation to 'do a Deakin', jump the gate and plunge into the water – would that be a fitting conclusion?

Two ladies rounding the corner of the path interrupt my fantasy as they bid me 'good evening'. The image of the wild swimmer dissolves into the pond weed. I move on along the path till it runs out into the quiet of the suburban streets of Slade Green and the end of this wilderness adventure.

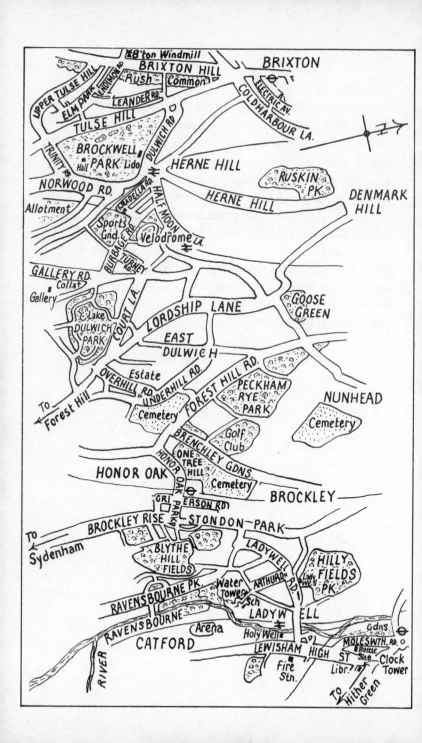

CHAPTER 4

BEYOND THE VELODROME
Lewisham to Tulse Hill

In the Olympic summer of 2012 cyclist Bradley Wiggins was one of the most celebrated people in Britain. He headed into the Olympics off the back of being the first Briton to win the Tour de France. His fame was so great that he relegated David Beckham to a walk-on role in the opening ceremony as he rang the bell that announced the commencement of the Games. It was a moment of pride that would have been keenly felt in a neglected corner of South London.

Wiggins was partly responsible for some of the Olympic spirit seeping through my pre-Games cynicism. Along with nearly seven million other people in the UK I tuned in to watch the road time trial, as interested to see how the streets of suburban south-west London presented themselves to a huge global audience as much as to cheer home another gold medallist. Buried amongst the deluge of praise poured upon the victorious Wiggins, somewhere in the social-media torrent I caught a reference to Herne Hill Velodrome, the cycling venue for the 1948 London Olympics and the place where Wiggins had learnt to race. There were photos of this ragged-looking public track, a world away from the new, multimillion-pound velodrome erected on the site of the old Lea Valley Cycleway. Although I struggled to fully buy into the hoopla taking place on my doorstep, this echo of the 1948 Olympics grew in romantic stature. Herne Hill Velodrome was under threat. Even though cycling was the new rock and roll, one of its seminal venues was being allowed to slowly fade into the past. To have seen Wiggins at Herne Hill would soon acquire the same mythic status as having witnessed Bowie at the Rainbow Theatre or Hendrix at the Marquee.

The question of the route to Herne Hill was easily settled. I had fallen in love with the Docklands Light Railway – the DLR. The affair was sealed on the return from Beckton, sliding through a glorious sunset as if levitating above East London on a magic carpet. Public transport has the ability to inspire strong emotions – mostly in men. Now I had become smitten. The outer limit of the DLR is at Lewisham, a terminus that sounds so distant from the brave new world of Stratford. And another place in London I had never been.

The options from Lewisham to Herne Hill seemed straightforward. Through Ladywell, Honor Oak, skirt Dulwich and into the velodrome for the conclusion of the penultimate race of the season – the Autumn Omnium.

Going out to Herne Hill would also place me within the orbit of Tulse Hill. There is a chapter in *Where London Sleeps* that claimed Tulse Hill had been the birthplace of astrophysics. It was too good to resist. What better way to round off an excursion to a sporting event than with a journey into a baffling area of science? The path seemed easily navigable on both my trusted *Greater London Atlas* and the One-Inch Ordnance Survey map of London pinned to my box-room wall. It would be a trek through a sequence of places completely unknown to me.

The DLR to Lewisham terminates at Loampit Vale at the confluence of the River Ravensbourne and one of its tributaries, the Quaggy. The Light Railway shadows the Ravensbourne from near the point where it empties into the Thames at Deptford. The river carves out the valley where Lewisham lies 'shaped rather like a full-blown rose with the side petals beginning to fall away'. Harry Williams's romantic description laid down in 1949 is not immediately apparent in the shadow of the vast new Renaissance development that dominates the approach. Whilst Renaissance promises to 'deliver an exciting future for Lewisham', the name of the suburb points to an ancient past. In his history of Lewisham, John Coulter speculates that the settlement was first established by a Jutish warrior named Lëof or Lëof-suna – which more or less means 'home of the dear son'. By AD 918 it had taken on the more recognizable form of 'Lieuesham' when Alfred the Great's daughter Elfrida made a gift of the area to the abbots of Ghent. In the 1600s it was phonetically pronounced 'Lusame', which is not far off how I imagine it's often spat out in the Wetherspoon's on the High Street.

I'm drawn into the centre of 'South East London's biggest shopping centre' by the bright hand-painted sign for Lewisham Model Market, lopsided yellow lettering on a crimson background, precariously hanging above a royal-blue set of doors.

I've been to London's flower markets, fish markets, antiques markets, meat markets (both varieties), old cattle markets, flea markets, craft markets, covered markets and numerous street markets – but never to a model market. The entrance to the Lewisham model market is at the end of Love Lane, a narrow passageway where the fruit vendor tells me the market has been closed for three years. Whilst there was a spirited campaign to save the trendy Columbia Road Flower Market, Lewisham Model Market seems to have died a quiet death.

It's a sedate September Sunday morning with a few early drinkers sucking on fags outside the Wetherspoon's. There's a gentility to the High Street hiding behind the identikit shopfronts – Currys, Primark and Poundworld all mask fine modernist-looking buildings. They seem to be maintaining a stately dignity despite the vandalizing of their façades by cheap chain-store signage. Poundworld took on its 'steel frame construction with stone-clad façade' from another bland high-street regular, Peacocks. Before that it was the flagship site of Chiesmans Department Store, opened in 1921 on the site of the original 1880s drapery shop. The Currys had been a large, elegant Woolworths that seems to have been cut in half over time.

Lewisham town centre suffered the single worst V-1 flying-bomb attack in South London, in July 1944, when 59 people died and 124 were seriously injured. A photo shows the devastation of the explosion, with a whole section of what had been a crowded market flattened. What was left standing was then hit again by the 'post-war blitz' of the 1960s.

Above a shop next to Primark the sounds of a loud, joyous

chorus of evangelical singing backed up by a pulsing rhythm section wafts across the High Street. A one-legged man sitting on a folding stool outside has the look of a fella who's seen it all. Perhaps he was here in August 1977 to witness the Battle of Lewisham.

In the year of the Queen's Silver Jubilee and the release of *White Riot* by the Clash, the National Front marched through Lewisham protected by 3,000 police officers, a quarter of the Metropolitan Police Force. The march was a deliberately provocative gesture in an area with a large black population.

When the National Front were met by an alliance of anti-racism activists, headed by the Socialist Workers Party, the scene quickly descended into a riot on a scale that makes the disturbances of August 2011 seem relatively well mannered. Bricks were handed out from the construction site of the Riverdale Centre that I'd passed on the way into town. The police responded by charging into the crowd in Transit vans and wielding riot shields for the first time on British streets outside Northern Ireland. By the end of the day 214 people had been arrested and 11 policemen hospitalized.

With the tense climate of the late 1970s, its high unemployment and wilting national pride, some people have compared resisting the racist National Front at Lewisham to the defeat of Oswald Mosley's fascist Blackshirts at the Battle of Cable Street in 1936. But whereas Cable Street has entered into the folklore of London, the Battle of Lewisham has largely been forgotten.

Lewisham was only meant to be the start point for my trek to Herne Hill and yet I'd managed to get bogged down in its beguiling architecture and social history. Although tempted to find where the brilliantly named Quaggy River ran through the town along a concrete channel, I needed to return to the Ravensbourne to find my bearings and get back on course.

The river leads me into Ladywell Road. On the corner there's an ornate, old carved-stone doorway that appears to open to nowhere, an urban enigma. There's a fine phalanx of Victorian redbrick piles formed by the Coroner's Court (1894) and Ladywell Baths (1884) with its circular tower. The baths were fed by their own spring but it's a different water source that's brought me into the lane – the site of a medieval holy well.

Within the leather-bound spine of *Old London's Spas, Baths and Wells* (1915) Septimus Sunderland M.D. noted that Ladywell 'possessed two springs, one of which was medicinal'. He went on to write that one of the springs was noted as being in existence at the time of Edward IV (1442–83) and was regarded as a holy well. Steve Roud's *London Lore* pointed me towards *The Legendary Lore of the Holy Wells of England* by Robert Charles Hope, published in 1893, which gives a fuller description of the 'holy well'. Hope recounted the story of how 'a poor woman afflicted with a loathsome disease' was recommended by her doctor to use the waters from the well, only because he had given up hope and she lived in the vicinity of the well. The woman was miraculously cured, the reputation of the Lady Well spread and 'The waters were given gratis to all comers.'

The more curious aspect of the story was what happened when they tried to sell the healing waters for profit:

An attempt to enclose the wells with a brick wall, and to give the profits of such monopoly for the 'Poor's use', was frustrated by the Divine hand in a striking manner. The water lost its virtue, 'taste, its odour, and effects', proving that 'in behalf of the Poor (incapacitated to right themselves) God sometimes immediately steps in for their assistance'. The scheme of enclosure was abandoned.

This sacred spot was apparently located where the bridge crossed the railway lines at Ladywell Station. I felt the need to mark this stage of the walk with more than a photograph and a scribbled line in my notebook. Two days before heading south I was wandering through Bloomsbury and passed Treadwell's Bookshop, London's leading purveyor of esoteric texts. They also sell the ingredients for magic spells.

Rummaging amongst the small packets of herbs and dried plants I plucked out lady's mantle, for the obvious name association with Ladywell, and mugwort because it sounds like 'Muggle' from Harry Potter – Treadwell's is like the real-life manifestation of a shop in Diagon Alley. I conferred with the charming lady behind the counter and a serene-looking woman whom I took to be either a witch or a palm reader (she may well have been the plumber but she had a certain glint in her eye).

I explained that the herbs were for a votive offering at a Lady's Holy Well and they nodded their approval – both would be suitable offerings. Lady's mantle is good for the female body. *The Folklore of Plants* tells us that 'Dewdrops gathered from its folded leaves were a highly esteemed beauty lotion.' Mugwort is 'a source of power and protective against thunder and witchcraft'. More useful to a man embarked on a series of walks with an unreliable left knee, William Coles in *The Art of Simpling* (1656) said, 'If a footman take mugwort and put it into his shoes in the morning he may goe forty miles before noon and not be weary'. I only had to cover eight or nine miles before the Autumn Omnium finished at four o'clock.

When I arrived home I proudly presented the 'magic herbs' to my two sons. The elder looked up from a baffling game on the Xbox and declared that I was in danger of turning into a 'hippy wizard'. Maybe he was right. I wasn't so bothered about being labelled a 'wizard'; it was the 'hippy' part that bothered me slightly. I got a haircut the next day.

Approaching Ladywell Station the coast was clear. I took out the small bags and sprinkled some of the contents to the breeze. My votive offering took about a minute to perform. It was hard to conjure up any great sense of ceremonial standing next to an Oyster card reader and a sign warning of a £20 penalty fare for not possessing a valid ticket on the station platform. There was no mention what the fine was for performing unauthorized pagan rituals.

Moving on up the hill that climbs out of the Ravensbourne Valley to Brockley and Hilly Fields I checked my notes to discover that the well had most likely been situated on the other side of the bridge. I momentarily considered going back to repeat the symbolic act of well-worship but thought, with the stiff autumn breeze that was blowing, some of the herbs would have made their way across the railway tracks to the correct location. In any case, I was now standing outside a smart Victorian house that bore a heritage plaque marking it as the site of the other well, a more prosaic medicinal spring.

Septimus Sunderland states that this 'chalybeate' mineral spring was the one that gave its name to the area. I whip out my bags of herbs and make another impromptu offering as two lads poke pizza leaflets through the door. The presence of other people makes me realize that not only could this appear a little strange but the small plastic bags of dried green plants to some eyes could resemble a more commonly consumed herb often rolled up and smoked rather than scattered to the breeze. I slip the mugwort into my running shoes, as recommended by both William Coles and my stoner mates, make sure that the handwritten label on the lady's mantle is visible and shove it to the bottom of my bag. If the frequency of police stop and search in south-east London is as bad as rumoured, I could have some explaining to do. Claiming to be a 'hippy wizard' might not be enough to get me off the hook.

This was the first of several hills that I would climb – although at this point I was blissfully unaware of the fact. I dropped down Arthurdon Road SE4 back into the river valley. A vast redbrick water tower rises from the rows of 1980s council housing. It's a majestic structure that overpowers its original function of servicing St Olave's Union Workhouse. It deserves great romances composed in its honour, bardic verses performed at an annual fayre. On the other hand it's been tastefully converted so that you can rent a one-bed flat for £725 per month.

In 1953 a young poet and activist, Ivan Chtcheglov, writing under the pseudonym of Gilles Ivain, produced an article called 'Formulary for a New Urbanism', in which he put forward this utopian vision: 'Everyone will live in their own cathedral. There will be rooms awakening more vivid fantasies than any drug. There will be houses where it will be impossible not to fall in love. Other houses will prove irresistibly attractive to the benighted traveller.'

This water tower could be seen as the realization of that romantic idea of urban living, not delivered by the French revolutionaries of the Situationist International of which Chtcheglov was a founder member, but by a sharp-eyed property developer. Chtcheglov's notion that architecture should 'play with time and space' seems to have been finally manifested in this quiet South London cul-de-sac.

Aside from the water tower, the institution's administration blocks and dining hall remain. A fella sat on a step smoking a fag outside one of the renovated buildings confirms its origins: '*Oliver Twist*, 'ent it!' he laughs.

St Olave's wasn't an ordinary workhouse but an infirmary for the old, sick and frail – one of the first of its kind, starting a new trend in geriatric care. There is an image from 1900 of the dining hall festooned in wreaths of flowers and lit by chandeliers. It defies the Dickensian and Orwellian image of the dark, hellish work-houses of legend. My nan was born the year Ladywell Infirmary opened – it looks much nicer than the old-people's home she ended up in eighty years later.

St Olave's Union Workhouse's converted water tower

After 'Formulary for a New Urbanism', Chtcheglov continued to propose new theories of how to re-imagine the urban realm, including the increasingly mainstream idea of psychogeography. Perhaps it's fitting that he was committed to an infirmary of sorts, an asylum in Paris. I hope the architecture was as inspiring as the Ladywell Infirmary.

On Ladywell Fields I pick up a yellowed leaf from the Lewisham Elm. The changing of the seasons brings with it a frisson in the atmosphere. A metal plaque next to the tree accords it the status of 'One of the Great Trees of London', a survivor of the Dutch elm disease that wiped out over twenty million trees in the UK. If you think of the image of a classical English landscape, a painting by Constable or Turner for example, the elm is there as surely as the rolling green hills and the spire of the village church. It was one of the enduring symbols of 'this green and pleasant land'. The decimation of the native elm was such a loss that it would be as if everybody suddenly stopped saying 'Mustn't grumble' or every curry house and kebab shop disappeared overnight. Luckily, this totemic emblem of England lives on in Lewisham.

From the trees lining the riverbank hang large mobiles made from plastic bottles that appear like gifts to the great Trash God that rules our cities. They form part of a performance piece that will take place in the park that evening, with music, lights and film projections powered by the waters of the Ravensbourne.

Across a patch of waste-ground I catch a view of the Catford Stadium sign. Greyhounds haven't raced at Catford since 2003. The 1930s buildings were gutted by a 'suspicious' fire two years later. The idea of a dog track in Catford almost sounds like a joke – a quip, a one-liner come to life. Say Catford Dogs quickly enough and it sounds like Cats 'n' Dogs. The large, rounded yellow letters of the sign keep alive memories of a track that was regarded as one of Britain's great sporting venues. In its pre-1960s heyday Catford drew big crowds, celebrities presented trophies, the legendary greyhound Mick the Miller raced here, and overfeeding and doping scams took place. Ultimately, Catford suffered from its lack of 'facilities to attract corporate clients, such as air conditioning and waitress services', the BBC reported at the time of its closure. Now only three of London's thirty-three greyhound tracks remain in operation.

As I climb out of the Ravensbourne Valley a boy sitting on a skateboard shoots downhill past me at great speed. The steep incline heads into Montacute Road. This could be crudely read as meaning 'Mont – acute' or steep hill, but more likely derives its name from Sir William Montacute, a founder of the Chivalric Order of the Garter, who was granted the land in the early 1300s. An alleyway leads between houses into Blythe Hill Fields with its incredible views northwards to the City, book-ended by the twin clusters of towers around Canary Wharf and the Gherkin. The vista stretches south over the rooftops from Penge to Croydon. The benches seem to be struggling with gravity and all decline wildly at one end, the kind of feature that would have tickled the Goonish comic mind of Spike Milligan, who lived at the bottom of the hill as a teenager.

Excavations in the back gardens of houses in Blythe Hill Lane revealed sections of the Roman road that led from London to Lewes in Sussex. The road branched off from Watling Street near Peckham and went straight across the top of the hill to the North Downs and the Weald of Kent. Sitting in the shade of a large ash tree I attempt to imagine the view the Roman engineers would have had when they stood atop this hill nearly 2,000 years ago.

The view north from Blythe Hill Fields

Scanning along the route of the Lewes Way is to look across a carpet of tree canopies dotted with patches of brown rooftops. It appears as a lush plain, irrigated from Catford through Sydenham to Beckenham by the River Pool, a tributary of the Ravensbourne. There are only a handful of other people in the fields to share the view, whereas over the river you'd be hard pushed to get across Primrose Hill without being garrotted by a stray kite or knocked over by a cavalcade of roller-bladers.

Leading off Blythe Hill sits Gabriel Street, where I stop outside the house in which Spike Milligan lived when he first returned from India with his parents in 1933. Milligan's manic comic genius still permeates through the strata of contemporary British comedy. Milligan and his *Goon Show* cohorts paved the way for a whole new comedic language – irreverent, surreal, quirky and mad. It was born here, in these unassuming streets.

Spike's early performances were at the Lewisham Hippodrome and Ladywell Baths. Various biographers have analysed how, having grown up in colonial India, the culture shock of 1930s Lewisham undoubtedly had a profound influence on his later work. The intense heat, colour, smells and vibrancy of the sub-continent were replaced by smog, tripe, Woolworths and races at Ladywell track.

The names of London suburbs punctuate Milligan's work as laughter points. In one monologue a prize in the most boring story of the year competition was a weekend in Neasden. A sketch takes place 'Live from Ruislip Lido', depicted as a muddy pond. The *Goon Show* character Major Bloodnok had a cottage on Clapham Common, and Croydon Aerodrome pops up in an episode called 'Wings over Dagenham'. In 1969 Milligan scripted a feature film, *The Bed-Sitting Room*, set in an absurdist post-apocalyptic Britain where the only surviving heir to the British throne lives at number 393A High Street, Leytonstone. He had an A–Z of London gags.

I try to imagine the impact it would have had on the listeners in 1951 Britain as the first *Goon Show* was broadcast on the BBC. Characters such as Harry Secombe's Neddie Seagoon, Spike's Minnie Bannister, Peter Sellers's Hercules Grytpype-Thynne, and Professor Osric Pureheart given voice by Michael Bentine crackled to life through the nation's wireless sets. Prince Charles was tuning in, as were John Lennon, the Pythons and Peter Cook. A small crack was driven across the staid, deferential world of post-war Britain through which the Beatles, Monty Python and the whole alternative comedy movement would emerge. Comedian Eddie Izzard claims that Spike 'changed the face of world comedy'.

There's no blue plaque outside 22 Gabriel Street; there's a blue van instead – Milligan could have made a joke out of that.

Further along the street the borough council *have* erected a plaque to Leslie Paul, 'Author and Founder of the Woodcraft Folk'. Paul started the Woodcraft Folk in 1925 after leaving another youth movement with a name that sounds straight out of an episode of *The Goon Show*. The Kindred of the Kibbo Kift, which Wikipedia tells us is 'archaic Kentish dialect for "proof of great strength"', seems to have been a quasi-pagan, anti-war version of the more militaristic Boy Scouts. They dressed up in Saxon jerkins and hoods, adopted 'Indian-style' names and held Tribal Camps. This wasn't just a bit of fun; its founder, John Hargrave, believed that teaching city-dwellers to embrace the great outdoors would usher in a new era of world peace.

By coincidence, Kibbo Kift wound up the same year as the first *Goon Show* broadcast, which was also the year Leslie Paul published his autobiography *Angry Young Man* – a phrase that would catch on in the 1950s to describe a clutch of writers such as Kingsley Amis, John Osborne and Colin Wilson, who wouldn't have been seen dead singing round a campfire in a jerkin.

As I pass Honor Oak Station I realize that now the race is on if I want to catch the Autumn Omnium, which might not be just the last race of the season but the last at Herne Hill. I need to get my head down and pick up the pace.

Where Honor Oak Park drops down to become Forest Hill Road, a great view opens up that stretches across the London Basin to the northern heights of Hampstead, Highgate and

Muswell Hill. This point by One Tree Hill marks the tip of the Norwood Ridge. It appears on the *Landscape of London* map as a dark smudge running in a slightly diagonal line from South Norwood Hill, standing at 367 feet, rising to Beulah Hill's 387 feet, Westow Hill, Sydenham Hill (390 feet) and Forest Hill.

I now start to see the physical shape of this part of South London, where the built environment appears merely as an uncomfortable rash. Thinking back to the previous walk, I saw the ascent of Bostall Hill and the seven miles of heath and meadowland that stretch along the uplands from Greenwich Park to Lessness Heath. The geology of that escarpment was laid bare as it descends to the Thames at Erith. And here was the Norwood Ridge, with the valleys of the Ravensbourne and Wandle-Effra on either side. It appears as such a landscape of peaks and valleys that I should have been accompanied by a Sherpa and a St Bernard.

Next I traverse into the territory of another series of hills that circles Dulwich. A 1920s essay by Alan Ivimey stated that Dulwich residents claimed it was 'surrounded, like Rome, by seven hills' – by my estimation Herne Hill, Tulse Hill, Brixton Hill, Knights Hill, Streatham Hill, Dawson's Hill and Dog Kennel Hill, with the peaks of the Norwood Ridge. Absorbing this is a grounding experience, standing before the shapely contours of Mother London.

One Tree Hill may form some kind of orifice in the landscape as a large posse of ramblers are disgorged from the Green Chain Walk on to the road, guided by a ruddy-cheeked walk leader. I want to implore them to break free – liberate themselves from the bondage of the led walk and go solo – but they are moving at such a rate that it is difficult to keep up. At that pace I could well invoke the wrath of my pugnacious left knee, forcing it to cramp up and send me on a tailspin headfirst into a lamppost, the ramblers guffawing in hubristic glee at the fate of the lone wayfarer. We hit Camberwell Old Cemetery at the same time after they are held up at a crossing by a stalled Smart car – I slip through the gate before them, sure that they will stop to admire the elaborately carved Victorian headstones whilst I now have about half an hour to get to the velodrome.

The path splits – I go to the right and they go to left, having heritage soundbites barked at them from the front of the party. My aim of reaching Herne Hill before the end of the race is substituted for getting to the cemetery exit before this Panzer division of gadabouts. In the zombie movie version of this scene they would get picked off one by one by the undead rising from the graves whilst I somehow emerge the sole survivor. However, they reach the gate before me, with the added humiliation that I have to stand to one side to allow the tired tail end to pass through.

It was a good time to slope into the corner shop and grab the customary vegetable samosa.

There were more hills and views to admire, river valleys carved out by unnamed tributaries. Dawson's Heights Estate zigzags off the peak of Dawson's Hill, sailing away into the clouds. Designed by architect Kate Macintosh when she was just twenty-six, English Heritage claims it 'possesses evocative associations with ancient cities and Italian Hill Towns' – an appropriate adornment for one of Dulwich's Roman hills. A Roman fort did stand on Dawson's Hill, which is also said to be the site of an Iron Age burial mound. The building of the estate revealed the remains of a temple dedicated to the worship of the Egyptian goddess Isis. I attempt to absorb energy from the ley line the Dawson's Hill Trust says runs through the London Clay but all I can feel is the chafing from the bag of mugwort in my trainers.

Dawson's Heights Estate

Dropping down into Lordship Lane I was tempted to take a detour to the Grove Tavern, which became famous in the 18th century for the waters that came from a spring in its grounds as Dulwich Wells took its turn to serve as a popular day trip for City weekenders. This time I could make a less exotic offering than my failed paganism in Ladywell and partake the medicinal waters served up in a frothy pint glass (Sunderland reports that it took five half-pints of the 'sulphurous'-smelling waters to experience their full 'purging properties'). But I owe it to Bradley Wiggins to make it to the velodrome on time. If he can win the Tour de France and four Olympic gold medals, surely I can get from Lewisham to Herne Hill before four o'clock on a Sunday afternoon.

I scoot past Dulwich Park, where a wedding party were having their photos taken with the newly fallen leaves blowing around the billowing bridal gown. Then through Dulwich Village at speed, ignoring points of interest I'd noted from Gordon S. Maxwell's 1927 account of the area, and turn into a long street where bank managers and dentists mow the lawns of their imposing double-fronted abodes.

For such a seminal sporting venue the entrance to Herne Hill Velodrome is nondescript to say the least. It sits at the end of a long drive off the sedate Burbage Road. It's 3.30 p.m. and the climax of the Autumn Omnium is about to begin. During the 2012 Olympics the new £93 million velodrome over in Leyton was the hottest ticket at the Games – it was the place to be as the stars of the British cycling team won seven gold medals. Riding on that wave of hype and hysteria I fully expected a big turnout today.

Instead, there's a scattering of people dotted along the two blocks of scooped plastic seats, no more than fifty in total. The cyclists wander along the edge of the track, a mixture of serious-looking competitors and youngsters. As soon as the starting gun for the last race goes off someone says, 'Fire up the barbie, there's plenty of sausages.' There's a family vibe, warm and convivial, what sport ought to be, and this isn't village cricket in the shires, it's one of the last major races of the season – a national event.

I wander the edge as the cyclists zip round the curved banks of the track. Watching archive clips of races from the 1920s and 30s the crowds were ten deep where I now walk alone. The annual Good Friday event regularly drew attendances of over 10,000 spectators to watch international stars such as W. J. Bailey and Lucien Faucheux.

The cyclists buzz round for another lap. The leading group are well-honed racers with legs like tree trunks, but the rest of the field includes teenagers, young women and an old white-haired fella bringing up the rear. 'It's amazing what speeds these cycling demons can reach as they pass and re-pass in a ding-dong struggle that's fascinating to watch,' goes the Pathé newsreel commentary from the 1938 ten-mile tandem race. It applies just the same seventy-four years later.

The tea lady, Jan, draws up beside me, pushing her granddaughter in a pram. Jan is a Herne Hill institution; she's been doing the teas for years, now serving them from a pop-up gazebo. During the Olympics she was sought out by news crews for anecdotes of the young Bradley Wiggins's exploits at Herne Hill. Her son-in-law is racing today; as a teenager he raced against Wiggins on this track and even beat him on occasion. She tells me it's quiet today to what it normally is. The Olympic effect, she tells me, can best be seen at the packed Saturday-morning open sessions, with even pensioners rocking up to get in on the action.

Herne Hill Velodrome's 'Save the Velodrome' badge

The future of the track now seems to be secure with a new lease, but the buildings from the 1948 Olympics stand crumbling and condemned, out of use. These were the only permanent structures that the IOC asked to be built for the 'Austerity Games'. As I admire the brickwork on the original seating Jan tells me that until last year one of the judges from the 1948 Games used to still come and act as a judge at every race, right up to the age of ninety-five. That is part of the spirit that keeps this place alive.

There is a crash on the track. One rider spins off the steep bank, taking out the cyclist directly behind. First-aiders dash across the grass centre yelling, 'Stay on the ground, stay on the ground!' Jan says she saw a twenty-bike pile-up once. With the race abandoned I tell Jan that I'm going to make a dash to catch the last admission at the Dulwich Picture Gallery. 'Hang on,' she says and grabs her husband, who hands me a 'Save the Velodrome' badge. I proudly pin it to my jumper and head back out on to Burbage Road.

I arrive through the side entrance of Sir John Soane's elaborate pile dead on the time of last admission. The staff are friendly and amused by my indifference to how little time I'll have to explore the gallery's impressive collection of Old Masters. Looking into the first series of rooms the image that comes to mind is the scene from Jean-Luc Godard's 1964 film *Bande à part*, in which the young and feckless characters attempt to break the world record for racing through the Louvre from one end to the other. They narrowly fail with their time of 9 minutes and 43 seconds. Taking my first real rest of the day on one of the plush sofas at the end of the gallery I roughly calculate that you could rush through this mini Louvre in under a minute.

Dulwich is Britain's oldest dedicated gallery, twenty-four years older than the National. Gordon S. Maxwell wrote that Turner was a frequent visitor and that the lauded Victorian art critic John Ruskin used to walk to the gallery from his home at Herne Hill to scrutinize the Old Masters and then tear into them through his critiques. It was through these walks to Dulwich, mulling over his writing as he went, that Ruskin paved the way for the Pre-Raphaelite movement. Maxwell also reported how the poetry of Browning was inspired by the pictures here and quotes a letter by George Eliot describing a day out at the picture gallery.

A cluster of paintings catch my eye and draw me away from the seat. I'm short-sighted so all I had really seen were blurred outlines and colours. First is Vernet's *Italian Landscape*, then *Jacob with Laban* by Claude Lorrain – both depicting hilly landscapes and river valleys redolent of the terrain I'd walked through on the way. Tom Lubbock, writing in the *Independent*, described Lorrain's painting as 'an idealised vision of the Roman Campagna', the land centred on the seven hills, just like Dulwich (although I'm sure Dulwich has more than seven hills).

Taking Banksy's advice to 'Exit Through the Gift Shop', I pick up a copy of *An Illustrated Map of Remarkable Trees in Dulwich*, 'compiled by the Tree Committee of the Dulwich Society and illustrated by Rosemary Lindsay'. It says a lot about Dulwich that a) it has a society; b) that society has a Tree Committee; and also c) that the Tree Committee has produced this brilliantly hand-drawn scale map detailing the English and botanical names of Dulwich trees. The list runs alphabetically from alder to wingnut via honey locust, mimosa and privet (Chinese).

Perusing the map laid on the gallery lawn, the music from Lambeth Country Show (an oxymoron if uttered any time in the last 160-odd years) drifts over the loquat and magnolia trees in Brockwell Park. It's been a day of catching endings so I decide to mop up the end of the fair.

My path ascending Herne Hill shadows the course of the submerged River Effra. Winterbrook Road that adjoins the arced strip of Victorian shops on Half Moon Lane possibly hints at one of the tributaries that would have run off the high ground into the river. In his definitive book *The Lost Rivers of London*, Nicholas Barton describes the course the Effra took at this point: 'Crossing under the main road near Herne Hill station, it ran along the north-east side of the park of Brockwell House' on its way to the Thames at Vauxhall. Barton lists fourteen 'lost rivers' and a further five 'dubious lost rivers', including the famous River Fleet, the Earl's Sluice, the Neckinger, Counter's Creek, the Walbrook, the Tyburn, Westbourne, Stamford Brook, Falcon Brook, streams at Wapping and Rotherhithe, Hackney Brook and the Black Ditch.

Along Half Moon Lane and through the gates of Brockwell Park I'm swimming against the tide of revellers leaving the Lambeth Country Show, face-painted children and cider-smelling adults tethered by balloons.

What is left in Brockwell Park at the end of the weekend festivities are the die-hards, those not wanting to let go of South London's premier event of the year. It's a fluid mass of Crusties, Rastas, green-wellied Clapham Sloanes, dads with one kid on their shoulders and another in a papoose – the whole London melting pot spilled out onto the grass. The music is an Afro-folk-dub hybrid that would struggle to survive beyond the park gates. In the spirit of the rural country fair there are tents for various homemade concoctions and home-grown produce, and prizes are awarded for monster marrows and colossal courgettes cultivated in Lambeth backyards and allotments. If I'd been here earlier I could have carried away organic jams from Camberwell, artisan breads from Stockwell and craft beers brewed in Brixton. It is a peculiar ritual recalling the rustic past of these lush uplands. The red faces and flailing arms around the live stage and the beer tent indicate that it has clearly struck a chord with the locals.

I'd originally planned to pack a swimming costume for this

walk – to take a dip in Brockwell Lido. It looks like a glamorous bathing spot on friends' Facebook pictures, an urban beach. Late one night in the mid-1990s the BBC broadcast a fantastic documentary about the lido; it seemed so exotic, like a rare treasure. Opened in 1937, relatively close to the open-air pool at Tooting Bec, it was based on the design of the lido at London Fields. Given the climate, it's a great endorsement of the stoicism of Londoners that there are any open-air swimming baths in the city at all. By all accounts, Brockwell Lido is thriving and as fashionable today as the Dulwich Springs were in the 19th century.

Leaving the festival stragglers behind I head out of the park towards Tulse Hill in search of the curious story recounted in *Where London Sleeps* of a Victorian observatory. Walter Bell described the private observatory built by William Huggins on Upper Tulse Hill, from where he pioneered the new science of astrophysics in the mid-1800s. From his house Huggins used the latest spectroscope technology to 'solve the riddle of the stars'. The Mars Rover pootling around the Red Planet as I scan the house numbers might not have been able to reach Mars without Huggins's discoveries about the chemical composition of the stars and their movements in relation to the earth.

No. 90 Upper Tulse Hill, possibly one of the most significant addresses in British science, is now part of a long terrace of 1980s council houses. I scan the clouds to look into the same skies from which Huggins drew his groundbreaking discoveries. It's an inauspicious spot, not even the highest point in the area. It's difficult to imagine Professor Brian Cox standing here delivering one of his breathy pieces to camera as he popularizes for a mass TV audience the science Huggins helped open up.

I sit down on a low wall and consider this as the conclusion to the walk. Back over at the velodrome the BBQ would be in full swing and hopefully the riders involved in the crash are back up on their feet and chomping into a burger. In Ladywell Fields the flowing waters of the Ravensbourne will be just starting to power the lights, projections and music as the festivities begin. Up in the heavens stars drift into alignment above Tulse Hill.

From Tulse Hill I follow the course of a tributary that according to Barton flowed along Leander Road into the Effra. A few turns and I find myself on Brixton Hill opposite the notorious prison built in the 1850s for female convicts sentenced to transportation. You know you're in Brixton when a woman casually walks past you with a blue carrier bag on her head. There's a tangible increase of energy as you approach the centre of Brixton – it closes in from all sides. I imagine a young Vincent van Gogh wandering this way when he lived in Hackford Road, SW9 – no wonder he want mad. The young Dutchman fell in love with his landlady's daughter, Ursula, who didn't return his affections, so it would have been a forlorn Van Gogh moping round Brixton for some of those formative years. When working at a school in Isleworth in 1875 he wrote letters to his brother Theo describing walks he took into the suburbs and long strolls to the City beside hedges of hawthorn and blackberry, noting the frequency of elm trees.

The traffic on Brixton Hill congests and congeals, sirens squeal as police cars snake through the fractured lines of vehicles. It's a rude awakening after seven hours of hill walking. But by now I can't seem to stop. In the end the walking becomes compulsive. Cresting Brixton Hill I'm still not completely sure where to terminate this schlep – the shimmering image of the Shard at London Bridge sitting perfectly in alignment with Brixton Road looks appealing. That is until I pass Electric Avenue.

'Electric Avenue' was a hit in 1982 by Eddy Grant – 'We're gonna rock down to Electric Avenue' (that's off the top of my head after thirty years). The song is apparently about the riots of 1981 that put the area on the front pages and to this day still define Brixton in the minds of the general public. When I worked in a small gallery on Brixton Station Road, local author Alex Wheatle did a memorable reading from his novel *East of Acre Lane*. The book tells the back story of the events leading up to the riots from the perspective of a group of young black men finding their way in the world. The central character, Biscuit, is in the market on Electric Avenue looking for his girlfriend when the call to action goes up and the trouble kicks off.

> Biscuit, who was in Electric Avenue looking for Denise, heard the commotion. He ran to see what was happening and couldn't believe his eyes as he reached Coldharbour Lane. Youths were hurling missiles at the police vehicles that were rushing to the scene. A car driven by a black man with a youth in the passenger seat, his T-shirt reddened, almost ran Biscuit over. 'Bloodfire!' he gasped. 'Revolution ah start.'

Brixton Market in full swing on a Saturday is one of the great sights of London and deserves to be the real reason for the area's fame. The fishmongers, butchers, fruit and veg traders, the noise, the banter and the bustle. And the arcades. Thank God they saved the Brixton Arcades from the brief threat of being turned into Xeroxed malls.

The influential German theorist Walter Benjamin created his seminal work, *The Arcades Project*, whiling away the hours in the covered precincts of early 20th-century Paris. The Brixton Arcades, in conjunction with the market, are every bit as beguiling and worthy of eulogy.

Market Row, Brixton

Benjamin saw the arcades as being like the portals to the underworld of ancient Greece, 'a land full of inconspicuous places from which dreams arise'. The arcades were 'galleries leading into the city's past' that we pass during the day not realizing

117

the wonders they hold. But then, 'At night ... their denser darkness bursts forth like a threat, and the nocturnal pedestrian hurries past – unless, that is, we have emboldened him to turn into the narrow lane.' In the gloom, as a solitary street cleaner shovels up rotten veg and the fishmongers hose down the pavements, I feel 'emboldened', largely by hunger, to enter one of Brixton's dream-like arcades.

The covered bazaar of Market Row has been jazzed up, made all cool and Hoxton-trendy. Open-fronted eateries play host to well-dressed twenty-somethings. Maybe this is a portal into Brixton's past as a Victorian middle-class enclave. The ackee and saltfish place that I used to go to ten years ago seems to have bitten the dust so I settle down on a self-consciously rickety stool in a tapas joint with a plate of bread and cured meat washed down by a bottle of Alhambra beer served in a fancy fluted glass.

It's difficult for any 'dreams to arise' as Blur's *Parklife* album is throbbing through the speakers. *Parklife* is a great London musical statement from the mid-1990s when London's greasy spoon caffs and greyhound stadiums were being rediscovered by popular culture. The album artwork features photos of Walthamstow Stadium, which, like Catford, has gone to the dogs. It looks as though the Brixton Arcades are still going strong, though, and Herne Hill Velodrome has a few years' reprieve to produce a new crop of Olympic heroes.

The hills of South London are behind me as I trudge through the crowded High Street with touts offering tickets to that night's gig at Brixton Academy. People ask for a pound with great eloquence and narrative aplom; there's none of that 'Can you spare some change?' on Brixton High Street. You get an entire dramatic monologue.

Outside the tube station a man dressed as a leprechaun in a skirt and holding a placard that says 'Jesus Will Soon Come and

Sweep All Politicians from Power' dances a jig in a wide circle. 'The costume and the dancing are just to get attention really,' he tells me. 'Music and dance are powerful things and have no barriers.' He then produces a business card from his emerald-green waistcoat before booting up his stereo for the next performance.

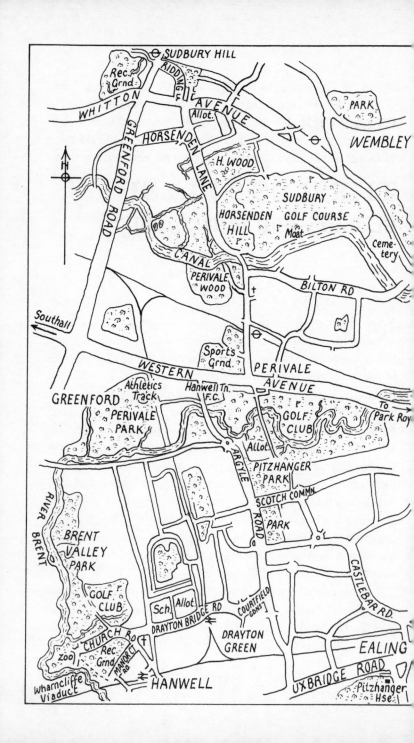

CHAPTER 5

THE 'LOST ELYSIUM'
Sudbury Hill to Hanwell

My regular commute usually started on the westbound Central Line platform at Leytonstone. Whilst waiting to travel the two stops to Stratford I felt teased by the ultimate destinations of the trains spelt out in orange dots on the display board. Ealing Broadway, West Ruislip, North Acton and Northolt urged me to abandon the tyranny of the day job and abscond to wander in the western suburbs, following my nose and being guided by the spirit of adventure. This was often my preferred method of travel; *Lonely Planet* and *Rough Guide*s always seemed intent on negating unscheduled journeys, herding legions of backpackers onto their well-beaten tracks. In my early years in London I would occasionally stand at a bus stop and catch the first bus that came along, or sometimes it would be the fifth bus, and ride it to the end of route. I seemed to send up in Crouch End and Elephant and Castle a disproportionate number of times.

This fantasy of actively getting lost at the end of the Central Line was still nagging me one lunch break rummaging around in Walden Books in Camden. I picked up Walter Jerrold's *Highways and Byways in Middlesex*, published in 1909, with its title

121

stamped into the deep-blue cover in gold Gothic lettering. Somebody once told me Walden was the inspiration for the sitcom *Black Books*. But the owner is a gentle, benign man, as opposed to Dylan Moran's scowling, depressive, dipsomaniac Bernard Black – although the interiors of the two shops are uncannily alike. *Black Books* or not, Walden is a treasure trove of topographical literature.

As I paid for my copy of Jerrold the owner handed me a complimentary pile of the *Transactions of the London and Middlesex Archaeological Society* to pass on to my friend Nick Papadimitriou, who used to work in the shop and spent most of his wages there (Bernard Black was reluctant to sell any books, let alone give them away). Volume 55 features '"Our Lost Elysium" – Rural Middlesex: a pictorial essay' by Michael Hammerson – a compilation of black and white photographs from the early part of the 20th century, a perfect companion to *Highways and Byways*. Knowing Nick would never relinquish any book about his beloved Middlesex I make photocopies of the pictures.

Later in the week, on a cold, wet Sunday night, I wandered up to the Wetherspoon's on Leytonstone High Road with the Jerrold, the photos and an A–Z. This is the pub that mops up the seekers of that last drink of the weekend with its midnight closing; the 'end of the world' feel as last orders approaches is one of the most poignant times of the week. I marked the sites of the photos on the A–Z, then read the corresponding pages in *Highways and Byways*. Mentally, a journey started to come to life. Standing at the bar, waiting for my pint of Terra Firma to settle, the faded pictures, the map and Jerrold's words converge. The anticipation of a walk to join them together becomes tangible.

With the maps, pictures and books spread out across the table, memories return of sitting in hostels planning the next move.

A trek into the Golden Triangle, a near-death motorbike ride on the way to the temple complex at Sukhothai, an overnight coach journey from Mount Bromo along treacherous, winding roads with a driver buzzed out of his skull on tiny bottles of Thai 'energy' drinks. With the *Lonely Planet* next to useless, the word of mouth passed around in hostel dorms and cafés popular with backpackers became essential. This compendium of traveller folklore was scribbled into the margins of the monsoon-stained travel guide. That life is necessarily transitory, a journey that has to end somewhere. Looking around the Wetherspoon's as the final pints are drained by Leytonstone's finest, the backpacker trail took a crazily circuitous route to bring me here.

I was ready to strike out west but had a full week's work to negotiate first before I could escape into the 'lost Elysium' of rural Middlesex. The five days of commutes were put to good use, making notes, finding references, looking for hints and trails, dangling from the orange poles of the Overground from Stratford to Kentish Town West juggling books and sheaves of paper. The excitement of the coming venture built with each day. I forget to scowl at hipsters boarding the train at Hackney Central with their oversized bikes. I endure meetings in which the gabble of bullshit sounds as if it's refracted through cotton wool, but the imagined gurgling of the River Brent through Greenford is crystal clear. I check BBC weather forecasts and tentatively see if I can interest the kids in joining me with references to Saxon burial grounds.

The day before the expedition I decided to abandon the plan to ride the tube to its terminus and randomly drift from there. The photos of the 'lost Elysium' and the sketches in Jerrold fixed my mind on certain locations. There is a rustic scene of a footpath leading from Horsenden Hill to Sudbury Hill Station (1915) – a man and woman in Sunday best and straw boaters stand either side of a five-bar gate staring into the distance, their bikes propped against another gate next to the white post marking the footpath. One is captioned, 'Cross Roads, Western Avenue, Perivale' (1937), showing the intersection of two roads flanked by tall trees, surrounded by muddy fields with the first sproutings of the white buildings that would soon overrun the area. There's a photo looking towards Perivale from Ealing taken in 1904, with Horsenden Hill rising above a landscape without a house or a factory in sight. Place a tower on the top of the hill and it could pass for the famous view of Glastonbury Tor.

Perivale from Ealing in 1904, from '"Our Lost Elysium" – Rural Middlesex: a pictorial essay', by Michael Hammerson, *Transactions of the London and Middlesex Archaeological Society* 55, 2004

Lining the photos up on the map, a course opens up on the page that follows an ancient trackway down through Ealing to Hanwell. A publication celebrating the jubilee of the now defunct

Middlesex County Council in 1939 describes the three Neolithic roads that ran from the crossing of the Thames at Brentford:

> The first ran eastwards through the districts known to-day as Strand-on-the-Green, Chiswick, Fulham and Chelsea to Charing Cross; the second led between Hanwell and Ealing over Horsenden and Sudbury Hills to Brockley Hill at Stanmore, where there was an encampment, and the third went by way of Hanwell and Hayes to the ford across the River Colne at Uxbridge.

*   *   *

It's Remembrance Sunday with brilliant clear blue skies when I find myself at the work-a-day tube platform. I'm heading west for the first time since the walk out to Hounslow Heath in May, when I'd been tempted by a turning to Hanwell off the punishing Great West Road but had, thankfully, resisted. Today, that would be where I'd hope to end up by the early 4.15 sunset to take in the glory of Isambard Kingdom Brunel's Wharncliffe Viaduct.

Clattering north on the Piccadilly Line to Sudbury Hill the tube driver announced that there would be two minutes' silence at 11 a.m., 'unless there is an emergency,' he reassures us. Tube drivers are amongst the great heroes of London, stately guardians of our daily travels. They're up there with late-night shopkeepers who serve after-hours booze and emergency Calpol (the two go well together), and the staff of sandwich bars who seem to remember how many sugars you take if you buy your coffee from them more than once.

The Wembley Arch appears over the rooftops near Alperton before I alight at Sudbury Hill. It's easy to take the architecture of the London Underground for granted. Most of the time you're in a hurry, the ticket machines don't work, you can't find your Oyster card, the carriage is packed and somebody is playing grime remixes through the speaker of their phone. But the stations on this branch of the Piccadilly Line are beautiful enough to induce Stendhal syndrome, the condition suffered by people when they are overwhelmed by the beauty of the art and architecture of a particular place. Sudbury Hill is another modernist jewel created by architect Charles Holden, who also built the University of London's Senate House, famous for its appearance in *Ghostbusters*.

Holden designed over 50 tube stations from the 1920s onwards, including the labyrinthine 'ambulatory' of Piccadilly Circus and the domed Valhalla at Gants Hill that was a tribute to the opulent Moscow Metro. The Royal Institute of British Architects stated that 'it was the largest building programme in the capital shaped by a single architect since Christopher Wren rebuilt the City churches destroyed in the Great Fire of London in 1666.'

Holden built Sudbury Hill in 1931 and according to its English Heritage listing it still sports many of its original features, including the casements around the tall ticket-hall window with its distinctive period roundel with enlarged U and D in UndergrounD. It's in the maligned corners of suburbia that the real architectural gems are hidden, like the early-modernist experimental housing block at Pinner Court and the Bauhaus-influenced Eastcote town centre.

In the early part of the 20th century London Transport actively encouraged commuters to head into Metroland through a series of beautiful underground posters. One from 1912 shows Constable-like chocolate-box scenery of a babbling brook – with overhanging oak and elm trees – winding itself through a lush green pasture with the caption, 'To Snatch Space in Green Pastures and Beside Still Waters Book to Alperton, Sudbury or South Harrow'. The 'New Suburb' of Sudbury Hill itself was advertised in 1916 with the slogan, 'Live Where It Is Only a Step from Your Front Door into the Country', then beneath this the more practical sell: 'Cheap Seasons, Cheap Fares, Cheap Rents, Special Trains for Workers Mornings & Evenings'. And the advert that I have responded to 103 years after it was plastered on District Line platforms: 'Book to Perivale, Sudbury or Harrow for Field-Path Rambles in Old-Fashioned Country'.

London Transport poster

The photos I'd looked at in the *Middlesex Archaeological Journal* date from the same era as the posters so they weren't the kind of over-hyped estate-agent spiel that has tried to rename Holborn 'Mid-Town' or sell Barnet as the new Camden Town. Only a hundred years ago there was open countryside just seven miles west from Marble Arch.

Sir John Betjeman wrote of the 'lost Elysium' in his poem 'Middlesex' in the 1950s. When Walter Jerrold wrote his *Highways and Byways* it was still a place of escape for the people of the crowded, smoggy city. Jerrold saw the coming development of Sudbury, noting the plots marked out for the planned 'garden city'.

The urban planners saw a different kind of Elysium rising from the Middlesex fields. The 'place of perfect happiness' would be an affordable home with a discounted season ticket. How many young couples lured out into the new estates by the swanky ads came to see the tidy rows of streets as the Elysium of Greek mythology, 'the place at the ends of the earth to which heroes were conveyed by the gods after death'.

A narrow, tree-lined lane opposite the station heading away from the parade of shops and semi-detacheds appears to be a trace left behind for those in search of 'Field-Path Rambles in Old-Fashioned Country', which would otherwise seem unlikely in Sudbury Hill at first glance. The lane leads in the direction of Horsenden Hill – could this be a remnant of the Neolithic trackway that led from Brentford to the encampment at Brockley Hill?

Young trees bend over the pavement that takes me on to Ridding Lane Open Space, which occupies a hill with views stretching across West London. A solitary tower block stands in the corner, far removed from the orderly villas of the inter-war expansion into the area. Allen Court has been selected for redevelopment by Ealing Council after the ten-storey block had fallen below the government's 'Decent Homes Standard'. A review showed that residents felt unsafe after dark and harboured 'concerns about drug use and drug dealing'. The block will be demolished and replaced with a mixture of social and private housing – utopia will get a second chance; the view that I capture stretching out behind a tall oak tree deserves it. The architects of the new scheme could look for inspiration in Christine Jackson's 1930 poster for the new suburb of Sudbury Hill, with its elegantly hand-drawn pipe-smoking men in cricket jumpers leaning against shovels as a child rides a scooter past picket fences and old men pushing wheelbarrows. The ideal of an English settlement is not so dissimilar to a Hobbit shire – a place of cosy conviviality and second breakfasts.

1930s 'villadom' is alive and well over the crest of the hill along Sudbury Heights Avenue and down Rosehill Gardens and Melville Avenue into Horsenden Lane North. It's a land of cheery Sunday car polishers who bid me a bright 'good morning'. The commuter-ville imagined by the Electric Underground Railway has survived into the 21st century, still serviced by Charles Holden's sleek modernist stations.

I feel like a tourist from the future with my digital camera, photographing the shadows of bare branches cast across the pebble-dashed row of houses. To a teenager growing up in a post-punk 1980s soundtracked by Wham's 'Club Tropicana' and Duran Duran singing 'Rio' on a yacht, 'pebble-dash' was as terrifying a P-word as prog-rock and peroxide-induced-hair-loss.

Walking down these streets in the new millennium the people of the pebbledash culture perhaps deserve a higher status – a century on from their birth these suburban outliers have come of age. Whilst people were scurrying off in search of the latest up-and-coming area following the blitzkrieg of regeneration schemes, the pebbledash people stood firm. They've placed their faith in an unfashionable mode of living, free of inner-city anxiety and the passing fads of the '*latterati*'. There's not a breezeblock or aluminium balcony in sight – the solid London brickwork is coated with a layer of sand and cement, and embedded with hardy little round stones. Maybe this pebble-dashed nostalgia is another symptom of turning 40, along with spending evenings building Airfix models of Second World War fighter planes and discovering games consoles for the first time.

Preparing for the ascent of Horsenden Hill I pop into Costcutter and optimistically enquire whether they sell takeaway coffee. My hopes are temporarily raised when the bloke thinks I mean 'copy', which we laugh off, and I settle for a banana and a tube of Murray Mints. If I were in serious need of a caffeine hit the Ballot Box Pub is open for business and advertising the freshness of its coffee, but I was raised to think it was an affront to the landlord of a pub not to drink alcohol – and there's a full programme of *Soccer Sunday* about to kick off that would almost certainly waylay me as effectively as the faery folk beneath the hawthorn bushes. The *Geographia Greater London Atlas* from the mid-1950s marks the area around the Ballot Box as Brabsden Green, a name straight out of Trumpton. The pub is all that remains of the village, the other buildings having been demolished after the war.

The wet grass sparkles with large pearls of dew as I climb the northern face of the hill. Two men fly a model aircraft in wide circles high above the rooftops. The summit of Horsenden Hill stands 273 feet high with views across four counties – north-west out to the Chilterns, Hemel Hempstead and Watford; south and west to Windsor Castle, Runnymede and the North Downs. It's a canvas so vast that the built environment is reduced to brown smudges and ridges of red tiles. You get a glimpse into a prehistoric London occluded at street level. There were settlements on Horsenden Hill dating back 7,000 years, and excavations have turned up flint tools and numerous potshards from the Iron Age through to the Romans.

The name is said to mean 'Horsa's Dun' – 'dun' being an Old English word for 'hill', the hill of Horsa, most likely a Saxon warrior and possibly buried within the summit. In *The Chronicles of Greenford Parva* published in 1890, John Allen Brown recounted a Mr Farthing's earlier version of 'A Legend of Horsenden Hill'.

The story goes that Horsa and his wife, a woman who 'was gifted with supernatural powers', had one daughter, Ealine, whose beauty and intelligence were famed throughout the region. For some reason she rejected the advances of all the suitors who came to ask for her hand until she married Bren, the chief of a neighbouring tribe. 'The joining of the hands over the holy stone over the magic circle was performed with great pomp and ceremony according to the rites of Odin, the Saxon Deity, and after a festival of many days' duration, Bren carried home his beauteous prize to his own castle.' So far, so fairy tale.

But the match wasn't a good one. Ealine was bookish and bright, Bren was coarse and crude, and soon he was fooling around with the local women 'whose tastes and sentiments were more in accordance with his own sensual disposition'. Feeling scorned, Ealine dispatched a starling she had taught to speak to carry the news of her faithless husband's philandering to her father. Horsa reacted as any self-respecting Saxon warrior whose daughter had been dishonoured would and promptly raised a fierce army to exact revenge. Bren got news of the impending attack and 'the two armies met and crossed at the ford which has ever since borne his name' – Brentford. In the ensuing battle, 'Bren was slain and Horsa mortally wounded.' He 'died of his wounds and soon after buried with great pomp, along with his arms and favourite war-horse' on the spot that 'has ever since borne his name'.

Ealine and her mother retreated into the forests of the vale, where they continued their learning and were worshipped by some of the local rustic people for their wisdom and knowledge of magic. After living to a grand old age the area where Ealine died was named Ealine's Haven, where today buses to Ealing Broadway terminate at Haven Green.

According to Farthing's story, even into the 19th century local people would try to avoid Horsenden Hill late at night, not because of footpads or highwaymen but because of the sound of Horsa's giant steed that restlessly roamed the land. 'And some go so far to as to affirm they have seen the shadowy form of the dead warrior when the pale moon illumines the hill, and the white mists curl upwards from the vale at its foot.' One morning large, blue-tinted hoof prints of a giant horse were found 'scorched' into the hoar frost, marking a path across a field at Greenford Marsh in the direction of Horsenden Hill. Allen Brown adds the note that it was 'undecided whether the difference of colour was due to the fiery feet of Horsa's steed or to unequal condensation due to causes that may be easily explained'.

The various excavations of Horsenden Hill didn't uncover the remains of Horsa or his mighty steed, just bits of pot and flints. The remains of seven Saxon warriors, however, buried with their spears and wrapped in hemp cloaks still fastened by bronze brooches, were found on Cuckoo Hill, Hanwell. The field where they fell in battle is near a bend in the River Brent and until recently was know as 'Blood Croft'. Did they die in the conflict between Bren and Horsa, and not in a clash with the local British tribes as some accounts claim? The path from Blood Croft to Horsenden Hill would cross Greenford Marsh where the spectral hoof prints were scorched into the frost. That is surely a better yarn than explaining it away as an odd pattern caused by condensation.

It's in the direction of Cuckoo Hill and Greenford that I now need to go if I want to take in the majesty of the Wharncliffe Viaduct at Hanwell in the last of the late-afternoon light. The dark winter evenings have drawn in since my last walk just six weeks ago – the autumn of the omnium has given way to early winter. I need to break the spell of Horsenden Hill with its myths and legends, and start to descend, walking over a carpet of bronze leaves beneath the denuded oak trees.

Any mental flights of fancy are rudely broken by a loud shout of 'Fore' as a Sunday-morning hacker shanks his drive off the tee in the direction of the Hanger Lane gyratory. Fancy building a golf course on a Scheduled Ancient Monument; before you know it there'll be crazy golf at Stonehenge. I turn towards the third tee and incredible views east towards the towers of the City of London and Canary Wharf open up above a green where a golfer sinks a ten-footer and clenches his first in celebration as if he has just won the US Masters.

The path over Horsenden Hill

Avoiding golfers and being chased by untrained dogs I end up walking along an avenue of spindly birch trees and young oaks. Through an alleyway and the distant past melts into more classic suburbia with little of the intervening few thousand years between. I crack open a packet of Cadbury's Snack Biscuits as I casually browse Google Maps on my phone to get my bearings. I nearly choke on a chocolate shortbread square when I see that after over an hour drifting around Horsenden Hill, rather than follow the ancient trackway to Hanwell I've taken a newly laid gravel path straight back to Sudbury.

Modern GPS technology guides me around the base of the golf course and along a narrow footpath ankle deep in mud. The trees form a tunnel overhead and this now feels like a true remnant of the ancient trackway. It wouldn't be much fun to go on a walk and not get lost – I've always thought that was the only reason to plot a route beforehand, so that you can deviate from it and plunge into the unknown.

It wouldn't be the unknown I'd plunge into if I continued to follow the red dot gliding over Google Maps but the Grand Union Canal, making its way slowly from Paddington Basin through Slough to Birmingham. Meeting the canal here prompts a memory of filming the writer Will Self walking along the towpath towards Heathrow with our mutual friend Nick Papadimitriou. I'd been busy trying to stay out of the murky waters as I shuffled backwards endeavouring to keep them both in shot and capture decent audio of their intense riffing, so I couldn't be certain that this was the section of the canal we'd walked along that day in June 2008.

Luckily the event was recorded in Will Self's book *Walking to Hollywood*, where I am played by the former *Happy Days* actor-turned-blockbuster-movie director Ron Howard. In the narrative of the book Will is deeply annoyed by the intrusion of the filming, and paranoid about being captured on camera. The 'Ron-John' character, a 'bat-eared sycophant in a letter jersey making up to Henry Winkler' (that's me all right) hands the Will Self character the camera so he can check he hasn't been filmed. 'When he offered me the camera for my inspection, rather than examining the playback, I simply removed the tape cassette and chucked it in the canal. He trudged away disconsolately over Horsenden Hill …', it says in the book.

I was wearing a 1950s-style red-checked shirt that day and I was called 'Ears' by Whiffy Smith at primary school, so the description is not a total liberty. The tape-tossing into the canal, however, was thankfully a fiction and I didn't 'trudge away disconsolately over Horsenden Hill', but made my way to Perivale Station, where I am again heading but this time with a much smaller camera that fits neatly in my pocket. The idea of a semi-fictional version of myself walking over Horsenden Hill before the real me seems in keeping with the mythology and industrial experimentation of Perivale. It is an eldritch zone, seemingly, with the ability to warp reality. From Horsa's wife's dalliances with fairies among the trees of 'Fairey Vale' in Saxon times to the peculiar glass box transparent car with inflatable plastic seats – the Quaser-Unipower manufactured here in the 1960s – you sense there are uncanny occurrences taking place in these streets and the industrial estates.

It was the perfect location for Sylvester McCoy's Doctor Who to plonk his Tardis down. The seventh Doctor's teenage tearaway sidekick, Ace, was from Perivale and throughout 1989 they kept dropping back in on the 'boring' West London streets that Ace had left to go roaming the solar system in a battered old police box. Ace may have experienced a 'Psychic Circus on Seganox' and licked the Kandyman on Terra Alpha, but back in Perivale she had to contend with a mysterious Victorian mansion called Gabriel Chase that had a Neanderthal butler by the name of Nimrod, and had all her old mates abducted by inter-dimensional Cheetah people who metamorphosed from vicious feral black cats at the local playground. In an echo of the legend of Horsenden Hill, the Doctor finds a strange set of hoof prints running across the hill, prompting another explanation for the phenomenon – neither condensation nor the ghost of a Saxon warhorse but the tracks of shape-shifting, otherworldly, horse-riding bipedal cheetahs. How could anyone say Perivale is 'boring'? Even the fly-tipping is imaginative.

I take a photo of an assorted pile of household goods left on the pavement topped by a single, carefully placed Ugg boot. Artist Bob and Roberta Smith has said that fly-tipping forms a kind of 'unofficial sculpture'. Bob and Roberta has occasionally used these discarded items in his sculptures and paintings, which have then been exhibited in major galleries – including the Tate – completing the journey from the kerbside to the cultural mainstream. However, I think it's doubtful a major British artist will pass by this afternoon to turn this creation into a Turner-nominated installation, so my photo will have to do.

I briefly linger to take in another great modernist statement by London Underground – Perivale Station, a 1938 design by Australian architect Brian Lewis and completed after the war in 1947. Its elegant concave tall-windowed exterior catches the

late-afternoon sun, which also casts long shadows from the traffic bollards. It's a building that suggests great things will happen
once you step into the high-ceilinged ticket hall. You could take
the Central Line east to admire Charles Holden's stations at
Wanstead and Gants Hill.

The station was designed as Perivale underwent the early years
of its transformation from what Allen Brown called 'a rustic,
deeply secluded hamlet', 'almost forgotten', protected by the
River Brent and its habit of flooding. In 1901 the population of
Perivale was just 60. Shortly afterwards came the Great Western
Railway, followed by the A40 road that linked Perivale to what
Professor Peter Hall termed the 'West London Industrial Belt'. By
1951, Hall tells us, over a quarter of a million workers were
employed in this area that stretched from Cricklewood and Colindale down through to Hammersmith, then out further westwards
to Slough and the tiny hamlet of Perivale.

The two old photos of Perivale that I'd examined in the pub
the week before the walk – one looking from Ealing towards
Horsenden Hill taken in 1904 with not a building in sight, the
other of the crossroads of the A40/Western Avenue in 1937 with
the first factories emerging from the fields – mark the points
at which 'Elysium' was lost. 'Parish of enormous hayfields/
Perivale stood all alone' wrote Betjeman in 'Middlesex'. As I
approach the junction of Horsenden Lane and the A40 that
could be the one from the 1937 collodion print, Perivale is certainly not alone but in the company of a herd of stampeding
cars careering between London and Oxford. Rather than enjoying the tranquil countryside of the London Transport posters
you are washed in great waves of sound, of tyres on tarmac and
engine whirr. This wall of white noise serenaded me to sleep at
night with my windows open in the redbrick inter-war council
house of my childhood, 18 miles west down the A40 – almost

exactly half-way between London and Oxford – cosy within its acoustic footprint.

When I was recovering from my knee operation a few years ago, my sleep disrupted by a bad reaction to opiated painkillers, I soothed myself back into a slumber by placing a mattress next to the open windows so I could hear the distant whoosh of the M11 link road. Apparently babies are calmed by white noise because it reminds them of the sound of the womb. My younger son would hug the stereo speakers whenever we put on a My Bloody Valentine CD. I listen to roads.

This dirty old highway was my first real tangible idea of London. As a child I travelled up to Ealing and Hillingdon for cricket matches with my dad, first in his battered old Hillman, followed by a green and then an awful purple Austin Marina (funny how you date your childhood by what car your dad was driving – Hillman mid-70s, green Marina late 70s, purple Marina early–mid-80s). Just after the war, Dad cycled up along this same road from Wooburn Green to Ealing with his friend Podgy Winch to visit an evacuee who'd stayed with Podgy. He had a brand-new three-speed racer bought as a reward for passing his 11-plus, and remembers that he hardly saw any cars the whole way there and back on the forty-mile round trip.

For me, these outer suburbs along the Western Avenue *were* London, the big, scary city with its London Transport bus stops as exotic as the Taj Mahal. When I started at polytechnic in 1989, that glorious puke-stained, feedback-drenched adventure began with a lift from my sister along the A40 in her car stacked with records, a guitar and a few clothes. When we passed over Notting Hill on the Westway with its white, high-fronted houses, my stomach tensed, I felt sick – a small lump in my throat – I was leaving home at eighteen years old. Cathy was playing some god-awful music that stemmed the flow of any authentic emotion and by the time we had emerged across the City on the Whitechapel Road I was raring to go. This road is the beginnings of my London – and also an asphalt umbilical link to the place of my birth.

On this day, any feelings of sentimentality and pangs for Bucks are outweighed by rumblings of hunger. The need for food and the desire to go inside one of London's most iconic buildings could potentially be dealt with simultaneously, now that Wallis, Gilbert and Partners' iconic Hoover factory has found new life as a Tesco superstore. Once again British art deco was sponsored by an American industrial giant, like the architectural gems of the Great West Road. As a kid travelling up from the sticks this was the first real statement that you had arrived in the big city – a vast, white-tiled slab adorned with flags. The angular lines of the pillars around the grid-pattern windows and the lanterns topping the concrete posts of the outer wall looked like Gotham City – it was easy to imagine the silhouette of the Caped Crusader swooping in front of the floodlit façade at night.

The Lloyds Bank opposite is a more understated modernist block, also tiled white with a green ceramic relief in the apex of the roof that looks like the spiky green ears of the young wheat that had once made Perivale famous. Above the main entrance to the Hoover Building next door, in a similar angular pattern, the wheat has ripened to a luminous gold.

However architecturally important the building might be, it is still a Tesco superstore and on Sunday afternoon it looked rammed – not with admirers of 1930s architecture but with all those thousands of people who decide to go to the supermarket an hour or so before the only time in the entire week when it closes early. I can't compete with these people; there's probably a healthy sprinkling of Doomsday Preppers amongst them, stocking up for the imminent government collapse, asteroid collision or zombie apocalypse. I cross the footbridge over the eight lanes of traffic, feeling like Philippe Petit tightrope-walking between the Twin Towers in *Man on Wire*, to the clump of buildings in the lay-by (it's a bit of an exaggeration but I suffer from slight vertigo).

Starvin Marvin's silver bullet 1950s diner seems the perfect eatery to complement the iconic architecture over the road, but it's so busy that even people with babies bawling in hand-held car seats are prepared to queue. The only place left is the Mylett Arms attached to the end of a Premier Inn.

Despite my ravenous hunger there isn't time to order any pub grub if I want to reach the Wharncliff Viaduct in daylight. Instead I settle for a pint of Bombardier in honour of Remembrance Day, and a packet of cheese and onion crisps. At a table with a 'road view' I am tormented by the 'Fayre & Square' menu with its photos of burgers dripping in cheese and bacon, and huge medieval roasts. If I order now that'll be the end – the second half of the Liverpool vs Chelsea match is about to start and the ale is going down very nicely, but another pint would write off the rest of the day. I wait for the alcohol to seep into my legs, then haul myself from the table.

Over the road from the Premier Inn car park a lichen-encrusted lychgate welcomes you to a glimpse of the 'Pure Vale' of legend. In a leaf-strewn alley stands 'The Ancient Church of St Mary the Virgin' that dates back to 1135 when the entire population of the parish could have assembled around a few tables in the Mylett Arms. The 16th-century brilliant-white weatherboard tower is dappled with leaf shadow. It's packed to the door for the Remembrance Day service so I wander into the churchyard to look for some of the tombs mentioned by Jerrold and for the 13th-century lepers' window on the south side of the chancel. A flock of green parakeets swoops noisily from the ash and pine trees over the headstones to Ealing Golf Club. Just as I'm trying to document what I think is a rare bird sighting on my pocket camera the vicar very politely asks if he can pass. I turn to see the entire congregation lined up patiently behind me outside the church; they smile as they pass on their way to lay a wreath at the war memorial.

St Mary the Virgin's, Perivale

Watching them walk through the graveyard makes me think of my grandfather, William Rogers, who fought as a teenager in the First World War, seeing action at the Somme and Vimy Ridge. He died two months after I was born. Following the carnage of the trenches he led a quiet life as a diligent shift foreman at one of the local paper mills, his leisure time spent playing dominos in the Barley Mow across the road and watching Wycombe Wanderers. My dad always says he was a quiet man; no wonder after what he had experienced at such a young age. And here I am yomping through old Middlesex searching for adventure. I reckon he'd be glad: I'm terrible at *Call of Duty*, would have been late for shifts at the mill and never got the hang of dominos – wandering around London is probably the best thing for me.

The scene outside St Mary's churchyard is ridiculously sylvan – a wooden bridge over the winding River Brent where weeping willows droop into the gently trickling waters. It would be nauseating if it weren't counterbalanced by the brutality of the Western Avenue. When Jerrold walked through Perivale, Ealing and Hanger Hill and saw the early signs of the suburban sprawl to come, he would probably have been surprised that this pocket of rurality managed to survive. This was the Middlesex countryside promised in the pages of *Highways and Byways* and advertised on the old London Transport posters. Perhaps Elysium wasn't lost after all; it just fell down the back of the sofa with the TV remote and some loose change.

Walking on past Pitshanger Allotments, the oak leaves glowing in the early rays of sunset, I take an added interest in the various models of homemade sheds on display that have been constructed from mismatched lumps of wood and pallets. I've just finished constructing a kit shed at the bottom of my garden that stretched my DIY skills to such a limit that it had a similar effect as the space race had on computing and dehydrated foods. My shed is a bit mamsy-pamsy compared with these proper working sheds. I have collaged the ceiling of mine with an A–Z bought in a charity shop for 99p – an odd experimental 1990s edition with lurid colours printed on overly glossy paper. It was too distracting as a practical object but as ceiling decoration it looks like a London-lover's Sistine Chapel. I've glued the pages at random on the roof so that Perivale morphs into Falconwood before moving on to Avery Hill and Black Fen, names worthy of any misguided heroic quest.

Thankfully, my path leads further through Ealing across Pitshanger Park and Scotch Common. Arthur Mee explains the name of Pitshanger as deriving from 'hangra, a wooded slope, and pyffel, a kind of hawk', neither of which are apparent as I head onwards down Argyle Road – the kind of street that made Ealing one of the more appealing suburbs thrown up by the westward expansion of the city. Such slumbering domesticity always seems to suggest a greater mystery lurking behind the respectable façades. Shapeshifting lizard people, retired assistants of intergalactic Time Lords, and Mossad assassination cells would never be seen dead in Knightsbridge or Shoreditch – but the streets of Ealing are the perfect environment in which to melt into the background. What could be more normal than Ealing? An advert for a Psychic Fayre at the Town Hall hints at more esoteric happenings in the area.

Somewhere nestled in this comfortable 'Villadom' will be an old person who'd be able to utter that blessed cliché, 'I remember when this was all fields.' A photo in Kate McEwan's *Ealing Walkabout* shows the junction of Scotch Common and Argyle Road from 1902 with two young women in Edwardian dress standing in a deserted country lane. McEwan writes that 'Argyle Road follows the line of the ancient "Green Lane" from Perivale' – the same trackway linking Brentford with Brockley Hill that I have been following from Sudbury Hill.

That path takes me across the bridge at Drayton Green, the pale-blue paint peeling from the iron walls exposing rust seams with rivets the size of your thumb. Drayton Green was one of the early-medieval hamlets of the area, now a convenient traffic through-route between Ealing and Southall. Cuckoo Lane and Manor Court Road sweep round Brent Lodge Park, the final approach to where the Wharncliffe Viaduct stretches across the skyline. Queen Victoria apparently used to request that her royal train slow down when crossing the bridge so she could admire the view. It's a true marvel of 19th-century engineering and also the kind of place Alan Partridge would take a lady on a first date. Initially, the most striking feature is 'Hanwellites 93' graffitied across the top of one of the arches – who were the Hanwellites? Were they a group of travelling players who took their name from a 1935 Will Hay film, like the Narkovers? A ska band who regularly played at the Railway Tavern? That'd fit. Or they could even be the local five-a-side football team.

Standing beneath the viaduct in the early-evening gloom you feel the full scale of this cathedral to the industrial age. The vast space overhead induces a feeling of religious awe. I read somewhere that shopping malls are consciously built with the same effect in mind: capture a void above our skulls and we instinctively fill it with metaphysical deities and higher powers – it becomes a portion of heaven captured on earth. But whereas Westfield gives me a migraine, my mind is calmed within the cavernous sanctum of the Wharncliffe Viaduct. Birch trees rise into the emptiness, bats swoop to their nests in the hollow brick piers, and the Brent snakes through the undergrowth as the 4.29 slides past to Bath. It put the 'great' in the Great Western Railway when it opened in 1837, and was the first structure in the country to be granted Grade I listing, before Buckingham Palace and Hampton Court. It's a recognition of the reshaping of the land that the railways brought about. In his groundbreaking book *The Making of the English Landscape*, W. G. Hoskins compares the building of the railways to the great prehistoric monuments: 'Nothing like their earthworks had been seen since the earlier Iron Age of pre-Roman times.' To fully appreciate the Wharncliffe Viaduct, he writes, you have to see it on foot.

Families make their way home from Connolly Dell and Brent Meadows through to Half Acre. I want to feel the full acoustic force of a train thundering on the tracks but when it comes it's more of a measured release of compressed air, a turbo-powered guff. I linger on a bench in Churchfields for a while watching the brightly lit carriages skim across the horizon. The bells chime out from St Mary's. It's one of those early-winter evenings when it is just cold enough to turn your cheeks a comfortable red. The kind of weather that dissolves in the warmth of a pub. Before I can settle down for a pint, though, there is one loose end to tie. To find the studio my sister lived in during her first year at Chelsea Art School. It sat round the back of an old thatched cottage somewhere near the church.

Before the walk she told me that the well that gave Hanwell its name was in the back garden. Despite having the address, the lanes around Hanwell Church (another possible site of pre-Roman settlement) are sheathed in the darkness of a pre-electric age. She barks directions at me down the phone from Maidstone and guides me to a Hansel and Gretel thatched cottage. Gordon S. Maxwell would have knocked on the door and asked to see the well. He might even have just bowled around the back and rummaged around in the garden. But I can't seem to formulate the opening words in my head and I don't want to alarm anyone on a Sunday with my walking jacket, ruddy cheeks, beer breath and wild hair. The journey feels complete – standing outside someone's house in a dark lane gagging for a pint and something to eat.

In the night fields beyond St Mary's the ghosts of Saxon warriors are stirring themselves to walk abroad and Horsa's steed polishes its hoofs for its midnight run to Horsenden Hill. I slope up the lane, through the streets that Jerrold described as having 'the appearance of the urban "hobble-de-hoy"' and jump on an E1 bus to Ealing Broadway, where a fairy princess lies resting under one of the bus shelters.

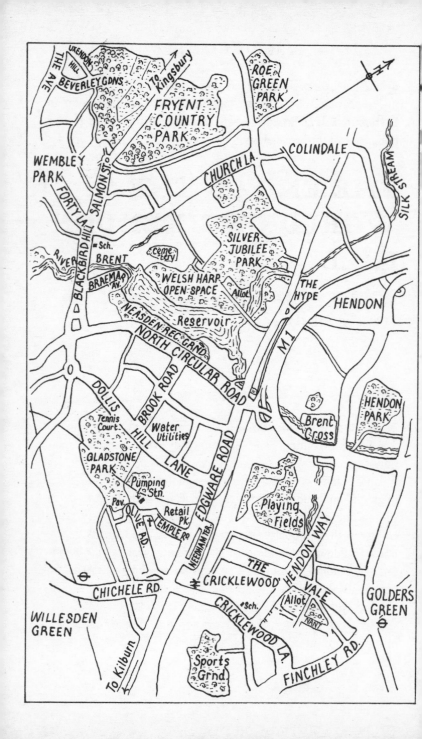

CHAPTER 6

THE END OF THE WORLD ON UXENDON HILL

Golders Green to Wembley via the Welsh Harp

My foray into rural Middlesex had made me think of my old walking buddy Nick Papadimitriou. Nick's greatest ambition is to somehow fuse with this now defunct municipal authority and in his own words, 'Become Middlesex'. So I had a tinge of guilt about heading out into his homeland without him. There was an unexplored section on the O/S map in my box room, an empty north-west quarter between Wembley and Golders Green, north to Edgware, Stanmore and Colindale – classic Nick country. It would be unthinkable to make a second incursion into these lands without him.

I also had the stack of *Transactions of the London and Middlesex Archaeological Society* to pass on from Walden Books, so I dropped him an email proposing a walk. There was no reply.

I sent a Facebook message. Again no response. I checked his Facebook activity and had seen that he'd left a comment on a photo of someone's cat saying it reminded him of Bob the Street Cat. When he didn't reply to two text messages and a voicemail I started to fear that he'd sensed my presence in the zone of Horsenden Hill and Sudbury, and had taken great offence. Had I stepped over some invisible line at Hanger Lane and was now engaged in a simmering topographers' turf war?

As a final act of reconciliation I sent him a postcard from the London Transport Museum. It was a 1924 painting by Edward McKnight Kauffer of *The Colne River at Uxbridge by Tram*. On the back I wrote: 'Feel like I'm trespassing in Middlesex without you.' If this didn't smoke him out I knew I was in serious trouble.

Sure enough, the day after sending it I received a call. He'd had his head down working on a series of poems and was also engaged in an intense wargame that was at a pivotal stage. 'Where did I want to go?' he asked. 'How about the Welsh Harp and Dollis Hill?' I tentatively suggested. 'Fine,' he said, and not much else. We set a date but two days before, he cancelled. I fretted he'd decided that the Welsh Harp was out of bounds and started to make other plans well away from his sacred territory: up the Lea Valley, across Leyton and Tottenham marshes – along the ancient territorial boundary between the Middle Saxons and the East Saxons.

Then another call – 'How about Friday?', and he'd show me Uxendon Hill. 'You'll like it, it has a superb view of Wembley Stadium.' The date would be 21 December 2012, the winter solstice, but also the day that millions of people fervently believed would be end of the world as it marked the end of the Mayan Long Calendar. So serious was this belief that both NASA and Russian President Vladimir Putin had made statements denying that the world was about to end. That really calmed the paranoid minds of the Doomsdayers – it just added more chuff to the already muddled conspiracy.

There was one place in which the Doomsdayers believed they would be safe from the coming apocalypse, Bugarach in the French Pyrennees. Thousands of nutjobs had converged on the pictur-esque village awaiting the end of days. Nick and I were going to watch Armageddon from Uxendon Hill in north-west London. This was a once in a lifetime event – you'd need a good view.

Nick lives in a tower block on Childs Hill, a seven-minute walk from Golders Green. A peculiar searing white light broke through the clouds illuminating the wet pavement as I worked my way along the Finchley Road, past the Hindu temple and down Wycombe Gardens. Nick's gleaming white tower stands backlit on a mound commanding views across all of North London and out into Hertfordshire. He has been religiously mapping this ground over the last twenty years or so, requisitioning the domain name of Middlesex County Council to publish his find-ings online. Here you'll find fine-detailed logs of the course of the Clitterhouse Brook, the Silk Stream and all the tributaries of the River Brent. Despite this he still receives several planning applications a week and various complaints about broken street lights and uncollected bins.

Nick was the perfect guide to the post-flood world. He'd carried out this research for Will Self to use in *The Book of Dave*, a novel set in a submerged London hundreds of years in the future. A map in *The Book of Dave* shows the surviving high land of the city around Hampstead and Mill Hill.

Nick greets me at the door holding one of the three feral cats he has adopted. I spot the postcard I'd sent propped on the light switch outside the bathroom. There is the wargame laid out on an old card table with worn green baize – he prevents me putting my tea down next it. 'It's the battle at La Fière Causeway, June 1944 between the 505th US Paratroop Infantry Regiment and the German 1057th Grenadiers – the Germans are winning. I'm going to finish it tonight after the walk.' The notorious French psychogeographer Guy Debord was also a wargamer and even created a game still played today, *The Game of War*, the tactical brain that helped inspire the Paris insurrection of May 1968 being put to a more recreational use. As far as I know Nick isn't planning an uprising but uses wargames as a distraction from his study of Middlesex.

I'm a bit late and today is the shortest day of the year, even if it isn't the last day ever, so I'm keen to get going. But Nick wants to chew the cud over a brew, talk a little about various book ideas he's been working on, but more about his observations of life in a North London tower block.

The previous evening I'd rewarded myself for the two hours' research with an episode of Sean Lock's sitcom *15 Storeys High*, a lost TV classic that got left out behind the estate bins. Lock plays a character called Vince, 'the most sullen man in Britain', who lives on the fifteenth floor of a South London tower block with his naively cheerful flatmate, Errol. It's a view of tower-block living that you rarely see on the telly. Vince has a job for a start, as a lifeguard at Ladywell Baths. The main storyline of each episode is broken up with surreal vignettes of the people living in other flats on the estate, like the table-tennis obsessed brothers, Billy Bailey's self-indulgent guitar teacher and Peter Serafinowicz's wannabe boy band manager. 'Good,' Nick says, as I tell him about it while admiring the view from his balcony. 'I'm glad someone has shown a positive view of people who live in tower blocks, so I don't have to.'

Finally heading out an hour later than planned Nick feeds the remaining two cats that live in the abandoned garages outside. We stop on the metal footbridge over the six throbbing lanes of the Hendon Way and take in the view northwards towards the *Book of Dave* landscape – the London that will endure if somehow the Mayans got it right and a biblical flood is on its way at some point in the afternoon before 3 p.m., after which it would be 22 December in Australia and the world would be able to breathe a collective sigh of relief. Nick points out the landmarks – tower blocks in Hendon, 'Mill Hill promontory' with the green-domed roof of the National Institute of Medical Research mentioned both in the *Book of Dave* and Iain Sinclair's *London Orbital*, the Hampstead Massif, or the Isle of Ham in *The Book of Dave*. Finally, far away, a blur in the distance above the rooftops, 'the North Middlesex/South Hertfordshire Tertiary Escarpment', the subject of Nick's book *Scarp*. This belt of high land in front of us has been as much an inspiration to the roadside prose writers of the 21st century as the Lake District was to the Romantic poets. Expect boarding houses and hearty weekend breaks on Scarp and Mill Hill in the next century.

The bridge takes us on to Cricklewood Lane, once the heart of Britain's aerospace industry. Handley Page aircraft manufacturer had both its factory located here and an aerodrome nearby. It was a Handley Page plane that made that first commercial flight from Hounslow Heath in 1919 (at that stage there were no customs facilities at Cricklewood). The Cricklewood Aerodrome was to have the unwanted distinction of being the site of the first passenger air crash in Britain. As far as I can tell the site of the factory is now occupied by a Virgin gym. In between it had a brief spell as a boutique film studio, where the cult horror flick *Hellraiser* was made.

Nick and I admire a crumbling factory next door. The date 1913 is stamped into the flue at the top of the iron drainpipe.

A slippery alleyway running down the side is littered with fly-tipped rubbish – the usual collection of mattresses and black bin-liners – not worthy of the Bob and Roberta Smith 'unofficial sculpture' tagline. It's a beautiful building, and would have been part of what was once a thriving industrial zone. There was so much creativity and production going on in Cricklewood they even had time to reinvent the humble potato into the nation's favourite snack food at the first Smith's crisps factory.

Cricklewood was also where theatre entrepreneur Oswald Stoll opened a film studio in 1919. Maybe he was drawn in by the 'Wood' in the name, simply substituting 'Crickle' for 'Holly', hoping some of the stardust would rub off along the way. Amongst the first productions was an ambitious early venture in colour film using a process called Prizma Color (the alternative to Technicolor). Made in 1922, *The Glorious Adventure* was a sprawling epic set during the Great Fire of London and co-starring the Duke of Rutland's daughter, who was reckoned to be the 'most beautiful woman in England' (by the Duke of Rutland). Stoll even brought over a Hollywood director to Cricklewood to take the helm, Sheffield-born J. Stuart Blackton, who had directed a whole string of studio pictures dating back to 1897.

Where the Hollywood moguls had built their empires in the California desert, the British impresarios headed to the industrial fringe of London. Around the same time, silent Shakespeare productions were made in Walthamstow and a young Alfred Hitchcock was starting his career at Gainsborough Studios in the backstreets on the border between Islington and Hackney.

Stoll continued building his movie empire by the Edgware Road with films such as *The Secret Kingdom* (1925), *Dick Turpin* (1935) and *Old Mother Riley* (1937). The epics and musicals left Cricklewood in 1938 and it says much about its legacy that the BBC recently produced a spoof documentary called *The*

Cricklewood Greats about an imaginary film studio parodying the earnest programmes about Ealing and Shepperton. There was no reference to the fact that a real documentary on the Greats of Cricklewood could have been made; Cricklewood was chosen as the last place you'd believe had been home to a venerable pillar of the British Film Industry. There's now a Matalan on the site where the studios stood – the memory erased and replaced with a mockumentary and a clothes shop. It's a shame Stoll didn't have the chutzpah to spell out CRICKLEWOOD in enormous letters across Dudden Hill.

From a thriving cluster of cutting-edge industries, Cricklewood became another of the London suburbs whose name worked as a punchline. The surreal sitcom *The Goodies* that ran through the 1970s both entertaining and baffling my young mind was set in Cricklewood, perhaps to act as a counterbalance to the otherwise bonkers nature of the plot and dialogue. Anything could happen in the Goodies' Cricklewood – the last dodo would turn up there, they'd fall down a large hole and get eaten by a *Tyrannosaurus rex*, a new army camp is built as a children's playground, and a kitten is accidentally given a growth formula, turning it into Kitten Kong.

Cricklewood is now being sucked into a regeneration scheme known as 'Brent Cross Cricklewood' – effectively an extension of the shopping complex by the North Circular Road. From telecoms, crisps, film production and the birth of the aviation industry to a retail park in the space of a century. It's not all doom and gloom, though – there's a new Travelodge on Cricklewood Broadway.

Nick and I duck into Tesco Metro for sandwich triple packs and bags of Walkers crisps, as Pepsico decided to rebrand Cricklewood's most famous product.

You can see that the Broadway once had a tinge of Edwardian glamour when it was the hub of the northern trolleybus routes. There's a fine modernist building with what looks like the original blue tiling and grid-pattern windows peering down on the plastic Argos and Subway shop frontages below.

The Broadway is part of the Edgware Road, which in turn is built along the route of the Roman Watling Street, which partly followed an existing Ancient British trackway linking St Albans to Canterbury. I've started to become blasé about walking Roman roads and ancient trackways in the way that I eventually got tired of Khmer temples and reclining Buddhas when I was backpacking in South East Asia. I'm far more drawn to the rows of Victorian railway-workers cottages set back off the road that look exactly like a street used in an episode of *The Goodies* I'd recently watched. Nick says the cottages have long since been tastefully converted and 'occupied by desktop publishers and charity fundraisers'. The one-time supposedly 'Loony Lefties' that put the London Borough of Brent in the national press have gone mainstream, like the ideals that they were previously derided for.

Brent was one of the London councils, along with Lambeth, Hackney and Haringey, targeted by the Tory press for their supposed bonkers policies in the mid-1980s. The red tops ached with fabricated stories of kids forced to sing 'Baa, Baa, White Sheep' and the banning of black bin-liners. When Brent East elected 'Red Ken' Livingstone as its MP in 1987 it was seen as being at the heart of this leftish scourge that believed in crazy things like gay rights, anti-racism and environmentalism – all ideas now adopted by the Tory party as conventional wisdom. Nobody even bothers to call Ken Livingstone 'Red' anymore. The genuinely bonkers Tory Boris Johnson, who replaced him as Mayor of London, merely painted Ken's proposed municipal hire-bikes blue. Next he'll replace them with penny farthings, and eventually space hoppers.

We pass near Ken's Cricklewood home as we make our way towards Gladstone Park. Nick poses outside St Michael's Church to recreate a scene from a video I shot on a walk we did together in 2005 that followed a water main running across the region. I'd only just met Nick and this had been the second walk we'd done together, joined by a friend, Peter Knapp, a talented photographer. It had been my habit to take a camcorder on walks to document the route and the landscape. I'd been this doing throughout a two-year Arts Council-funded project with my sister in our home town of High Wycombe and the footage had been essential in justifying to the Arts Council what we'd done with their money. But every time I raised the camera to grab a few seconds of a view or a manhole cover Nick would step in front of the lens and deliver a burst of his philosophy of 'deep topography'. Here outside St Michael's he'd talked about how he was making legal 'psychogeographic claims' on areas of London that would include the walk along the water main, Bedfont Court Estate and the sewage treatment works at Rammey Marsh near Enfield. My artful shot panning across the Brent Valley to Harrow had been photo-bombed by Nick talking about mysterious 'storage vats of regional memory'.

There was a strange atmosphere in the London air that afternoon. It was the day after a series of failed suicide attacks on the bus and tube network two weeks on from the devastating 7/7 bombings, and three of the attempted bombers were still on the loose. Jean Charles de Menezes had been executed by armed police officers at Stockwell Station that very morning. I'd felt particularly self-conscious carrying a rucksack on the Overground up to the Finchley Road.

The walk seemed like a way to get a different perspective on the city at a time of collective trauma – a means to peer behind its cloak of intense paranoia. Walking removed us from the troubled psyche of the city as we engaged in a slightly ludicrous trek following an underground water pipe. For a few hours whatever else was going on felt distant – the logic of the quest was all that mattered.

We eventually ended up behind an abandoned industrial unit somewhere near Stonebridge Park in the pitch black, using Pete's camera flash to peer into a chasm that had opened up in the tarmac revealing a large pool of water – it looked like the kind of environment in which Gollum would happily thrive. Nick was over the moon. We've been walking together ever since.

Excerpts of the video footage went on YouTube when it was still a relative novelty and soon 'deep topography' was being discussed at academic conferences held at provincial former polytechnics. I decided to give up attempting to film the landscape and just shoot Nick over the course of the year. I pitched it to the BBC as a 'psychedelic Wainwright'. They turned it down. Commissioning editors at Channel 4 looked at me sympathetically, shaking their heads whilst worrying about the state of mine, but I made the film anyway. That's how I'd ended up trying not to fall into the Grand Union Canal at Perivale and being portrayed as a 'bat-eared sycophant' played by Ron Howard in a Will Self novel. Russell Brand, Iain Sinclair and Will Self contributed in-depth interviews to the film. But mostly it was just me and Nick schlepping around. The final shoot was my first attempt at walking further than the end of my road after the knee operation, trudging out to Mogden Purification Works on a freezing December afternoon.

The resulting film, *The London Perambulator*, was shown at festivals to sell-out audiences and had a special screening at the Curzon Soho. I sat down in the back row of the auditorium and reflected that if I hadn't made the film I'd be in the audience myself. In the bar afterwards Nick was offered a lucrative publishing contract.

We made a radio series for Resonance FM. BBC's *Newsnight* asked permission to use clips from the film in a profile about Nick and deep topography. Since then I'd made another self-produced documentary profile, this time of the artist Bob and Roberta Smith, had worked on a multimillion-dollar project (not my own), and in an odd throwback to the plot of *Walking to Hollywood* had been dogged by a film crew for a week in Los Angeles.

Now we were back where that journey had started, itself a stop-off on a longer backward journey to the project with Cathy in High Wycombe in which I'd first used old walking guides to open up a seemingly familiar landscape. That project was also part of a regression as I returned from my travels abroad finally realizing that the true adventure would be closer to home, itself a direct link to childhood walks with my father.

As Nick strikes his pose in front of the church he assumes I'm taking a photo, but in fact he's being captured in full 1080/24p HD video frozen in a rare moment of silence. After ten seconds I tell him I'm shooting video. Without breaking his stance, holding the distinctive green metal railings, he says, 'We're nourished by the Metropolitan Water Board Water Main. If they ever dug it up we'd shrivel and die; we'd end up working at Walmart for £4 a year.'

St Michael's was also the scene of another performance from the past. The church hall had been the home of the École Philippe Gaulier theatre school, famous for its clown training. This is where Sacha Baron Cohen learnt to become Ali G and Borat. Household names such as Helena Bonham Carter made their way to this nondescript suburban street to rediscover the secrets of the craft from the notoriously cranky old French maestro, Philippe Gaulier. I enrolled here to study Clown in 2000. It was a revelation.

This wasn't the Zippo's Circus or kids' party clown – Gaulier preached an intense philosophy of comedy based on revealing your humanity and sensitivity. 'Complicité' was at the heart of the skill – this was learnt through a simple exercise involving garden canes; it seemed like a kind of magic. He told us that the clown had travelled far and suffered much, that's why he always carried a suitcase around. I may have done the travelling bit but the suffering was to come over the course. If he thought your performance was boring he would quietly lead the rest of the class out of the room. 'You don't love us enough,' he would say as they departed, 'you may as well stay here alone, your performance will be just the same in an empty room.' That was on good days. Other days you would simply be dismissed as a 'cretin' but then told to be 'a superb cretin'. 'The clown is an idiot with one idea.' 'When a clown is in the shit we love him.' 'Enjoy your flop and think you've done something amazing.' These mantras were drilled into the class that had come together from all over the world, including some experienced professional actors and comedians, but in Philippe's class we were all beginners.

Making him crack so much as the faintest smile was one of the greatest feelings of achievement I'd ever experienced. I wish I'd bought my red nose along on the walk to hang on the gate. It's a nursery now and kids are natural clowns; somehow most of us forget this skill in the rush to grow up.

We stop in front of Cricklewood Pumping Station. It's a building whose architecture by far transcends its function – it dwarfs St Michael's in both size and ambition. The tall, arched windows that flank the sides must flood the engine hall with brilliant sunshine at this time of day, illuminating the polished steam pumps. It was used as the engine room of the *Titanic* in the original 1958 Pinewood film, *A Night to Remember*. Nick had described the pumps in the grounds as 'inlet valves for unmediated cosmic energy'. Its day-to-day job is much more prosaic – passing the water supply across North London, irrigating the homes of the ever-expanding suburbs. Even in the digital age we're still dependent on these steam-punk fantasies to provide our most basic needs.

Further along Olive Road it's sad to see Cricklewood Library boarded up, the 'Save Cricklewood Library' sign still optimistically attached to the metal railing outside. The *Kilburn Times* reported that once Brent Council closed the library it reverted to its former owners, All Souls College, Oxford, who have been in possession of land in the area since at least the 15th century. There had been a determined campaign to run the library as a Community Space, and for a while neighbouring Kensal Rise Library was squatted in order to keep it alive. Local campaigners ran a successful pop-up library at the Cricklewood branch.

Lately, the *Kilburn Times* reports that All Souls have decided to sell the land to a developer to build flats. There's a bitter irony to a great and privileged educational institution selling off a library in a less affluent area. It's somehow worse than the alarming rate at which pubs are being bought up by supermarkets: at least you can still buy beer and crisps at a Tesco Metro. I wouldn't fancy your chances of borrowing a book from the people living in the new flats and using their internet for an hour, then picking up some leaflets for local Zumba classes before having a quick browse through *Auto Trader* on your way out.

We move across Gladstone Park. As a gardener's son I take umbrage at the naming of this former garden after a prime minister who merely used it as a place to unwind, whilst the nameless gardeners who tended and nurtured the grounds remain unhonoured. The house where Gladstone stayed has been demolished while the park prospers, so perhaps the gardeners have had the last laugh after all.

The green parakeets I'd seen at Perivale churchyard are also here, roosting high in the bare boughs of a plane tree. A lady walking her dogs tells us that they escaped from London zoo in the 1960s and that there are now 40,000 breeding pairs. Nick instantly contradicts her: 'I'd been told they escaped from Jimmy Page's private aviary.' They argue about this for some time, neither one backing down, and I'm willing Nick to concede that the zoo story is more plausible. His version sounds like yet another example of the colourful mythology surrounding Led Zeppelin. Next thing we know 'Stairway to Heaven' will have been written about this steeply ascending path through the park and John Bonham is buried on the summit of Dollis Hill (hence the litter of empty vodka bottles). The one thing they both agree on is that the parakeets are found all along the course of the Brent, the river seemingly providing these exotic tropical birds with an ideal habitat.

Looming over the park and the city below is the GPO Research Centre at Dollis Hill. This is a huge, grey, 1920s building dominating a high ridge. Once the cutting-edge centre of telecommunications research for the Post Office, it has inevitably been converted into 'luxury' flats.

We slip through the automated gate behind a departing car and reckon we have a few minutes to explore the grounds before security kick us out. 'To Strive To Seek To Find' is carved on one side of the entrance. On the other, 'Research Is The Door To Tomorrow'. Officially opening the site in 1933, Prime Minister Ramsay MacDonald spoke of his pride that 'Today, London is most conspicuous of all the capitals in the progress and the application of electric science.' This was no idle boast. When Apple was still just a seasonal fruit, the world's first digital electronic computer was built at Dollis Hill. The Colossus, designed by Tommy Flowers, played a vital role in the breaking of German codes during the Second World War. The speaking clock and transatlantic telephone cables were also developed here. But this was not only a place of innovation; it was also a place of secrets. There was a door marked 'Post Office Special Investigations Unit Research', which was allegedly an MI5 laboratory and interception centre.

Dollis Hill was the site of a subterranean 'citadel' constructed as an emergency war-time Cabinet retreat, codenamed PADDOCK. The Whitehall planners had built the underground Cabinet War Rooms in Westminster but, realizing that they wouldn't survive a direct hit, decided that a 'purpose-built totally bomb-proof war headquarters' was needed. This was the bunker at Dollis Hill, 'a last resort Citadel' in the words of Winston Churchill if the government was unable to continue in Westminster. PADDOCK contained thirty-four rooms over two floors beneath layers of reinforced concrete. There was a private apartment for Churchill, with rooms for his staff and accommodation for the War Cabinet. As Ken Valentine points out in his book *Willesden at War*, the morning after the heavy bombing of the docks in the East End in September 1940 that marked the start of the Blitz, 'the first thing Churchill did was not to visit the battered East End as one might infer from his biographer's account. Instead, he hurried out to Dollis Hill to see for the first time the emergency war HQ.'

The bunkers are still there. Photos and footage online show the old dials and valves, the air-raid warning lights and apparatus for purifying contaminated air. The perfect place to hide out in the event of a doomsday scenario.

After five minutes we are still at liberty in the grounds, not a soul around. Maybe they have retreated to the bunker in preparation for the coming apocalypse. It's actually a disappointment not to be apprehended – security guards are often an excellent source of information and would have been our best chance of a view of PADDOCK.

Outside the gates we take in the expansive view north across what Nick insists I write down in my notebook as the 'Valley of the Sulis'. 'Don't explain,' he says, 'just put that down, Valley of the Sulis,' and he walks off ahead as I write it down and take a photo of the silver ant cars crawling along the twig of the M1 motorway. Sulis was a Celtic goddess associated with healing adopted by the Romano-British at Bath, who merged the deity with the Roman goddess Minerva. Only Nick knows what relationship this has to the valley containing Hendon and Kingsbury, and he isn't telling; all he'll say is that the area is also known as Oxgate and Coles Green.

The view over the 'Valley of the Sulis'

This was the type of exchange that characterized the radio shows we produced for Resonance FM that centred round a field recording from a walk just like this one. From hours of audio I'd recorded on a handheld device a significant portion would be debating about which route to follow, realizing that we were lost and Nick yet again berating himself for not bringing a compass, even though neither of us know how to use one.

Today's walk has been fairly typical – several hours of unbroad-castable banter. I haven't done enough research but am clinging on to the few factoids that have lodged in my befuddled brain, so I keep going on about trying to find the underground passage that leads from Uxendon Farm to the hill. Nick is dismissive of this and spends much of the time talking about the novel he's just started writing, none of which I can repeat (nor record for possible future use). In between that I'm recounting funny things my kids have said and trying to explain *Call of Duty: Black Ops II*, which I'm sure Nick would love.

After walking alone for the best part of the year it's just a pleas-ant change to have any chatter to accompany the sound of your own footsteps. As eagerly as we chuntered on we both openly acknowledged the fact that we preferred to walk alone – Nick was even planning on writing a whole book on the subject. This walk is therefore a welcome interlude before we return to our solitary schleps. I'm already ruing that we by-passed the Fred Kormis-sculpted memorial to concentration-camp victims in Gladstone Park because of the argument about the origins of the green para-keets. I try to raise this with Nick but he's too busy telling me about the central plot of his novel.

I've only just noticed that Nick isn't carrying a bag; he just threw on a jacket as we left the flat. My permanent mental image of Nick is of a man wearing a Russian hat with a canvas satchel containing a large notebook and an old Bartholomew's atlas. Here he is, hands in pockets, hatless with a woollen lumberjack coat. Meanwhile, I'm not only rugged up in a thick fleece and waterproof jacket but packing a messenger bag containing a camera, field recorder, travel tripod, spare batteries and memory cards, water bottle, 1950s Geographia atlas, sheaf of notes, archaeological report of the excavation of Dollis Hill (unread), first aid kit, BlackBerry, knee strapping and spare cap. And I feel quietly proud for packing light. Nick tells me he stopped writing up his walks some time ago whilst I find even more methods for documenting almost every footstep.

I knew all this electronic clutter annoyed Nick on one level. Waiting for a train at London Bridge when we were heading off on our previous walk together he'd told me I that he'd once thought of me as an artist but I was now 'just some sort of media type'. It's still one of the most offensive things anyone has ever said to me (even including the indirect 'bat-eared sycophant' dig via a description of Ron Howard).

Since that first video we'd made together I'd started working for a small independent production company. Aside from the doomed pitches of well-meaning documentaries to BBC4 and More4, I had inevitably been sucked into the meat-and-drink world of the TV Moloch, writing up generic formats for dating, cookery and clip shows. I'd worked up passion projects for Saturday-night shiny-floor-show presenters and beloved soap actors – all of which were thankfully never made. Slowly some of the twisted logic that justified this pile of dung being spewed out into the public domain through the idiot box had seeped into my own worldview. I'd seen behind the curtain and caught a glimpse of the tired, toothless old bloke pulling the fraying strings.

My response was to develop a dating format in which people were hooked up with their ideal match on every characteristic apart from the caveat that they followed an opposing religion, which would be revealed to them in the presence of their families after a perfect date. *Inter-Faith Dating* wasn't the kind of 'edge and jeopardy' the broadcasters were after. *Was JFK My Dad?* speaks for itself. *Mind Control Live*, in which contestants were locked in shipping containers on an abandoned airfield and subjected to government mind-control experiments wasn't the type of reality show E4 were thinking of, apparently. *Made in Chelsea* took that slot instead.

Nick had seen me go from the idealist outsider who thought that *National Psychogeographic* could be the prime-time Channel 4 replacement for *Location, Location, Location* to a battle-scarred bloke cutting a taster tape for a *TOWIE* make-over show – and thinking it would be great telly.

My final week in the job involved an excruciating meeting in a floor-lit, glass-walled room where the cold-blooded vice president of the channel made repeated references to not being interested in making TV for men with beards. Nobody had suggested making TV for men with beards. Looking around, I was the only man in the room and the only person with a beard – I'd clearly rubbed her up the wrong way. Maybe she didn't like my idea of *Dead Celebs*, in which we faked the deaths of the nation's favourite celebrities to see what the reaction would be whilst the 'dead celeb' looked on. I was quite proud of that one. I hadn't managed to redeem myself with *Zombie Wasps*, either. The passionate plea that this was a pressing global issue probably put the final nail in the coffin.

The thing that had hurt me most about Nick's jibe was that perhaps he had been right – up to a point.

Not long after the final radio show had been broadcast I'd been working in Los Angeles, and found myself at some glitzy event stood chatting with a famous comedienne and one of the new rising stars. For a 'media type' this should have been a big moment – for people in film and TV, working in LA is like an oil man landing a job in Saudi Arabia. But as she nattered away about something I was mentally plotting a walk along Hainault Road, round the back of Whipps Cross Hospital and up to the Royal Oak pub at the top of Lea Bridge Road. It had just dawned on me that I'd never been there, and here I was glazing over in front of two charming, funny, pleasant Hollywood stars as I took an imaginary walk on a wet Tuesday evening through Leytonstone to the Walthamstow border.

Now I was back walking with Nick. My head was full of the meaning of the journey, of how it was fitting in with previous treks, of the ever-evolving portrait of the city that was forming.

We crossed the North Circular via a footbridge. Twentieth-century urban planners were obsessed with ring roads and radials – they couldn't get enough of them. Looking at the 1943 *County of London Plan* you start to wonder where they were going to find space for all the schemes: 'Radial Road No. 1, Radial Road No. 19 Streatham By-pass, The A Ring-road, The C Ring-road (North and South Circulars), Sub-arterial radial roads Nos. 3, 4, 7, 9, 10, 12, 14, 17, 18 and 20'. That's just a sample. It seems the road-building was left in the hands of a group of over-excited young boys with a pile of plastic track and a box of shiny new Matchbox cars.

Ken Livingstone came up with a more sensible use for the North Circular when he was canvassing in Leyton in 2011 – build a tram-line along it, swiftly linking east and west. I alone applauded this brilliant plan whilst the rest of the room looked distinctly unimpressed. The next question was about what he would do to reduce parking restrictions.

Nick splays himself across the concrete plinth near the base of the bridge, laid out like a sacrificial victim to the car cult, and insists I take his photograph. 'Why?' I ask. 'I've just always wanted to be photographed like this,' he says, still lying flat on his back, arms and legs spread wide whilst the traffic zips past on the other side of the chainlink fence. I oblige but also pull the trick of videoing instead of taking the photo so I capture the moment when he breaks his melodramatic pose to ask if I've taken the photo yet.

Nick on the bridge plinth

We brush past tall, brown stems of teasel to a bench beside the Welsh Harp Reservoir. One of the features of these patches of wilderness near the edge of the city has been the lack of people. From Hounslow Heath, through Crayford Marsh, Ladywell

169

Fields and Horsenden Hill there has been barely a soul around. Nick and I are alone – we don't see so much as even a solitary dog walker. Only two hundred yards away cars whoosh along the North Circular Road. The hills rising out of the valley are thick forests of redbrick houses and yet two blokes are sitting on a bench alone in 170 hectares of open space. There must be some sort of inbred aversion in the city dweller to these seemingly untamed places. Perhaps it's the fear of getting muddy feet or folk memories of the bear that escaped from the Welsh Harp menagerie in 1871.

The Welsh Harp was once so popular with day-trippers from the East End that it had its own railway station. In 1969 Harold P. Clunn wrote about how 'The craze for sun-bathing has been freely indulged in on the shores of the Welsh Harp lake,' but prudish locals complained and the sun-seekers were moved on. The Swinging Sixties clearly didn't make it this far round the North Circular.

The lake is formed from the damming of the confluence of the Brent with two of its tributaries – the Dollis Brook and the Silk Stream – the latter explaining Nick's cryptic reference to the Valley of the Sulis. Plugged into the Grand Junction Canal it forms part of a substantial body of recreational waterways that flow through London. It's a designated Site of Special Scientific Interest on account of the number and variety of its wildfowl population. In *London's Natural History* (1945), R. S. R. Fitter lists 'squacco heron, the night heron, the little bittern, the ferruginous duck, the avocet, and the grey phalarope' among the birds found bobbing around on the water with the less glamorous ducks, gulls and waders.

With the light fading Nick doubts we'll make it much further than Kingsbury Church on the far side of the lake. We move off across the marsh grasses to choruses of coots and moorhens.

Checking Facebook on my phone, several friends in Australia joyously mock the Mayans as 21 December passes with the world still seemingly intact. This is all a bit rough on the Mayans – if being brought to the verge of extinction by the Conquistadors wasn't bad enough, now a bunch of New Age fruit loops have misread one of their most precious ancient documents. The end of the Mayan Long Calendar only meant the start of another – not the end of time itself.

Welsh Harp Reservoir

We emerge into the kind of streets on the far side of the reservoir that earned Neasden the reputation as being a 'typical suburb' in the post-war years. Dapper lines of bow-fronted houses with wood-panelled roof gables, where the cream and white-rendered exteriors outnumber the pebbledash people. There is a vague whiff of Prozac and mothballs carried on the breeze. But unlike other London punchline suburbs Neasden fought back in 1970, after being regularly mocked in *Private Eye*, with a 'Stop Knocking Neasden' campaign. Angry letters were written to newspapers and posters put up at tube stations. It might be time to revive the campaign but this time with the addition of some Hollywood glamour. The ITV drama *Mr Selfridge* was recently filmed here, prompting chat-show host Graham Norton to describe the choice of location as 'cruel and unusual'. Lead actor and Hollywood star Jeremy Piven, famous for his role as Ari Gold in *Entourage*, defended the area, saying it was 'exciting' and mooted the possibility of buying a house in Neasden. The next day the *Evening Standard* reported 'Norton Knocks Neasden'.

On Blackbird Hill a group of men stand on the pavement in their vests; one is holding a jacket in his hand but doesn't look like he has any intention of putting it on. This is usually a bad sign when the temperature is hovering not far above freezing. There's an angry air mingling with the exhaust fumes and although Nick points out the row of terraced houses that now forms a conservation area, my instinct is to push on rather than stand taking tourist snaps. The traffic coming off the North Circular heading to Wembley is relentless. If the pollution doesn't get us, whatever is keeping the vest men warm might inspire them to take a closer interest in this pair of gawping wanderers.

We do, however, stop to take in the views: first of the narrow canal feeder hedged in by neatly mown grass verges, then of the

Brent with its wild banks of trees and shrubs cutting a broad course through the suburban sprawl. There's been a bridge here for eons and such is the vibe in the area I wouldn't be surprised if there was a fat troll lurking beneath it.

The River Brent at Neasden

We trudge up Salmon Street in the last of the daylight, feeling the steep ascent of the 'nose-shaped hill' that apparently Neasden means in Anglo-Saxon. Nick strides ahead like a Polish infantryman marching towards the River Vistula, or perhaps like an impatient man in his mid-fifties. He stops abruptly to admire a 1960s post-box on top of which some wag has placed a Coke can as some kind of statement of symmetry. Nick used to say that he was developing methods of communicating with objects in the built environment so he could unlock their secrets. Reinforced-concrete posts were usually his favourite inanimate conversation partners. I assumed he was chewing the cud with the post-box but he tells me he was just admiring the design. Further along there is a 1920s junction box with chipped blue paint – Salmon Street seems to be an outdoor museum of 20th-century public-utility architecture.

Nick issues the terse instruction that we need to move on and then powers off once more as I'm still fiddling with the contents of my bag. From Salmon Street we turn into another Roman road, Fryent Way, which becomes Honey Pot Lane, and you do have to wonder whether the Romans needed so many roads given that they only had chariots and a relatively small population. There was already the Edgware Road and the track that leads from Hanwell to Brockley Hill heading north. They would have got on famously with the authors of the *County of London Plan*.

We turn off the pavement to urinate in the trees near the sign announcing the new name given to the site – the banal-sounding Fryent Country Park. Uxendon Hill sounds far more exotic and less like the product of an uninspired brainstorm of the local government development agency. We trade our favourite piss stories. Nick easily trumps my tale of needing a wee on a twenty-hour non-stop bus journey across Sumatra with his epic four days without passing water when he was locked up on remand in Brixton with some vicious-looking squaddies. He's led a colourful life and reels off the crimes he was banged up for in his early twenties that sound like they've come straight from the *Beano*.

We plod on in the dusk through the ankle-deep, wet London clay that tops the hill covered by denuded spindly birch trees. The rooks and crows are making a hell of a racket and a woodpecker is enthusiastically nutting a tree. A half moon shines brightly over the white stone obelisk trig point that appears like a pagan monument. It's a site of worship for that curious breed – the map addicts. Humphry Repton's 18th-century pond absorbs the moonlight, adding to the mystical feel. This should also draw adherents to that greatest of British cults – the gardeners. Repton was one of the key landscapers who created the idea of the English garden. I have visions of Alan Titchmarsh and Diarmuid Gavin turning up later to dance naked around the water before offering up sacrificial copies of their latest garden-make-over books. Before us is the orange glow of the mother English temple – Wembley Stadium.

The lights of Harrow twinkle across the valley – the only higher peak in the area, with Uxendon Hill standing at 288 feet, marginally higher than Horsenden Hill.

We sit on the bench, now in the pitch black, admiring the pumpkin glimmer of the curved lines of street lights. 'It's a roaring beauty, Middlesex,' Nick declares. I concede that I finally see why he has dedicated himself to venerating his home county. It's a region of bounteous wonder largely overlooked by the rest of London, written off as humdrum suburbia.

The first time I met Nick we bonded over our shared love of *The Fringe of London* by Gordon S. Maxwell, published in 1925. Maxwell is the patron saint of the urban rambler, codifying the art and the practice. There is a chapter in the book about Wembley Park written in the year of the Empire Exhibition that ran from 1924 to 1925 and drew twenty-seven million visitors. It gave us the old Wembley Stadium, not the new luminous spaceship below, suggesting perhaps we were right to choose Uxendon Hill as the spot to be saved by aliens from the apocalypse.

The trig point on Uxendon Hill, with the moon above

Maxwell came to the park to explore the old Wembley before it was swept away by development. Like us he arrived at this spot at dusk: 'The lights of the great City of Empire shone brightly beneath me,' he wrote. We stay taking in the tranquillity of the high ground that had also been deserted when Maxwell was here eighty-seven years before. After a while the cold starts to seep in through my hands and face so we make our way down the hill, sloshing through mud to the Christmas-lit houses in the streets below where we find possibly the greatest legacy of the Empire Exhibition – a curry house. Working our way through plates of rogan josh, aloo paneer and chicken jalfrezi we recount the highlights of the day not knowing when we'll walk together again. It'll be soon, I think – I just need to return east to survey the wreckage of the latest grand jamboree over in the Lea Valley.

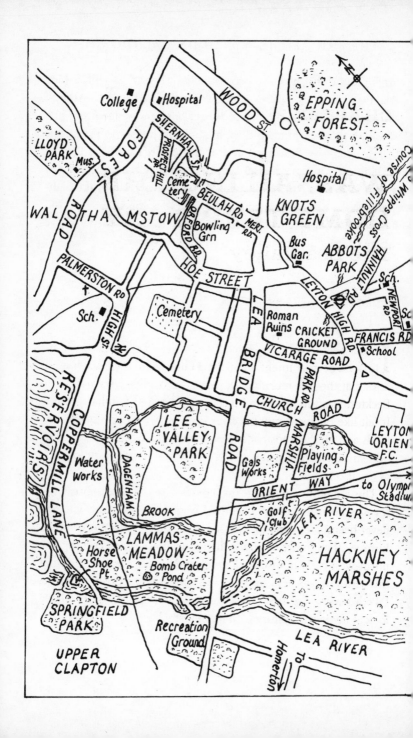

CHAPTER 7

WASSAILING THE HOME TERRITORY
The Lea Valley

It had been some time since I'd done a decent walk on home turf. I'd been so intent on pushing out beyond my usual boundaries that the July morning six months ago when I walked out to Beckton was the last time I'd seriously covered familiar ground. It felt like I'd spent months away – my mind occupying the new lands and obscure postcodes I was exploring. There had been the odd stroll across Wanstead Flats but nowhere near as frequently as usual.

This is a natural dynamic that comes with the urge to break out for new horizons. In my twenties I went from someone who had never been on a plane to a person who'd seen more of Asia than Europe, then more of Italy than England. After reaching the north-west passage with Nick on Uxendon Hill, the outer limit of this series of journeys so far, it was time to start closer to home. Like a backpacker fresh back from Bondi I was ready to take a look at my local territory with new eyes.

*   *   *

A tramp over Leyton Marshes had been on my list since the summer. It's a great expanse of wilderness beside the once mighty River Lea that you don't expect to see so close to inner London and it's a glimpse of the 6th-century 'Tun by the Lea' of the Anglo-Saxon settlement. I had instantly fallen in love with it upon first sight of the horses grazing tethered beneath the great electricity pylons that straddle the Lea Valley, the long, swaying marsh grasses and vast skies.

When I first moved to the area I'd seen an ad in the local paper for a 'Beating of the Bounds' – I figured it would be a good way to orient myself after the move across from the Angel. Despite the persistent rain throughout the day around twenty hardy souls turned out to be led around the ancient Lammas Lands by a local vicar and Katy Andrews of the curiously named New Lammas Lands Defence Committee.

As we waved willow wands and symbolically honoured the parish boundary markers, the history of the Lammas tradition was shouted out whilst we jovially traipsed over a patch of land I had previously never known existed. I'd missed the first ritual act of bouncing a child's head on a boundary marker by dangling them upside down because I'd got lost on the pitch and putt, and then fell head first into a bank of stinging nettles when attempting to jump across a ditch.

The idea of Lammas Lands is based on the Celtic system of cattle grazing. Parishioners had common rights to graze cattle on these fields from Lammas Day on 1 August till the old Lady Day on 6 April. People stopped grazing cattle here some time ago, after the railways carved up the area and there were the first encroachments by land-hungry speculators. In 1905 a determined group of local people got together and fought for the Lammas Lands to be 'devoted to the purpose of an open space in perpetuity.'

The right to free access to the land was still in place in 2006 but, with the 2012 Olympics on their way, the London Development Agency had their acquisitive eyes on all the spare land around the designated Olympic site. They'd decided that a chunk of the Lammas Lands would be a good place to relocate allotments from Manor Gardens in Hackney.

There had been a real mood of protest and defiance that day on the Beating of the Bounds, however twee we must have looked with our ribbons fluttering in the wind. All along the way there were reminders that our common-land rights were under greater threat than ever. And people had vowed to defend the ancient rights of free access to the land for the people of Leyton.

Over the ensuing years there has been a steady stream of calls to action, some initially successful but ultimately futile in the face of the Imperial-scale power of the Olympic Delivery Agency. First, Manor Gardens lost their fight to remain in Hackney and were relocated behind a metal fence at one end of the Marshes on top of a site where the rubble from bombed-out houses in the Blitz had been buried. There was every chance hard-working gardeners would be pulling up shrapnel and roof tiles with their potatoes. Then, in the final months before the Games, a chunk of Leyton Marshes was annexed to build a practice court for the American basketball team. The Vikings had tried to take this land with longships, silly helmets and battleaxes, when in fact all it took was a large bouncy ball and some hoops on poles.

I received the first positive news regarding the marshes for some time in an email from Katy Andrews. A group of Hackney tree musketeers was organizing a wassailing of the community orchards just over the river in Clapton. I had no idea what a wassailing was but it sounded vaguely pagan and would reconnect me with the area through a ritual that would probably involve some form of embarrassment again. I'd be more careful of jumping over ditches this time. It was taking place on Twelfth Night as dictated by tradition, a perfect time to embark on my first significant walk of 2013. I could see what had become of Marsh Lane Fields and Leyton Marshes before joining the wassail to head further along the Lea Valley.

Another beloved local feature had also been placed under threat by the Olympics – Leyton Orient Football Club. With either West Ham or Tottenham lined up to move into the Olympic Stadium just an over-hit pass away, the Orient had legitimate fears for their survival once a Premier League club moved into the area. I'd never been to watch the Os despite the fact that their Brisbane Road ground was just a short walk from my front door. Before I ventured back across the marshes on the Sunday I needed to check in with my local professional football club for the first time, to tie the ancient traditions together.

Attending your first football match has in some ways replaced the Beating of the Bounds as the means of learning your local boundaries. It's a rite of passage in which the young, predominantly but not exclusively boys, are introduced to a sense of tribalism and clan loyalty. I remember the FA Cup clash between Wycombe Wanderers and Bournemouth more vividly than my first kiss, even though that happened significantly later. Travelling by bus with my dad, Uncle Stan and my older cousins Robbie and Dave. The crush as the crowds funnelled into the turnstiles. The sound of the 2,000 people crammed into the wooden stands of Loakes Park. The smell of the wintergreen on the players' legs as they came out of the tunnel. The tea so strong it could support a spoon standing upright. And the fish and chips back in town after the match.

My elder son had a half-introduction into this at West Ham's Upton Park. But it came via a friend who had use of a corporate box for the day, so Ollie consequently spent three-quarters of the match watching CBBC on a TV inside whilst being waited on hand and foot. After the match I insisted we walked home in the rain across Wanstead Flats in order to get his feet back on the ground.

Patrick Brill, otherwise known as Bob and Roberta Smith, or simply Bob to me, lives two streets away and had mentioned he wanted to take his son to a match so I pinged him an invite. He didn't hesitate to accept. Bob's first and last match had been Reading vs Millwall in 1984. This would be his son's first match as it would for my younger boy, Joseph. It was a big responsibility – there'd be no going back for them after this – Leyton Orient vs Crewe Alexandra would be forever carved into the narrative of their lives. There was every possibility that after this intense exposure to the Brisbane Road faithful all three could end up supporting the Os FOR THE REST OF THEIR LIVES. How many other Saturday afternoons out carry such profound implications? They could find themselves in 30 years time yelling vile curses at TV screens as their team inevitably let them down, AGAIN. How many half-time burgers and stewed teas will they consume from here on in because of this day? Parties, weddings, even births will be carefully cross-referenced against fixture lists in order to avoid a clash. This was heavy – but the boys seemed ready for it. But the question remained, was I?

It's a freezing-cold January Saturday with snow forecast to coincide with the three o'clock kick off. The boys and Bob are wrapped up in coats, scarves and double socks. On Leyton High Road the Royal Café is packed with Orient fans loading up with huge fry-ups. There's a tabletop sale in the Trinity Methodist Hall where you can buy enormous pairs of off-white second-hand bloomers. It's interesting to see how the much-vaunted makeover of the High Road stops abruptly on the corner of St Mary's Road.

Almost overnight in the summer run-up to the Olympics the strip of chipped-plastic shop fronts had been transformed into an ersatz Notting Hill urban village of cheerily painted boutiques and delicatessens. On closer inspection the fried chicken and phone-card shops were still there beneath the stripy awnings. Suddenly the *Guardian* captioned photos of the High Road with the phrase 'continental café culture'. The Royal Café never made it into the Sunday supplement features as far as I know.

We reel around the fountain in Coronation Gardens to the streets of terraced houses that hug one side of the ground. Smart apartment blocks have been built into the backs of the stands – luxury flats with season tickets compulsory. This dual use of the ground was part of boxing promoter Barry Hearn's strategy to save the club from the financial mire that it found itself in during the mid-1990s when the chairman famously offered to sell the club for a fiver. A compelling observational documentary was made following the club through the trauma of the relegation season from the old Division Two under the management of the heroic John Sitton, spitting eloquence and threats of violence at his ailing team as they sloped out of the division. During one half-time rant Sitton uttered the sentence that would be his lasting legacy. He offered to fight two of the players at the same time and told them to 'bring your fucking dinner, 'cos by the time I've finished with you you'll fucking need it'.

There's none of that kind of language in the Family Stand, with a sign warning that 'foul and abusive language will not be tolerated.' Consequently I warn Oliver and Joseph to be on their best behaviour. They'd watched a double bill of *South Park* the night before and had been recounting it word for word to Fergal and Bob on the way down.

Leyton Orient Football Club

The gold pom-poms of the cheerleaders rustle in the freezing wind as Leyton's reserve keeper is caught in the sprinklers and the two teams are politely applauded on to the pitch. The players applaud the crowd back. It all seems so well mannered.

'Who's going to win, Dad?' Joe asks.

'Well, Crewe are known for playing good football but Orient are at home, so that's an advantage.'

'What did he say?' asks Ollie.

'Crewe are going to win,' Joe brutally summarizes.

Orient start with a series of hopeful long balls, tactics straight from their days playing on Hackney Marshes as Clapton Orient. But soon both teams settle into a fluid passing style and the sounds of negated celebrations of near misses, elongated

'Oooooooooooooooos' and shouts of 'Stay strong, Orient' bellow out around us. This is the atmosphere I'd promised Bob and the boys, who are rapt in the action.

The half-time whistle sounds and despite this being his first ever match Joe doesn't miss a beat. He's down the steps to the kiosk for footie nosh – one of life's great luxuries. He'd sat there patiently for forty-five minutes enjoying the football but also waiting till he can fill up at the snack bar. He and Ollie are more excited about what to eat and drink than they were when Orient midfielder Lee Cook rifled the Os into a short-lived 1–0 lead in the twenty-sixth minute. Ollie gets a hotdog the length of his arm and Joe goes for a jumbo sausage roll. This is on top of the bag of Maltesers they munched through during the first half and the promise of post-match pub grub at the Heathcote Arms.

The second half tos and fros, the floodlights come on and the pocket of supporters who have travelled down from Crewe are in fine voice isolated in a corner of the east stand. Bob cracks out a Thermos of hot chocolate and a hip flask of brandy. Despite a late Orient rally the game ends in a draw. Joe suggests they should do 'Ching-Chang-Walla' in the centre circle to decide the winner (this is what kids now call Rock, Paper, Scissors). The boys are impressed with the spectacle, both Ollie and Joe already asking about the next match. I take the opportunity of their high spirits to see if I can finally corral them into coming on a walk with me.

'You must be joking,' says Ollie. 'Not on one of your walks.'

'Come on, let's get to the Heathcote,' says Joe, who is already giving me his order for a BBQ chicken baguette. The rite of passage seems to have been successful.

Next morning, with the boys ensconced in the warm playing Lego *Star Wars* on the Xbox, I head out alone for the rendezvous with the wassailers at Millfields in Clapton. I stop at Dennis's Corner

Shop to pick up ceremonial offerings of Bahlsen biscuits and a can of Strongbow cider to toast the trees with. There are stacks of Sunday papers and a Turkish soap opera on the TV above the door. Dennis is always ready with a half-moon smile and a hearty 'Hello, brother, how are you?' Even though he appears to work ungodly hours his cheer never diminishes. He gives the biscuits and cider a mildly quizzical look but doesn't enquire further, in the spirit of the non-judgemental confidence a person shares with their local shopkeeper.

Dennis's shop sits at the bottom of a steep gully carved out by the now submerged Philly Brook that can still be heard gurgling beneath the street irons along its course. Until the late 19th century it would have been a picturesque stream winding down from Epping Forest through the fields past the few large houses that made up the area. Once the fields gave way to the rows of houses that still stand, the passive watercourse became a menace that frequently flooded. W. G. Hammock, writing in 1878, melodramatically described the area as the 'doomed valley'. Even when this gentle brook was buried in a concrete pipe its waters still burst into cellars and backyards as a reminder of its presence. Whenever work was done on the waterways that run through the Olympic Park in preparation for the Games, computer models were generated to predict the risk of the Philly Brook flooding once again. Even the world's greatest spectacle had to acknowledge this tiny stream flowing beneath the streets of Leytonstone.

Few people know the stream is here apart from those in the houses where it still occasionally breaks through into their basements. The only reminder is the name of a street that takes its name – Fillebrook Road – and even that was nearly erased when the M11 link road was gouged across the face and soul of Leytonstone. This hugely contested scheme prompted one of the most prolonged and creative urban insurrections in European history.

The Siege of Claremont Road lasted from February 1993 till the last residents were brutally dragged from the roofs of their homes in December 1994. Those who took refuge in the network of tree houses and rope walks that threaded across the street had the boughs of the trees cut from beneath them with chainsaws by imported private security operatives guarded by a force of around five hundred police.

Over pints of IPA in the Heathcote, life-long Leytonstonian and film-maker Ian Bourn recounted his memories of the pre-link road Leytonstone.

When Ian moved into Claremont Road in the mid-1980s, Leytonstone had the largest population of artists in the UK. The houses along the proposed route of the road had been bought up by the Department of Transport in the 1950s then gradually been blighted. An artists' housing association let them out at minimal rents and a flourishing scene blossomed. Ian talked of how the Northcote Arms became an 'unofficial art school'. Its alumni include Turner Prize nominees, professors of fine art, grandees of the art world. During the Whitechapel Open crowds of people flocked east to the open studios held in the houses condemned to make way for the road.

Ian and fellow filmmaker John Smith (now Professor) made numerous films shot around the area that were broadcast on the new Channel 4 and shown in the great London cultural institutions. The houses themselves became artworks. Ian formed Housewatch with a group of artist neighbours in Claremont Road. When they performed their *Cinematic Architecture for the Pedestrian*, an hour-long film performance that transformed the façade of Ian's house into a series of vignettes projected into the windows, it was reviewed in *The Times* and featured on *Newsnight* and ITN. Forget about Hoxton, Shoreditch, Mayfair and the Serpentine – for a period of time Leytonstone was the centre of the art world in London; it was London's Left Bank.

Then the Thatcher Tory government went on a road-building binge, green-lighting hundreds of schemes. Opposition to the road that would link East London to the M11 motorway resulted in an official inquiry held at Stratford Town Hall. An army of Department of Transport lawyers lined up against a phalanx of some of the country's most creative minds. Proceedings opened with one of the activists arriving with a carrier bag over his head weighted down with a bunch of keys on each corner. He was thrown out. Ian presented a slide show containing pictures of every tree, house and bush that would be destroyed by the road. His performance/presentation, with accompanying commentary, lasted an entire day. Without the benefit of an expensive legal defence team, delaying tactics were the best weapon they had. Noticing that the judge was being less than attentive when they delivered their evidence, one day the protestors, upon a precise cue, all put on animal masks. The judge looked up and impatiently pointed out that 'This isn't a pantomime!', leading to the inevitable chorus in reply of 'Oh, yes it is!' An eighty-year-old lady danced across his desk. This litany of stunts and pranks is dutifully recorded in the official transcripts.

When this failed, discussions took place over whether to form a microstate called Leytonstonia. A two hundred-year-old grove was occupied and borders erected. Long debates were held over what to use as the official currency. The militant vegans present always seemed to win the argument in favour of using carrots.

As the streets started to be demolished one by one, a last stand was made at Claremont Road. The bulldozers smashed their way through, obliterating over a thousand houses, and left behind a six-lane highway sitting in a deep cutting that creates a continuous drone of white noise.

The community was scattered across London and beyond. Some stayed in the area but Leytonstone's heyday as an artistic hub had been ended by a motorway. Bob's Leytonstone Centre for Contemporary Art, a shed in his garden not far from the road, continues the legacy of the E11 avant-garde.

Studying the 'zincographed' 1881 O/S map in the local archives at the Vestry House in Walthamstow you can see that where Dennis's shop is today was once a large pond in open fields fed by the brook. The houses I walk past at the end of Newport Road first appear on the 1894–6 map. But the first settlers came this way in the Neolithic, leaving behind some finely knapped stone implements that were dug out of the fields of Bent's Farm in the 19th century.

Turning into a built-up Francis Road, it too came into being some time in the period between the two maps but only with the first few houses and the police station. The Northcote Arms pub had been built along with a mortuary and a sewage works near the end of the stream in Leyton. The suburb that I now walk through had grown out of the fields in the space of ten years. Chicken2Eat is open, as is Pizza on Demand and the Sklep Polski, but the Bengali International Centre is closed, and the shutters are down on most of the other shops and smorgasbord of small businesses.

An eagerly contested football match is taking place on Leyton Cricket Ground, home to Essex County Cricket Club until the 1930s. Essex beat the Aussies on this ground in 1905 and England played a Test match here when a well-struck six would have landed the ball on the trams passing along Leyton High Road. Herbert Sutcliffe and Percy Holmes would have tonked a few of those in their record-breaking partnership of 555 playing for Yorkshire against Essex in 1932. A home to first-class cricket isn't necessarily the immediate association people make with Leyton.

In 2006 Labour Home Secretary John Reid chose the cricket club as the venue when he came to lecture the Muslim community about making sure their children were not being radicalized by extremists. The meeting came to national attention when one local character took objection to Leyton being singled out as the source of radical Islam and told Reid as much from the back of the hall. The media leapt on the 'heckling of the Home Secretary' by a supposed 'well-known Islamic militant'. Nowhere in the acres of news reports did it mention the heritage of the site, nor the role of the Muslim community in keeping it alive as a cricket ground.

Six years later, those Leyton and Leytonstone kids that the government was so concerned were being groomed for suicide missions were at the heart of the Olympic effort as part of the ebullient and brilliant brigade of volunteers. The biggest terrorist target in the world was in an area the Home Secretary had previously designated as perilous as Baghdad or Kabul, having denounced its people as dangerous radicals. Instead, they acted as perfect hosts to the international community. John Reid, now Baron Reid of Cardowan, possibly owes the people of Leyton an apology.

The area around the cricket ground is the heart of old Leyton. In the early 1700s workers carrying out 'extensive gardening operations' in the grounds of Leyton Grange unearthed remains of a substantial Roman building with arched doorways, pavements and polished Egyptian granite. A moated encampment was also discovered in nearby Ruckholts – later famous as the back door to the Olympic Park – that was also identified as having Roman origins. Stone coffins with Roman lettering were dug up in Temple Mills. Some of the old Leyton historians put the pieces together to suggest that this was the Roman station of Durolitum marked on the Antonine Itinerary (a Roman version of an *AA Road Atlas* of all the roads in the Empire) on the route between London and Chelmsford.

In his beautiful 1921 *Story of Leyton and Leytonstone*, W. H. Weston places the Saxon settlement of the Ley-Tun in the area where Church Road cleaves from the High Road. He has visions of folk-moots taking place on a green now built over with shops and housing and that serves as a rat-run through to Lea Bridge Road and Walthamstow. It is one of the least auspicious parts of Leyton, with any former significance long forgotten.

Evidence of Late Bronze Age occupation dating from the 10th to 9th centuries BC was found during the building of an estate in Oliver Road that splits from Church Road. A field report in *London Archaeologist* notes 'a large circular ditched enclosure … Many pits, postholes and other cut features were recorded both inside and outside the enclosure. Possible structures located internally included a roundhouse, a palisaded screen, four-post structures and hearths.' Evidence of 12,000-year-old Leytonians.

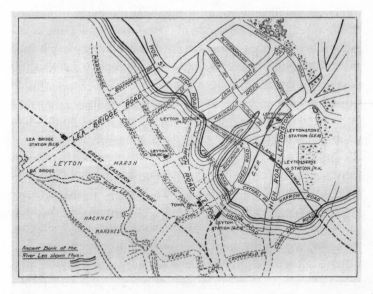

**A map showing the banks of the old River Lea, from *The Story of Leyton
and Leytonstone* by W. H. Weston, 1921**

What deserves to be a cherished part of the borough is apparently not so welcoming in the 21st century. The *Waltham Forest
Guardian* has reported that the estate built on the site is plagued
by drug dealers, the houses sprayed with bullets from a drive-by
shooting. This hasn't deterred the building of yet more apartment blocks around Weston's Roman Durolitum and Saxon
Tun as the continuous occupation of Old Leyton advances from
the Bronze Age to the Age in which the new structure on the
Green looks like a plastic spaceship held together with staples
and electrical tape.

It has taken me an Age to cover a short space of ground. The
clock is ticking down till the 1 p.m. meet with the wassailers on

Millfields and I'm still not even sure what wassailing is. The sun breaks through on Vicarage Road. There's a house in one of the roads leading towards Marsh Lane with tall, swaying pampas grass in the front garden, allegedly a sign that the people in the house are swingers. Although I've yet to test the veracity of this persistent urban legend by ringing the doorbell in a pair of tight jeans with a bottle of chilled Chablis and a glint in my eye, I have no reason to doubt it. It's so English to combine gardening and illicit sex.

Crossing Church Road I'm reminded of an archaeological excavation of my own whilst rummaging around in the Grot Shop on Hainault Road. I unearthed a 1980s Marks & Spencer's carrier bag full of old photos dating from the 1920s up to the near present – a whole life dumped in a plastic bag and left outside a Leyton junk shop among the mouldering books, broken pushchairs and listing shelves. The pictures that had caught my eye were of a group of young cyclists sitting on their bikes outside 'Graystone's Cycle and Radio Engineers', Church Road. It looks like summer in one photo taken directly outside the shop; they have their arms around each other's shoulders, smiling at the camera. Another is taken in winter in the street beside the shop; they are wrapped up in warm coats and gloves astride their bikes in a line appearing to be heading out on a ride. They seem to be a cycling club made up equally of men and women, none of them looking much above 20 years old. The date on the back is 1938. On the wall behind them plastered with fly-posters a newspaper headline reads 'HANGED BY HIS OWN FATHER'.

They look such a jolly bunch – you wonder if they were worried about the events in Europe. At the beginning of 1938 the government announced that all British schoolchildren would be issued with gas masks. Maybe it never crossed their minds – they were too busy flirting and showing off, discussing the best route to take through Epping Forest.

Capworth Street, then and now

What happened to this happy bunch during the war? The owner of the photos served in the navy and collected snaps of the ports around the Mediterranean – Malta, Alexandria and Nathanya Leave Camp in Palestine, November 1945, where he took a photo of a band called WE THREE sitting outside tents holding their instruments – a desert-skiffle combo rocking the casbah.

Graystone's has gone, converted into a house. The street beside seems little changed – although a large group of cyclists posing for a photo in the middle of the road would soon be shunted out of the way by an aggressively driven customized car. Crossing Church Road there are no cyclists, just a No. 58 bus to Walthamstow.

There was also a photo of a dog standing on Marsh Lane Fields with a full gasometer behind, taken in 1953, *The Goon Show* on the radio in the front rooms nearby. As I walk to where the photo would have been taken 60 years ago my stride is broken by a large, bright sign announcing the council's plans for Marsh Lane and Ive Farm Fields that include renaming them – Leyton Jubilee Park. 'The name has been chosen to mark the Queen's Diamond Jubilee' –pointing out the blindingly bloody obvious then mutates into the sneeringly patronizing – 'an event hundreds of you celebrated with street parties of your own.' All I remember about the Diamond Jubilee was the rain. I took Ollie to watch the flotilla on the Thames and got soaked to the skin. However, a couple of cancelled kerbside cake binges seem to have been taken by Waltham Forest Council as a mandate to strip this patch of ancient common land of any local distinctiveness and lumber it with a moniker that will have already been foisted on countless parks and open-air dog toilets the length and breadth of Britain, to add to the profusion of mind-numbingly banal Millennium Parks everywhere from Landkey to Market Harborough. But that's OK because at least it won't get confused with the wildly different name of the Queen Elizabeth Olympic Park, just a drop-kicked obsequious councillor away.

Marsh Lane

As I'm absorbing this quango'd travesty local historian David
Boote ambles over the bridge across the Dagenham Brook – which
seems both appropriate and fortuitous, as what David doesn't
know about the area isn't worth knowing. David has written
numerous publications, including booklets such as *Cinema in
Leyton and Leytonstone*, and *When Leyton Was a Village*.

We stand chatting outside the Eton Manor Athletics Club.
David has just been surveying the state of the post-Olympic
marshes and seems moderately satisfied that things have been put
back as they should be, but retains a note of healthy scepticism.
Three runners jog up the lane and invite us into the clubhouse
for tea. They are preparing to celebrate the centenary of Eton
Manor Athletics Club in 2013. I tell them I have to get a move
on to go wassailing, pronouncing it phonetically, 'way-sailing'. All
four people correct my pronunciation in unison: 'woy-sailing',

they declaim. 'I thought your Anglo-Saxon would have been better than that, John,' says David, and heads into the clubhouse.

There is a sign above the door of the Eton Manor cottage commemorating the Lammas Day protests of 1892 when thousands of people from Leyton descended on the marshes to protect their ancient commoners' rights. The East London Waterworks had dared to fence off land that had been drained by Alfred the Great and given to the local people (again Alfred obviously didn't do any of the backbreaking labour himself but graciously granted permission and then took all the credit). The fences were pulled down and the land put into the protection of the Borough of Leyton 'for all time'.

When I returned here in winter 2006 to join the protest against yet another encroachment on the common land – this time by the Olympic Delivery Agency – there was only a score of people and no riots. We walked around the threatened area followed by a BBC documentary crew and stood in a circle singing the Lammas Land Song:

The ground on which we stand
We will not be robbed while there's a ballot in this land
This is the land of the people.

The lyrics were a bit optimistic. It was the councillors we had elected with our ballot who had enthusiastically offered up a portion of the fields to the ODA, whereas in 1892 it was the council leaders who had torn the fences down.

With the furore largely behind us the flora has started to claim the green metal fencing around the allotments that had caused such uproar. The grazing horses that gave this place such a bucolic feel seem to have been moved but otherwise it wasn't the horror-show we'd feared. In summer the boys had run through chest-high, swaying grasses. Dragonflies darted between purple loosestrife, yarrow, black horehound and burdock. They looked for caterpillars on the stems of marsh ragwort. Elderberry trees were pregnant with ripe fruit. Now starlings arced through the sky, gathering for migration to Siberia. Hopefully, there is a wildness inherent in this soil that refuses to be tamed by ambitious bureaucrats.

I again lose my bearings on the pitch and put beside the large network of Eurostar railway sidings over the road from Marsh Lane. It's probably just as well that I've retired from trekking into rainforests and climbing volcanoes if I can't find my way across a flat, featureless nine-hole golf course. The cold weather has left the course to the dog-walkers. A path wraps around the legs of the electricity pylons, objects too fantastic to be mere functionaries in the urban infrastructure. As works of art they shame Anish Kapoor's Orbit sculpture in the Olympic Park, which is visible on the horizon from this vantage point looking south across the raised white staples of goalposts pinning down the turf on Hackney Marshes. It could have been worse – Antony Gormley modestly proposed a 390-foot steel cast of himself that would have stood among the vista of tower blocks like an impotent giant.

Finches flit through the brambles climbing the banks of the River Lea that benignly trundles beneath the Friends Bridge. At the time of the great rivers, long ago BC, the eastern bank of the river reached beyond Leyton High Road, submerging land occupied by Leyton Orient, the grand old Town Hall and thousands of homes. It was a mighty watercourse that flowed across the land-bridge connecting Britain to mainland Europe, joining a vast network of rivers. Weston wrote that by comparison the modern Lea is 'a puny rivulet'.

I find myself stranded on a peninsula formed by the Hackney Cut branching off on the other side towards Docklands. It's an area described by a Lee Valley Regional Park leaflet as being of 'swampy scrub communities' with 'natural glades providing an ideal habitat for the resident colony of speckled wood butterflies' – and reed warblers. A moss-covered concrete embankment lurks beneath the undergrowth like an ancient relic. There's the temptation to brush aside the moss looking for an inscription. It would read 'MIDDLESEX FILTER BEDS'.

A raised concrete path passes over the reed beds in their bleached-out winter state. The sluice gate cranks and sand trolleys have been preserved like religious artefacts. The stillness in the air adds to the sense of reverence as the path takes you up a set of steps to a large central dais sitting prominently in a clearing of tall, bare, spindly trees. The grooves cut into the face of the rotunda are given green highlights by the moss feeding into a smaller central circle. To somebody from a remote tribe unable to read the Lee Valley Regional Park interpretation boards this site has all the signifiers of an important temple complex from an ancient civilization. There are even the charred remains of a fire that had been lit directly in the centre of the circle as if part of some kind of esoteric ceremony.

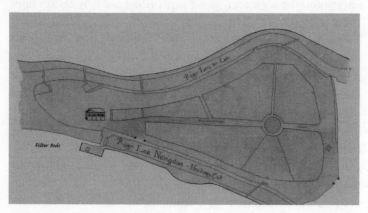

Diagram of the Middlesex Filter Beds

It's an incredibly powerful site, as mysterious as anything I saw in South East Asia or India. It deserves an annual ritual like the floating of candles on the waters of the ruined Thai capital of Sukhothai during the Loi Krathong festival. The celebration of this Victorian monument would have to involve the downing of copious quantities of cheap gin whilst performing some kind of symbolic vanquishing of the cholera epidemics that these water treatment works were built to combat. I settle for sucking on a Murray Mint whilst keeping an eye out for kingfishers – and I have a real ancient rite to attend with the Wassail.

The Hackney Cut is lined with brightly coloured residential barges. This off-shoot of the River Lea was made to serve the industrial area that ran along its banks down to its confluence with the Thames. Industry has now largely given way to amenity. Cyclists buzz along the towpaths built for horses to draw working barges to and from the timber yards.

The Millfields Community Orchard sits in the shadow of an old coal-fired power station, now a throbbing electricity substation. This isn't one of the ornate substations that seem to proliferate around the area, such as the one I had passed in Leyton built from large white blocks making it look like an Egyptian tomb. I became so seduced by these curious buildings that I contacted London Electricity with the proposal for a photographic project mapping them, prosaically titled 'Electricity Substations of East London'. Surprisingly, they replied with helpful information about where to locate more detailed notes on their architecture. There were clearly great minds at work in the construction of these nodal points in the urban grid, built at a time when the electric age was an exciting new era giving birth to the modern tube network, the light bulb, radio and television. The Lea Valley was at the very heart of this 'technological revolution', from the invention of plastics, the first light bulbs (long before Thomas Edison

got in on the act), Thorn's radio components, to the first television broadcast from Alexandra Palace. The modern world crackled into life along this strip of water. It's an interesting place to
witness the revival of an archaic rural tradition.

The wassailers arrive from Hackney Downs, a procession of
about a dozen people, mostly women, some pushing bikes loaded
with provisions for the picnic at the end of the walk. There is some
debate about which tree to wassail; tradition dictates that it should
be the King Tree but this is Hackney so we gather around the
Queen Apple Tree. The Wassail is a form of fertility ritual once
performed in rural communities to sing and drink to the fruit trees
to ensure a good harvest, *wassail* being Anglo-Saxon for 'be well'.

Song sheets are handed out and we all gather around the
wooden wassail cup containing cider. Toast is dipped in the cider
and hung symbolically from coloured ribbons on the boughs of
the apple tree to remind it of last year's fruit and as a gift 'for the
robin', otherwise known as the 'Orchard God'. This is carried
out with enthusiasm and good cheer, helped by the passing
round of hot mulled cider and spiced rum. The onward march of
the technological revolution into the digital age hasn't dampened our tendency to believe in the mystical. The more gadgets
and information we have grafted on to our brains just increases
the urge to seek out visceral and communal experiences – it's just
a shame it has to involve singing. Why do these local customs
always involve standing in a circle singing your heart out – or in
my case mumbling into my scarf?

The Tree Musketeers have been practising and are in fine voice
as they launch into the Apple Tree Wassail – '*Old apple tree, we'll
wassail thee.*' The singing is hearty and mellifluous for such a cold,
damp day. It ends with loud cheers of '*Wassail! Wassail!*' to scare
away the evil spirits and awaken the slumbering, benevolent
orchard-god. The libation is poured onto the ground around the

roots and a good harvest is assured. The flask of delicious mulled cider is on its rounds again in the company of the spiced rum and you can see how this would have been an excuse for a Twelfth Night end-of-Christmas piss-up when it was carried out around the village orchards at dusk. The farmer would have fired his shotgun in the air with the 'wassails' to make sure the evil spirits were banished. In Clapton that happens all year round.

As the circle around the apple tree breaks up for the walk to Springfield Park Community Orchard I notice Katy Andrews amongst the group. I try to ask her what she thinks about the state of Leyton Marsh but she gets on her bike, shouting back that we can talk about it at Springfield.

The group moves along the towpath past the new apartment blocks that are another phase in the gentrification of Clapton. It's an ambitious act to take an area up-market that was best known for its 'Murder Mile'. But the evidence is there on the riverbank, with the wax jackets and designer jeans tucked into the expensive wellies of clear-skinned people walking bijou dogs.

We cross Kings Bridge, spanning what was once the boundary between the counties of Middlesex and Essex, to Sandy Lane that runs along the edge of Leyton Marshes. Before the Norman Conquest this crossing would also have taken you from the land of the Saxons on the Middlesex side to that of the Viking Danelaw in Essex. Now it merely separates the London Boroughs of Hackney and Waltham Forest.

Looking east over the windswept marshes is almost to look back in time – if you could screen out the pylons. The Lee Valley Regional Park recently re-introduced a herd of grazing cattle to maintain the natural heritage of the grasslands. The authority talks of how this is 'a landform which is little changed since the glaciers retreated north many thousands of years ago'. This is also part of the Lammas Lands.

The other side of the Lea Navigation is a more recognizable 20th-century vista of council blocks wedged tightly together on the slopes rising up to Clapton Common. The Anchor and Hope pub perches on the towpath with a barge pulled up outside. It has seen many of the changes from the industrial working river to the leisure zone/amenity space it has become. I ask the lady walking beside me pushing a heavy bike bearing the picnic provisions what it's like. She ruefully notes that it is 'reflective of the area it serves'. I check that this means a crossover between estate geezers and the designer wellie mob, and she nods with a smile.

We are called to stop beneath the brick arches of a railway bridge where aviation pioneer A. V. Roe built Britain's first working aeroplane. The fragile-looking wooden-framed triplane was pushed out onto Walthamstow Marshes and in July 1909 Roe became the first Englishman to fly in an English-made machine. This historic event was described by Roe's assistant, Mr Howard-Flanders, as 'not much of a flight, just a hop with a minor crash'. Only ten years later they were flying from Hounslow Heath to Australia, in some cases still hopping and crashing but over longer distances.

Our tribute to Roe is to sing 'Here We Come a-Wassailing' gathered in his railway arch, but chosen for its acoustics rather than the historical resonance. '*Bud and blossom, bud and blossom, bud and bloom and bear/So we may have plenty of cider all next year.*' Again the singing is tuneful, reverberating around the arch – aside from my low-droning monotone sounding more like a tribute to Roe's broken propellers.

Over in Springfield Park we gather round a tall old pear tree, the oldest fruit tree in the park we are told. More revellers are waiting. It's now closer to the dusk of tradition. A rook '*waaarks*' loudly in a nearby tree as toast dipped in cider is hung on to the branches once more. A dog cheekily takes a drink from the wassail bowl and we again run through the repertoire of songs, swelled to a hearty rustic choir of thirty or so. The mulled cider and rum are passed around, hitting the spot. Springfield Park has the added pagan significance of being a place of 'springs', as its name suggests.

The final wassails go up into the freezing air, then Katy stands forward to announce another wassailing later in the evening leading off from the Nags Head in Walthamstow. I'm all wassailed out and leave the party to their picnic under the bandstand with the sap rising in the fruit trees.

Standing on the sixth bridge of the day, I look north along the Lea weighing up my options. This needs to be a circular walk for both symbolic and practical reasons – to form an alternative beating of the bounds but also to take me back to my front door on foot. One option is to push on along the riverbank and cross the Lea at Ferry Lane where Mark Duggan was gunned down by police, triggering the riots of 2011. The sun is cresting the hill behind the trees towards where mythology tells us Queen Boudicca set up camp near Copped Hall from where she variously either marched on London or made her last stand. I've no intention of making my last stand further up the Lea Valley; this cold could well seize my Homerton-knee despite my long-johns and so I march onwards to Walthamstow.

The bridge leads into Springfield Marina where the Coppermill Stream forms a small basin as it empties into the Lea. Mallards glide over a carpet of apple-green algae and reggae plays from one of the moored houseboats. The Coppermill is one of the Lea's main tributaries, being part of a designated Site of Metropolitan Importance. Three varieties of reeds grow in tall wands from banks that also sprout willows, hawthorn, elder and Russian comfrey. A flock of birds whirls into the air.

The stream takes its name from the mill that had been here prior to the time it was mentioned in the Domesday Book. Before copper it produced linseed oil; now it is Gate 4 of the Lea Valley

Reservoirs with its grand Italianate tower worthy of the Renaissance towns of Emilia-Romagna that inspired its architecture. The reservoirs form an immense body of water over seven miles long. The millions of gallons from this network of twelve reservoirs are heading straight towards where I'm standing outside the gates of the Coppermill Advanced Water Treatment Works. Here the murky aqua will be cleaned up and pumped out into the bathrooms and kitchens of London. It's an awesome location even though the buildings of the Treatment Works look like a regional tax office. What they do behind the green wire fence separates us from the age of cholera and typhoid.

The journey along Coppermill Lane into Walthamstow High Street mirrors the transition of Walthamstow from rural hamlet into busy market town absorbed into the railway-sponsored expansion of London. The market stretches the length of the High Street and lays claim to being the longest open-air street market in Europe. As it isn't trading today people stroll down the empty boulevard like an Italian Sunday-evening *passegiatta* past Argos, Superdrug and the 99p shop. Ricco's elaborate coffee lounge with its velvet chairs and gilt mirrors is full with a well-dressed crowd.

I've continued my habit of missing lunch. The Riverside Café had been packed and all I've had to eat is a couple of the Bahlsen biscuits bought at Dennis's shop. The locally listed L. Manze's Pie and Mash Shop is closed – pie and mash would have been perfect for a day like this. A plaque on the shop front tells the story of how the Manze family emigrated from Ravello in Italy in 1878 before building their pie and mash empire. This is an off-shoot, established by one of the brothers, Luigi, who opened it in 1929. Such a core London tradition perpetuated by Italian immigrants. I took my half-Italian, half-Australian wife to the

Manze's in Chapel Market when we first moved to London together. She politely declined the liquor and quietly chomped through her solitary dollop of mash and one pie – and never went back again.

My rumbling belly is taunted by the smell of roast meat from the Lord Palmerston pub on Forest Road but I've resolved to get to the William Morris Gallery for a first look before it closes. I'm tired and hungry climbing the rise with the dark ridge of Epping Forest ahead. I pass Pumps Gym – 'Walthamstow's Premier Hardcore Gym' boasts a sign propped up against the wall behind a stack of broken cardboard boxes and a three-legged armchair.

With the gallery in sight forty minutes before closing time I bump into the lady on her bike from the wassail; she urges me on to the gallery by telling me that there's a good café there.

The William Morris Gallery occupies the childhood home of the eponymous artist, designer and writer. It's a stately Georgian half-mansion set in landscaped grounds. Morris was a prolific and passionate polemicist as well as a designer of lovely wallpaper. Quotes from his works are painted on the walls. 'I do not want art for the few, any more than education for the few, or freedom for a few.' It's a sentiment that I imagine Bob would heartily endorse. As a trustee of the Tate Gallery he has tirelessly campaigned for the democratization of art and against the coalition government's cuts to arts education that he fears will return us to the days of art schools as establishments of the elite few who can afford the escalating fees. Bob was asked to contribute a piece of work to the gallery. Sensing a certain paradox in Morris's socialist beliefs and his multimillion-pound bespoke interior design and furniture company, Bob spelt out his reservations about Morris in one of his distinctive colourful text paintings.

WILLIAM MORRIS TOGETHER WITH PUGIN IS RESPONSIBLE FOR THE APPAULING LACK OF TASTE OF THE ENGLISH.

EVERYONE COVERTS GASTLY PEROCHIAL VICTORIAN HOVELS AND THEN DECORATES THEM WITH SICKLY FLORAL WALLPAPER.

LIKE MOST SOCIALISTS MORRIS WAS DELUSIONAL. HE THOUGHT OF HIMSELF AS A WORKING MAN WHILST EMPLOYING PEOPLE TO SLAVE FOR HIM METICULOUSLY HAND CRAFTING HIS RUBBISHY KITSH.

IF PUGIN AND MORRIS HAD NOT LIVED WE WOULD ALL LIVE IN DECENT ACCOMODATION IN UP TO DATE MODERN CITIES LIKE PEOPLE DO IN EUROPE.

DAMN BOTH OF THEM.

Morris's most enduring legacy does seem to be his floral designs printed onto wallpaper and gift-shop notebooks rather than the Utopian socialism he discovered later in life after the failure of his marriage. Before he decided to emancipate the working classes his principal mission was to bring what he saw as beauty into dowdy, cluttered Victorian homes – a crusade against poor taste rather than inequality and injustice. It's a bit like Laurence Llewelyn-Bowen joining the Workers Revolutionary Party following a midlife crisis.

The gallery shows us how Morris was an enthusiastic medievalist who swanned around in plate armour and chain mail posing for paintings by his Pre-Raphaelite chums whilst dreaming of an Arcadian past. Wandering around the exhibits, from the lush baronial interiors he created for the wealthy – his Romantic desire for an age of chivalry – to the radical slogans painted on the walls, Morris's credo comes across as a peculiarly English form of poetic radicalism in which the revolution not only promises liberation for the oppressed but really nice soft furnishings as well. Was there something about growing up in 19th-century Walthamstow that inspired this medievalist socialism that owed more to the Icelandic sagas that he translated than the works of Karl Marx? I ponder this as I buy a copy of his seminal work, *News from Nowhere*, and a roll of signature Morris print gift wrap to wallpaper the inside of my shed door.

As I emerge into the early-evening dark on Forest Road the bells toll from the illuminated clock tower of Walthamstow Town Hall, an imposing 1930s Portland stone structure. It reminds me of Mussolini's fascist architecture in Rome, much of which was built at the same time that Philip Hepworth designed the Town Hall. Hepworth had been on a scholarship at the British School in Rome before Mussolini came to power. The sculptor he commissioned to carve figures into the building, John Francis Kavanagh, had also been at the British School in Rome in the early 1930s. And by a spooky coincidence Bob and Roberta Smith won a scholarship to study there in the 1980s. Kavanagh's sculptures stand in the car park round the back of the Town Hall above loudly humming extractor fans – the angular modernist figures representing 'Work, Education, Fellowship, Motherhood, and Recreation' looking northwards over Chestnuts Fields.

I sit beside the oval fountain that magnifies the majesty of the setting. A young couple take photos of themselves posing in front of the plumes of water. The girl, tall and blonde, is wearing a tight black outfit. There must have been something in that mulled cider, because for a moment with my short-sightedness and the refraction caused by the water droplets she is Anita Ekberg in the famous scene from Fellini's *La Dolce Vita* in which she wades into the waters of the Fontana di Trevi.

Adjacent is the Assembly Hall, built in the same style. Engraved high above the entrance is the inscription 'FELLOWSHIP IS LIFE AND LACK OF FELLOWSHIP IS DEATH' – that's quite an intense message to absorb on your way in to a performance by the Forest Philharmonic Orchestra. It's taken from William Morris's *A Dream of John Ball*, his ghost still haunting the area.

The venue has played host to more seminal players in British musical history than the Forest Philharmonic. Ian Bourn told me that in the 1970s Pink Floyd had played there, and in June 1976 he went to a triple bill of the Sex Pistols, Ian Dury and the Kilburns, and the Stranglers, which drew such a small audience that Ian Dury refused to perform – Walthamstow wasn't ready for punk, it was still hooked on coiffed guitar heroes and keyboard solos. The gig was a kind of homecoming for Dury. He studied at Walthamstow Art College just a Johnny Rotten spit away next door on Forest Road, where he was taught by legendary pop artist Peter Blake, famous for his *Sgt. Pepper* album cover.

I lumber on along Shernhall Street, one of Walthamstow's oldest roads, past more pampas grass (there had also been some in Coppermill Lane) and drop down to Church End, the centre of what must be the most unlikely village in England. Say 'Walthamstow' and people will conjure up images of boy band East 17, the dog track used in thousands of mockney gangster movies and TV shows, and news reports of arrested terror suspects (the cognoscenti may associate it with Turner Prize-winning 'Tranny Potter' Grayson Perry who has his studio in the area). St Mary's Church, with the 15th-century timber-framed 'Ancient House' opposite, the quaint path leading past the 18th-century almshouses to the Vestry House built in 1730, is as incongruous to the popular idea of Walthamstow as finding a KFC at Buckingham Palace. It would be perfect for an episode of *Midsomer Murders* or another unnecessary Jane Austen dramatization.

In keeping with village tradition there is a pub at the heart of communal life. The Nags Head is rammed and a jazz band is 'ppptooping' away in one corner. I manage to push through to the bar and get a pint of ale. As I turn, my arm is grabbed and I'm exhorted to 'toast in Anglo-Saxon' – it's Katy Andrews. I'm perplexed. 'Wassail,' she says, 'it's a toast.' The wassailers that had meant to leave at 4 p.m. are still sitting in another room munching on pizza at six o'clock. It's a young, cool, hipsterish crowd in the Nags Head that you can't imagine toasting fruit trees in an old language on a biting cold evening. Not when there's a jazz band playing.

Katy is just starting to tell me what she thinks of the state of the marshes after the Olympics when the Walthamstow wassailers head out of the door. She gathers up her bags and dashes off after them.

A waitress passes carrying an obscenely large calzone that reeks of garlic – a reminder that I still haven't eaten. It provokes an uncomfortable memory from the time I lived in Modena, Italy, working as an English teacher, when I caused uproar in my local bar while ordering a calzone. I accidentally omitted the letter 'l', proudly and confidently ordering a '*cazzone*'. There were astonished belly laughs all round, coffee was spluttered across tables, knees were slapped, ribs ached. 'Can you say that again please?' the barman managed to ask through his sniggering. Adopting the principle that they would understand me if I just spoke louder I said again in a raised voice, '*Vorrei un cazzone, per favore.*' The laughs were even louder this time. I had politely ordered a 'big dick'. I'd go hungry for a bit longer. I wasn't going to take any risks that the waitress in the Nags Head spoke Italian.

I've inherited Katy's table and seatless hipsters are eagerly eyeing my under-occupied space. It's an odd assembly. Over-thirties, with good haircuts and serious faces, the men with sculpted facial hair, the women in designer vintage clothes. A Twitter acquaintance quipped that Walthamstow Village has been officially annexed by Stoke Newington. It becomes clear that I don't belong here in my Clarks boots caked in marsh mud and fleece from Sports Direct, although I note a few admiring glances towards my beard, which I'd recently attempted to trim when the battery ran out half-way through and had decided to leave it as it was.

The only thing that stops me getting on a W15 bus now is my dedication to completing the journey on foot and the desire to sup a couple of pints of Brodie's beer at the William IV at Bakers Arms, Leyton, which is en route.

The vibe in the William IV couldn't be more different from the Nags Head. It's a beautiful old London boozer with large, painted mirrors that in my eyes rival anything William Morris produced. The bar is edged with framed Victorian prints of country scenes mounted on a wooden border like a suspended gallery. The back room has a domed glass roof and roaring open fire. And best of all, in the back yard Brodie's Brewery turns out some of the finest ales ever to pass your lips.

The punters are a bricolage of locals of all varieties: young smartly dressed Eastern European couples, old fellas on their own, blokes left over from watching the Tottenham vs QPR game on the large screen, men with long hair and tattoos. A woman comes in pushing a pram. This is more my scene.

The barmaid greets me with a broad, friendly smile and I trust her to serve me the best ale they have on. At times there are upwards of ten different Brodie's on draft, ranging from Pomegranate Pale Ale through to the treacly Elizabethan ales five times the normal strength and served in one-third-of-a-pint glasses. You could drink your way round East London with their Bethnal Green Bitter, Shoreditch Sunshine, Whitechapel Weizen, London Fields Pale, Hackney Red IPA and Mile End Mild.

A little later she brings over the burger and chips I'd ordered served on a platter with a big side salad for less than the price of a Big Mac Meal. I tell her what a good choice the ale was and add how much I love Brodie's beers. 'It isn't a Brodie's. It's one of our guest ales.' Oh well, you can't have it all, I suppose.

The last leg of the loop takes me past the Grot Shop where I found the old photos of the cycling club and back down into the valley of the Philly Brook where Dennis is still behind the counter of his shop. I buy a bottle of Young's London Gold ale for the final libation and head home.

Ollie has just emerged from the bath so is politely dismissive of my call to wassail the pear tree in the back garden. Joe has his puffer jacket and wellies on in an instant. I empty the spent batteries and Lego blocks from a red Celtic goblet on the mantelpiece and we go out into the pitch black, Heidi bringing the bread without a single word about what we're doing and why. I still have the unopened can of Strongbow from the morning and Joe pours that into the goblet. He and Heidi dip in the bread and skewer it on the branches of the pear tree. We sing two verses of the Wassail Song led by Joe, who gives it his own tune. I ask Joe to pour the libation under the tree.

'You mean the cider?' he says.

'Yes, that's it,' I say.

'I poured a coin as well by accident,' he reports as the Strongbow soaks into the soil.

'That's OK.'

I feel a deep sense of satisfaction and completion, that I have somehow connected with the ancient spirit of place that sits beneath the pavements that we walk over daily and that stretch back into the Ice Age.

'It'll grow nice pears now,' I tell him.

'Just because it had cider and bread?' Joe shouts out incredulously.

'That's all it takes, and the singing, because anything that may have been stopping it growing has been banished.'

'Dad, you know that's hippy talk,' he says, before going back inside to his Lego.

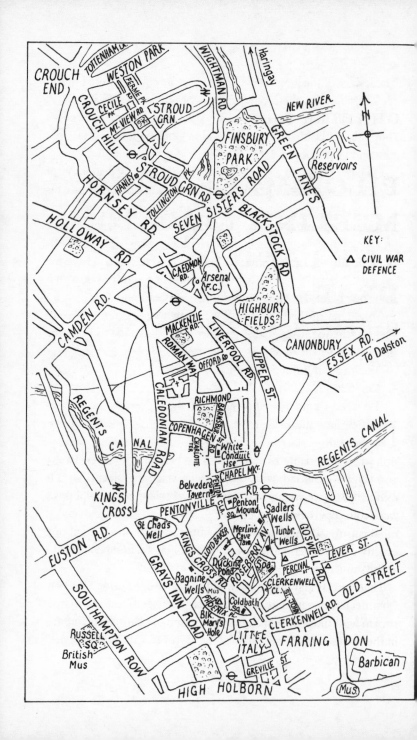

CHAPTER 8

PILGRIMAGE FROM MERLIN'S CAVE TO THE LAND OF THE DEAD
Saffron Hill to Hornsey

I first became aware of Hornsey as a student living in a large house on the Harringay Ladder, the name given to a succession of streets strung between the upright struts of Green Lanes and Wightman Road, with the New River dangling through the middle like a stray length of watery rope. It was a time when we were collectively trying to get our heads round the idea of postmodernism and there was much debate in the household about exactly what it meant aside from EVERYTHING and NOTHING at the same time.

Then one Friday night we were sat watching *Sean's Show* on Channel 4. The set-up was the traditional scene of a studio-based sitcom with the principal character, the eponymous Sean Hughes, in the living room of his flat. Sean broke off from his monologue, made a reference to the script, then walked across the studio set, past the balsawood scenery of the exterior of his lounge, said hello to the cameraman and entered the clearly visible 'set' for the next scene taking place in the corner shop. The penny dropped – that would do for us as an explanation of postmodernism.

But what left a more enduring impression after this deconstructed conceit wore off were the posters for the *Hornsey Journal* that decorated the 'exterior' sets. It added to the allure of the show for our raggle-taggle polytechnic mob that Sean's world was not located in fashionable Notting Hill or Camden Town but in Hornsey, a mystical land that happened to lie just the other side of the railway tracks at the bottom of our garden.

It was during these years that I really discovered my love of suburban exploration. I had a light timetable in my final term and used this time to go on long schleps around the streets of Hornsey, up through Crouch End to Muswell Hill and Alexandra Palace, then back down to Wood Green Shopping City. This realm beyond the reach of the tube became a dreaming space for me. As Bruce Chatwin had yearned for Patagonia, the deep furrows of Victorian houses laid out on the slopes of the northern heights seemed to be holding back precious secrets.

I'd stretched my horizons – west to Hounslow Heath, south-east to Crayford Ness, across the Norwood Ridge, up to Uxendon and Horsenden Hills. Coming home to the Lea Valley brought up the desire to return to further old ground. For a few years I had lived just off Penton Street at the Angel and walked to work every day to and from the South Bank. In those four years I walked everywhere from that high ground that rises up from the valley of the Fleet, barely ever moving by any form of mechanized transport.

Thoughts, feelings and associations become engraved into paving slabs and brickwork through the process of repeatedly tramping the same route again and again. There were fragments of unfinished research from the daily foot commutes that I wanted to attempt to connect, ambulatory thoughts and mobile-phone photos posted to my blog. I look back on these posts in a similar way to how I flick through my travel journals. One question I'd toyed with was what traces were left behind by the lost pleasure gardens of Finsbury and Islington that grew up around natural springs? Long before Islington became shorthand for a certain type of designer faux leftie and the birthplace of New Labour, it was famed as a verdant land of hills and magical pleasure gardens on the city's outer limits before travellers entered the dark and dangerous Middlesex Forest.

There was also the romantic mythology attached to Penton Mound, legends of Merlin and London's earliest foundation. And Hornsey had gained a new kudos as the setting of the greatest zombie comedy ever made in an area already drenched with stories of the undead. It began to feel like one of William Morris's Icelandic sagas. It was time to re-explore this once familiar landscape – to crack open some of its secrets that I had only previously skimmed across – and gather up some of the memories I'd deposited on those daily walks.

The departure point for this epic was over wet pavements and on the Underground to Chancery Lane, where a vicious wind whipped through the tunnels. A mile-long subterranean city lies beneath the platforms in a Second World War deep-level air-raid shelter. After the war it became a top-security telephone exchange that carried the 'hot-line' linking the leaders of the USSR and the US. The staff entered this secret world via a nondescript door on High Holborn.

The escalator up to the street is decorated not with adverts for West End shows and David Beckham pants but for diamond merchants in Hatton Garden. It was a decidedly unromantic work-a-day Wednesday scene as bunches of suited men beat fast footsteps along High Holborn – you can see why nobody suspected the secret life contained beneath the pavement. There's an easy escape from this mercantile city that doesn't involve descending down a deep shaft; it's a left turning through a barrier by the beadle's watch house and into a sequestered street that for centuries was part of Cambridgeshire.

Ely Place is one of London's curious anachronisms. The mighty City of London has no authority over this terrace of Georgian buildings – technically speaking even the police need permission to enter. It's a peculiar mini city state, a micro-Vatican. It was the London home of the bishops of Ely, who built their palace here after falling out with the Knights Templar. Shakespeare used it as the setting in Richard II where John of Gaunt makes the famous scepter'd isle speech:

This royal throne of kings, this scepter'd isle,
This earth of majesty, this seat of Mars,
This other Eden, demi-paradise ...

This other London that set its own rates and where the beadle would call out 'the hour and the weather like the old watch', the man in the top hat was the source of law and order. Aside from the beadle in his brick cabin by the gate there are only two other people about – a man sauntering back to his office with a takeaway coffee and a woman languidly sucking on a fag.

A dark passageway leads into Ely Court where Elizabeth I danced with one of her 'favourites', Sir Christopher Hatton, around the cherry tree at the door of the Old Mitre pub. They may have been jiving in celebration of his acquisition of the bishop's garden, which Hatton gained through coercion with Queen Bess's help. The *Ingolsby Legends* suggest that his wife, Lady Hatton, engaged in sorcery, summoning the help of hobgoblins and sprites to 'inwiggle' the queen and obtain the land. Hatton built his own mansion in the grounds and today Hatton Garden is one of the world's most famous diamond districts.

A doorway in the wall blocking off the end of the street leads through to yet another world, away from Cambridgeshire and beadles into the rough cobblestone courtyard of Bleeding Heart Yard. This is where the *Ingolsby Legends* tells us Sir Christopher's dancing took a more sinister turn when Lady Hatton engaged with the devil 'in terrible circumgyration'. The next morning she had completely disappeared but a still-bleeding heart was found by the water pump in this yard. Her ghost was said to be seen by the pump, working the handle to no avail.

Dickens recounts a different version of the legend in his novel *Little Dorrit*. He writes of

the legend of a young lady of former times closely imprisoned in her chamber by a cruel father for remaining true to her own true love, and refusing to marry the suitor he chose for her. The legend related how that the young lady used to be seen up at her window behind the bars, murmuring a lovelorn song of which the burden was, 'Bleeding Heart, Bleeding Heart, bleeding away,' until she died.

The wind rattles the metal sign of the Bleeding Heart Restaurant. A chef empties the bins. I check to see if they have heart on the menu but it looks as if it's out of season.

Emerging from Bleeding Heart Yard on to Greville Street the sun starts to crack through the grey clouds. A pretty redhead checks her hair in the window of a jeweller's as she walks along the street that descends into the River Fleet running beneath Farringdon

Road. The buildings obscure the steepness of this western bank of the 'Holeborne Vale'. Clear them away in your mind and to the east you look down upon the twin hills of the old City of London divided by the Walbrook. Walter Besant wrote in 1893 of the prosperous town that the Britons built on the western hill that pre-dates the Roman city, 'a high earthwork ... with a stockade'. Stretching from Farringdon Road to Walbrook it sat atop Ludgate Hill, now dominated by St Paul's Cathedral. Ludgate Hill is supposedly named after the British King Lud, credited by the 12th-century historian Geoffrey of Monmouth with building the first walls of this early London. On the western banks of the Walbrook the Romans later built their Temple of Mithras, where 'the Pompeii of the North' has recently been discovered. The slopes that I make my way along towards Leather Lane would have been open fields and fenland fringing the great forest of Middlesex.

There's a strong breeze from the east that would have brought a terrible stink from the open sewer that the 'Fleet Ditch' became before it was filled in. The International Precious Metal Co. bullion dealers occupy a shabby-looking building above a café. The entrance to Elite Jewellery is similarly inauspicious. This is the business end of the trade away from the swanky stores in Hatton Garden with their burly, black-suited security guards prowling the pavements.

The traders in Leather Lane street market ply their trade on a decidedly different scale. Hollywood studio fodder on DVD knocked out for £2 a pop, plastic BB guns, rails of sweatshirts and onesies with the word 'Geek' emblazoned across the chest. They look like a taunt aimed at the Department of Coffee and Social Affairs on the other pavement. There are stalls of socks and pants, fruit and veg, long lunchtime queues at the Mexican and Mediterranean food stalls, and plenty of empty pitches.

Leather Lane street market

When H. V. Morton visited one lunch hour in 1926 he reported a more vibrant scene and no onesies. A jazz band appeared, a man dressed as a chef demonstrated handy kitchen implements. The stalls stretched the length of Leather Lane on both sides 'from which the connoisseur of old bed knobs, rusty keys, or stray lengths of iron piping can recognize many rare specimens'. You could witness 'the decapitation of live eels and the head refuses to die'. It was so crowded that 'a two-horse dray delivering acid in big glass bottles is hopelessly marooned.'

The brisk trade in Leather Lane today is not among the jumbo knickers and socks for a pound but the effortlessly cool new coffee bars and healthy eateries offering thimbles of rare Amazonian cloud forest dew and crushed berries from the Tree of Knowledge. The smell of ground Guatemalan coffee beans is so intoxicating that I wander into Prufrock's where your espresso is made by an official world champion barista and the staff are as likely to have an MA in fine art or an album playing on Xfm as a food hygiene certificate. There are also a lot of men with beards so I feel oddly at home, but sadly can't get a table.

I loiter in the hope that my membership of the 'fellowship of bearded men' will get me moved up the queue. Admittedly, my own beard is not a fashion statement but a facial manifesto on laziness – put simply, I can't be bothered to shave. So when I see legions of otherwise stylish young men with great, bushy, Taliban beehive beards I can't help wondering if it's an accidental fad that grew from one particularly lazy but cool bloke who just happened to be the trendsetter amongst his group of impressionable friends. They were probably having a coffee here at Prufrock's and got photographed by *Vice* magazine and before you can say 'Nathan Barley' fashionable males all over the urban centres of the western world are sporting these hairy conical growths on their chins.

It didn't work. I didn't get a table, so moved on. The horologist just around the corner in Portpool Lane seems as if it could be a vestige of H. V. Morton's London. A fantastic collection of old watch parts and the insides of precision instruments are displayed in glass cases. Inside, the man offers me a book of footballer's haircuts for £3.50. A few of them have beards but the fashion in those days was more for Burt Reynolds moustaches, so I decide to leave it.

This was once an area of specialist trades – organ grinders, barometer makers, glass craftsmen – knotted together in the nest of streets that formed London's 'Little Italy' in the 19th century. A notorious rookery once existed in these dark, narrow streets between Gray's Inn Road and the Fleet. It was a lawless land that lay outside the jurisdiction of the City and the Crown, one of the 'liberties of Holborn' where criminals could seek sanctuary for forty days. Fagin's den in *Oliver Twist* was located in Saffron Hill, which runs parallel to Leather Lane. Portpool Lane was at the end of a murky waterway known as the 'Kings Ditch'. The high walls of the Bourne Estate restrict the sunlight and squeeze the lane, casting a Victorian gloom. Through the gated arch is Baldwin's Gardens, one of the dodgiest parts of the old ghetto.

Today, Saffron Hill is a development opportunity: loft apartments offering a zippy urban lifestyle, offices for design and web companies. Aside from two joggers in fluorescent vests and a delivery man there is no one around. No plank walks strung between the upper floors of the tenements making this a malefactor's safe haven, a labyrinth of crime, a no-go area, bandit country, where barely a word of English was spoken. The only criminal thing round here now is the £2.9 million for a two-bed flat in the Ziggurat Building.

Going by a map in the *Camden History Review* showing the houses occupied by Italians in 1871, the heart of Little Italy lay on the other side of Clerkenwell Road in the tight cluster of streets that fall away behind the Italian Church of San Pietro. The Vespa showroom and deli on Clerkenwell Road extend the Italian presence in the area beyond the church, which was established in 1863 by a missionary who came to London with the blessing of the pope to build a Catholic church for the Italian diaspora settled around the 'teeming and fetid alleys of Saffron Hill'. It was built as a bridgehead to bring England back into the Catholic fold after centuries of persecution. Building a Catholic church in mid-Victorian London was a radical act and correspondence from the pope in Rome to his London missionaries urged caution and discretion.

Although the Italian community spread out through London – further into Islington along the Caledonian Road, around Highbury Fields and beyond to Hertfordshire – St Peter's remains at its heart. The interior of the church is wrapped in scaffolding but I venture inside anyhow. When I lived in Modena our explorations of the neighbouring towns always began in the *duomo*. Departing the station it was my practice to drift, follow scents and moods, traverse the narrow streets peering into gated palazzo courtyards. No matter how many twists and turns you took, how random the route, we always ended up at the doors of the *duomo*. I never remembered to take my hat off when entering until I was rebuked by a warden, '*Signore, cappello, cappello, per favore.*'

Thankfully, the scaffolding in San Pietro doesn't obscure the frescos depicting St Peter and St Paul by the Piedmontese artists Gauthier and Arnaud. As I crane my neck to look at the painted saints ascending to heaven I realize I've yet again failed to remove my hat. I quickly whip it off just in case any of the scaffolders happen to be particularly pious. The clanging of metal brackets and joists being lobbed from high up echo round the cupola. They probably don't realize there's anyone down below; I start to fear for my life, divine retribution for my atheistic woolly hat-wearing in a place of solemn worship. I make my escape along Clerkenwell Road and into Eyre Street Hill.

The map of Little Italy shows a dense pattern of icons representing the houses of 'street musicians, figure makers, ice makers' in these streets that sharply decline from Clerkenwell Road. At night around Herbal Hill, Back Hill, Vine Hill and Eyre Street Hill some of the former ambience escapes from the brickwork. No longer a squalid slum but a media ghetto, something dank still clings to the fabric of the buildings.

Moving under the viaduct beneath Rosebery Avenue you enter into Black Mary's Hole, a basin formed by the course of the Fleet and Mount Pleasant. On chill winter evenings you can smell a muddy odour that manages to work its way up through layers of concrete and paving stones. There's an account by Chesca Potter of a psychic visiting Black Mary's Hole and reporting that 'she felt that it was a sacrificial pit to a goddess.'

I bought a bumper book of mysteries in a pound shop in High Wycombe one summer holiday and read about the seemingly plausible idea that ghosts are nothing more than tape recordings. A Cambridge don, T. C. Lethbridge, made the connection between ghost sightings and water – often underground streams that people didn't realize were there. Tragic events, like death, would make people emit strong discharges of electrical energy that would be recorded in the water, then 'replayed' like a video cassette under the right conditions. Apparently this is why ghosts are always in black and white – LCD colour technology won't run on water.

I don't believe in ghosts but I have great faith in VHS. Black Mary's Hole is like a great big video-cassette recorder. Encoded in the underground watercourse could be the murder of John Etheridge that took place here in 1766. Etheridge was driving cattle through the area and one of his bullocks strayed into a field belonging to a William Floyd. Thomas Plymmer, an employee of Floyd, came out of a smith's shop, struck Etheridge once above the nose, thinking he had dodged paying at the turnpike, whereupon Etheridge collapsed and died.

Potter also speculates that Black Mary's Hole could have been a place of worship of the Isis cult via the Black Madonna. The more likely explanation of the name was recounted by William Thornbury in his *Old and New London* (1878), citing an earlier account of a black lady called Mary who sold the waters that came from the spring. The Fleet was known as a 'river of wells' before it became what Thornbury described as a 'sluggish and plague-breeding sewer'. Pentonville and Islington became famous for the pleasure gardens that grew up around its springs. Bagnigge Wells on the higher ground where King's Cross Road runs gained fame as the house of Nell Gwynn, actress, mistress of Charles II and Restoration 'It Girl'. If there had been paparazzi in the 1660s they would have been parked up on the pavements outside.

Black Mary's Hole—there stands a dome superb,
Hight Bagnigge; where from our forefathers hid,
Long have two springs in dull stagnation slept ...

wrote the Grub Street hack William Woty in *Shrubs of Parnassus* published in 1760. These lines were written some 56 years before Samuel Taylor Coleridge published his famous opium-inspired verse:

In Xanadu did Kubla Khan
A stately pleasure-dome decree:
Where Alph, the sacred river, ran ...

Coleridge's description of the Mongolian capital with its springs and fertile pastures and a sacred river running between hills echoes the spring-fed grazing uplands of Islington on the slopes of the River Fleet. Woty recorded a 'dome superb' on the pleasure garden where Coleridge, off his nut on drugs, saw a 'stately pleasure dome' not where the filthy Fleet slithered through Mount Pleasant but 'Where Alph, the sacred river, ran'.

On this cold, bright, late-winter lunchtime people scurry through Black Mary's Hole, over the submerged river, to grab a spot at one of the 1950s formica tables at Andrew's on Gray's Inn Road, or up along Phoenix Place to Muratori, a favourite with the postal workers at Mount Pleasant Sorting Office. My great aunts Edie and Ethel worked at Mount Pleasant when they returned from South Africa in the 1920s. It has always fascinated me, this enormous building labouring away twenty-four hours a day processing the mail. I used to pass the polyglot queue of uniformed postal workers that stretched down Rosebery Avenue at the end of a shift, waiting for the No. 38 bus. It seemed like a world within a world. It's one of the great centres of London knowledge – every address in the city has a connection linking it to this building. Imagine the local knowledge contained in the combined brains of all those posties. Collectively they form a major part of the hive mind of the city itself. Maybe that's why it was targeted with a devastating incendiary bomb in 1943 that destroyed the parcel building, leaving a bombsite that is now used as a rough, open car park.

Black Mary's Hole

Climbing over Mount Pleasant I duck down a passage leading off Exmouth Market into Spa Green Fields. In the 1800s this was the site of great political gatherings, including a mass meeting in 1816 by followers of the radical Thomas Spence. Spence advocated that all land should be publicly owned by autonomous 'democratic parishes' and called for the abolition of the aristocracy. Spa Fields today is largely a piece of public art where workers chat and chew sandwiches rather than plot the overthrow of the established order, but I suppose you can't be completely sure unless you start eavesdropping on every bench. Lenin lived in exile not far away in Holford Square planning the Russian Revolution – perhaps there was something in the water here. Islington Council have taken precautions against further insurrection by screwing 'No Dogs' signs into the grass verges. The ruling class can sleep safely in their beds.

Guy Mannes-Abbott talks about the area being part of a 'utopian enclosure' formed by the fortifications erected by the New Model Army of Oliver Cromwell during the English Civil War. There was a defensive line across Finsbury that included Black Mary's Hole and Waterford Fort, on the site where the Spa Green Estate stands in defence of another ideal – the more practical utopianism of Finsbury Borough Council. Whereas other modernist housing projects are used as icons of urban decay, Berthold Lubetkin's Spa Green Estate was built to specifications that the Clerkenwell loft builders of today could scarcely match in their million-pound condos.

Finsbury Town Hall now moves to the rhythm of a dance academy after being saved from a Liberal Democrat plan to commit the historical travesty of converting it into luxury apartments. The McDonald's in Red Square was bad enough – yuppifying the home of municipal socialism would be have been the final insult. I head across Rosebery Avenue to the former ducking ponds in Wilmington Square and take a rest in the bandstand.

Somewhere around here there was the entrance to a cave deep in the heart of this hill that ascends up to Pentonville Road. According to one of the most beguiling London books ever written, *Prehistoric London: Its Mounds and Circles* by E. O. Gordon (1914), this was not just any old cave but Merlin's cave. Whether this is the surly, spotty teenage Merlin of the BBC series or the bearded, old, Ian McKellen/Gandalf-lookalike wizard of legend, it's too incredible a claim to be dismissed by a lack of serious historical evidence to back it up. Did Romulus and Remus really build Rome? Was Athens built by a half-man, half-snake creature? Was the Cavern Club actually crap? None of this matters to these cities.

E. O. Gordon's London is a city dominated by four principal 'sacred mounds': Tothill at Westminster, Bryn Gwyn or the White Mound (which is now the Tower of London), the Llandin at Parliament Hill and Penton Mound at the top of Pentonville Road (now the New River Head Upper Reservoir). Gordon believed that the Penton, which means 'head of the sacred mound', was the 'probable' site of a Druidic College. Despite warning of the 'mean streets' that are traversed on the approach to the hill she recommends that 'it is well worth a pilgrimage if only to appreciate the magnificent site of the "Holy Hill".' She was writing at a time when the now desirable Georgian squares laid out across the Lloyd Baker estate on the slopes leading up from King's Cross Road were considered one of London's more seedy suburbs. The idea that this is one of the most significant sacred sites in London, if not Britain, still seems fanciful on a cold and cloudy winter afternoon.

The top of Amwell Street, on the crest of the mound, still has a grubby look to it. In my experience, Filthy McNasty's pub is aptly named. But in the four years of walking across here at night nearly every day, the only time it seemed even remotely mean was when the youngest member of a mob of youths flashed his Stanley knife in front of my face. When I stopped to tell him he should go home to bed his hooded mates quickly intervened, told him off and issued me with a profuse apology for his rudeness and explained he was visiting from out of town. One night at this spot I passed Boris Johnson, when he was just an opposition MP, pushing his bike and yelling into his mobile phone, 'So much for the intellectual powerhouse of the Labour backbenches.' The sweaty crowd spilling out of Filthy McNasty's gave him worried looks as if he were some kind of nutter.

Penton Mound

I have performed my own pilgrimage twice on the summer solstice, walking an upside-down number 7 from Westminster across to Waterloo, along Druid Street to Bermondsey over Tower Bridge, up to the Penton and then on to Parliament Hill. Describing a walk as 'a ritual perambulation of the prehistoric mounds of London' is a good way of getting friends to join you on an all-day London ramble – it sounds more dramatic than 'fancy a stroll?'

Whereas you can barely take three strides on Chaucer's path to Canterbury without tripping over a wandering pilgrim there doesn't appear to be any fellow holy travellers on this religious trail. That might have been a different story if the Penton had retained the stone circle that Gordon believes 'crowned' the summit. Rather than take the inconvenient trip to Stonehenge tourists would merely have to hop on a bus to the Angel.

Going further, she speculates that this megalithic monument, aligned with the May sunrise, was probably 'the principal observatory of Caer Troia', the 'New Troy' established by 'Brutus' when he arrived in Britain following the Trojan Wars. Bearing in mind that Gordon was writing not long after the existence of Troy as a real place beyond the Greek myths had only just been established, she could legitimately have held out hope that the same would happen to the myths of the Welsh triads that she drew from. Gordon records that the underground passageway leading from the cellars of the Merlin's Cave Tavern to the cave deep within Penton Mound had only just been bricked up. It did exist. There have been 'prehistoric' artefacts excavated around the New River Head and Sadler's Wells – pointing to the presence of some kind of camp or settlement based around the springs.

The New River Upper Head was also the site of 'a large fort' in Vertue's map of Cromwell's civil war defences of London – the bulwark of the defence of Guy Mannes-Abbott's 'utopian enclosure'. This patch of land from Pentonville Road down to Clerkenwell Road that I have just spent two hours forensically criss-crossing, gathering up the deposited memories of years of walking, has been a continuous draw to visionaries, radicals, pleasure-seekers and poets. Why not add a wizard to the list?

I'm prepared to give reason and rationality a day off and take Elizabeth Gordon's glorious book as gospel. Every city needs its myths and legends, and the 'sacred mounds' theory deserves its place within London's mythology. I'd have it taught in schools. Moreover, the Penton *is* capped with a large, grassy mound protected by iron railings. You just have to by-pass the fact that it is a covered reservoir at the end of a four hundred-year-old, twenty-eight-mile-long aqueduct built to bring fresh drinking water into London from Hertfordshire – which is noteworthy in its own right, but nowhere nearly as romantic.

'Many a solar and lunar festival has probably been celebrated upon the summit of the Penton, in which British kings have played their part,' Gordon records. After this a procession of 'Bards and trumpeters', Druids and 'Ministers of the Sanctuary' made their way along Maiden Lane (now York Road) to the Llandin at Parliament Hill. My pilgrimage takes me in a slightly different direction north, but first of all to Chapel Market in the hunt for a quick lunch.

On the other side of Pentonville Road a pleasure garden still stands. The traffic thundering on the east–west route makes it hard to see how this would have been an area where, as Charles Harper wrote, 'the sweet meadows afforded country rambles.' The Belvedere Tavern was known for its games of rackets and 'men with learned horses, musical glasses, and sham philosophical performances, gave evening entertainments'. It's now called the Lexington and offers 'Live music, rare bourbons, American beers, Home Cooked food, Sexy Bartenders'. People are a lot more easily pleased these days than they were in the 18th century.

The Belvedere Tavern, also previously known as Busby's Folly, stands on the corner of Penton Street, the first part of the Pentonville development of the early 1800s by Henry Penton. Gordon might argue that his name drew him to Penton Mound but killjoys will tell you that Pentonville was named after him. Whatever Penton's vision for his 'new residential suburb' built on the fields of white saxifrage celebrated not only for their springs but for the dairy herds that grazed here, the Pentonville that grew up around this first row of houses became notorious as a grimy, insalubrious district. Harper describes it as covering 'from the congested squalid commercialities of King's Cross to the less congested, but still squalid district of the "Angel", Islington'.

To me this was home when I returned from a bout of travelling to finally plant roots and start a family. The sweeping westward views that drew city clerks on their days off are still there in the breaks between the buildings. Hordes of pleasure-seekers continue to make their way to 'Merry Islington' for the bars and restaurants. Early-morning pram walks used to involve slaloming round unconscious revellers and puddles of vomit.

I'd been hoping to pick up a new fold-out cabbies' map of London that I'd bought in the Knowledge Point opposite the Public Carriage Office, but it's no longer there. This intimidating grey building is where black-cab drivers come to be tested on the Knowledge – a comprehensive mental map of the roads of London that every cabbie must master. Learning the Knowledge sounds like an initiation rite for entry into a high-powered sect – the London Taxi Drivers. Lawyers practise law, doctors study medicine, freemasons observe 'the craft', but cabbies master the Knowledge. Imagine if you could fuse the hive mind of the Mount Pleasant Sorting Office with the Knowledge of the Public Carriage Office – it would form a London Mega-Brain, a super-consciousness of postcodes, rat-runs, open-spaces and one-way systems. We could ask it the answer to the question, 'Does London Exist?' The answer could well come out as 'Gants Hill', leaving us all none the wiser.

I move on quickly into Chapel Market where I can sate the desire for Manze's pie and mash that had been stirred in Walthamstow. I order a small pie and, with a dollop of mash smeared around one side of the plate and swimming in parsley liquor, it is placed on the marble counter top. The tea comes in a glass mug with the spoon standing upright. I settle on a wooden bench in one of the booths under the glow of a line of petal-shaped lights reflecting in the mirrors. It is a gleaming, working-class food palace. The white-tiled walls are broken up with brown borders containing a band of decorated green tiles embossed with a chain of ribboned flowers.

It's the kind of detail that would have caught the attention of Geoffrey Fletcher, author of books and pamphlets on overlooked London, his most famous being *The London Nobody Knows*. The film version surreally features James Mason in the sunset of his Hollywood stardom in 1969 wandering around abandoned theatres, street markets and an 'egg-breaking plant' in Southwark, wearily pointing out oddities and eccentricities. There is a sequence shot in Manze's – live eels are sliced into chunks, tooth-less oldies and mucky-faced toddlers stir bowls of green liquor and fork blobs of mash into their gobs to a weird early-electronic *Star Trek*-sounding music track. It makes eating pie and mash look like a trip to the Twilight Zone.

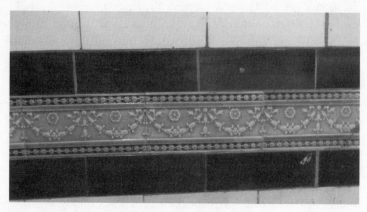

The decorative tiles in Manze's Pie and Mash shop

The market has resisted the endemic gentrification of Islington. There's something resolutely proletarian about the Chapel even though they've opened a Waitrose on the site of Woolworths.

The Chapel is all about designer T-shirts for a fiver. Pot-boiler romances third-hand by the box. Pot-smoking paraphernalia (I regret not buying the Bin Laden spliff-holder even though I've never smoked). The Arsenal merchandize stall. And, of course, fruit and veg and fresh fish – the backbone of the market. The attempted farmers' market only lasted a couple of weeks before they realized the taste for over-priced unicorn cheese and loaves of artisan breads costing a quarter of a dole cheque didn't stretch this far from Barnsbury. When you're on a tight budget, to pay triple price for a pound of broad beans they'd have to be magic of the Jack variety, rather than organic à la Jamie. The popular image of Islington as the fiefdom of self-satisfied 'fauxhemians' smugly reading the *Guardian* in a hot tub of caffè latte, whilst true of a percentage of the local demographic, is by no means a fair representation, as the farmers' market found out.

Past S. Cohen's emporium of wonderful clutter and through Sainsbury's car park leads to one of the most significant of the old pleasure grounds – White Conduit House. Tolpuddle Street, named in honour of the mass march that mustered here in support of the martyrs, brings up a memory of another famous convict. One afternoon in 2005, with a baby Ollie strapped to my chest in a sling, I wandered into a large throng of photographers and TV crews penned in behind a barrier outside the police station opposite White Conduit House.

'What's going on?' I asked the bobby at the door.

'We've arrested a celebrity.'

'What type?' I probed, whilst the media throng listened for any snippets of info.

'A singer.'

'Any particular singer?'

'Pete Doherty.'

'Ah ... Who's he?' I asked with my sleep-deprived baby brain.

The policeman looked stumped. A cameraman eagerly jumped in to fill the silence.

'He's the lead singer of the Libertines.' He then turned to the journo next to him, meekly saying, 'That's right, isn't it? That *is* the name of the band?'

Fame is hollow and transient in all its forms but White Conduit House held on to its for far longer than the Libertines or any of their spin-offs. It lives on as a Georgian restaurant, Little Georgia, but, high up, letters carved just beneath the eves spell out its former name. *The Book of Days* records that it marked 'the extreme verge of London', famous across the city for its hot loaves. There were firework displays during the week, balloon rides drew huge crowds and boxes for tea drinking hung with pictures were cut into the hedges of the long walks. A ballroom was built and archery practised in the extensive grounds.

White Conduit House

The small playground and Culpepper Community Garden behind Little Georgia could lay claim to being the true home of cricket. The nobility of London used to play cricket on White Conduit Fields until one of their bowlers, Thomas Lord, found a new ground in Marylebone and the world-famous MCC was born at Lord's. The Georgian restaurant is closed so I can't check to see if this famous connection is celebrated. When it was the Penny Farthing pub there was a framed blazer on the wall and near the fag machine a kind of dusty cricket monument made from a bat and pads resting on a leather kit bag. I only went there a couple of times; like White Conduit House of lore it became a haunt for ne'er-do-wells and eventually closed.

I stopped to tie my shoelace on a low, circular brick wall topped with an iron railing that I'd never previously given much thought to. Its sole purpose seems to be to protect a patch of weeds, and gather fizzy-drink bottles and chocolate wrappers. It now strikes me as odd. Chambers has a sketch of the old stone casing of the conduit that gave its name to the pleasure grounds. It's mentioned in 16th-century documents as feeding water to the Charterhouse in Clerkenwell via an aqueduct. By 1827 the conduit 'was in a pitiable state of neglect'. Could this be it, the source of the spring, an oddity on the pavement? White Conduit House is holding on to its secrets.

I pop into the cornershop across the road that kept me supplied with cans of beer and packets of Pampers during the years I lived on the Barnsbury Estate. Today I'm just buying a Twix. One day on the run to get the gas card charged up I walked in whilst a group of boys were excitedly regaling Borat behind the counter with the story of the suitcase they had just fished out of Regent's Canal, which runs past the bottom of the estate. 'There was a leg with half a bum,' one said matter-of-factly. A torso and other limbs were recovered from the water. The police initially thought the victim had been murdered in a ritual killing. The *Evening Standard* headline ran 'VOODOO FEAR OVER BODY IN REGENT'S PARK CANAL'. 'RIPPER KILLING HORROR' screamed the *Islington Gazette*. It turned out to be a young Somali woman, Nasra Ismail, who had been living in a homeless shelter in King's Cross and working as a prostitute. She was murdered by an unemployed 53-year-old punter by the name of Daniel Archer who lived nearby in Conistone Way, close to the old Caledonian Cattle Market. I made a note on my blog that however much I loved the area we would move before the kids were old enough to go fishing.

All is quiet as I slowly wander through the estate car park. Its pre-war U-shaped blocks felt like a comforting brick embrace in those skint but happy baby years. We lived in a one-bed ground-floor flat by the lift. In the days after we brought our first newborn home from the hospital people we'd never seen before came to the door with gifts and money. Bin-liners full of brand-name baby clothes were regularly left for us outside. After sleepless nights of crying, neighbours gently approached us the next day with suggested remedies and reassurances that everything would be all right. On warm evenings we put a fold-up table outside the front door, turning the paving slabs into a *terrazzo*. Friends came and sat on the ground, music oozed from flats above and met in the air, forming impromptu remixes. They were good times.

Our flat was sold by the landlord and the new owner has raised a high fence around the front door. There's no sign of Brian, who used to sit outside his front door like a sentinel, even in cold weather like today. It strikes me that I'm walking on the path to the toddler playground where Ollie took his first steps outside. As soon as he was confident on his feet he insisted I take him on night-time laps of the estate, stopping to examine every cigarette butt and snail that we passed. Kids are natural urban explorers.

I'm tempted to follow the toddler trail down to Regent's Canal, where it emerges from the tunnel running from the other side of Angel. But that would take me on a wholly other drift – I have my sights set firmly on Hornsey.

The end block of the estate on Copenhagen Street is called Copenhagen House – both take their name from Copenhagen Fields, which now lies under the Market Estate, further north off the Cally. In 1795 a crowd of 40,000 people gathered at Copenhagen House Inn in support of the London Corresponding Society, which was committed to the idea of universal suffrage and parliamentary reform. It was from here that up to 100,000 supporters of the Tolpuddle Martyrs marched.

The inn had been one of the original pleasure gardens that drew city folk north. 'Sex workers use the park and accost people on Market Road,' warned a bulletin put out by the Friends of Caledonian Park in 2005. The working girls had been pushed north by the development of King's Cross. The pleasure grounds and old cattle market were taken over by pimps, prostitutes, kerb-crawlers, and undercover police surveillance twitching in the bushes. Men reading their papers on the park benches were approached for business. The *Islington Gazette* carried the gruesome story of a prostitute picked up in Market Road then pushed out of a seven-and-a-half-tonne lorry and crushed to death under its back wheels after rowing about the cost of oral sex. The estate deteriorated badly over the years and residents were quoted in the *Gazette* describing it as 'hell'. The tall Victorian clock tower left over from its time in the Caledonian Cattle Market stuck out as an incongruous remnant of its momentous past life. Pock-marked murals in the courtyard were further echoes, along with the gin palaces in the undergrowth. The estate was eventually demolished and rebuilt from the ground up.

Heading into Barnard Park I pass the dodgy Irish boozer where I'd seen a pre-fame Russell Brand perform to an audience of three people, including the staff. Russell had been part of that group of comedians I'd met in the rehearsal room above a pub in Hounslow. Whilst others had gradually fallen away he'd steadily refined his craft over the ensuing years and here he was headlining the gig. As I'd walked in the door the barman had passed me on the way out with a bleeding head. When Russell arrived the MC announced that the gig had been cancelled because there wasn't an audience, assuring him that he'd still be paid. This didn't deter Russell. Not only did he perform for the few that were there but he put on a bravura extended set. The barman's blood and broken glass on the floor were quickly forgotten. He performed the same material two years later to a packed Albert Hall live on Channel 4 as he was being catapulted into the national consciousness. Some of the seeds of that triumph had been sown in the empty pub on Copenhagen Street.

Barnard Park was a schizophrenic place. Islington has such a paucity of open spaces that it can ill afford them to suffer from such mental instability. At night teenagers engaged in bacchanalian frenzies. Next morning, pushing Ollie and later baby Joe to the swings in a pram, you'd have to dodge burnt-out scooters and clear up the smashed Smirnoff bottles. Once it was safe, Oliver would hold us hostage in the playground for up to five hours straight, gleefully moving from the geodesic climbing frame to the concrete sandpit (the sand had been removed because it was full of broken glass) and on to the Zebedee things, round and round, Joe watching him from the pram with a Zen-like gaze.

Seven years later a man in an anorak on his own wistfully gazing into an empty children's playground probably looks odd but there's nobody around so it doesn't matter. I'd been hoping for an early shot of spring but instead it's been bitterly cold. In the time that I'm standing reminiscing about a pre-Xbox era the sun breaks through and the temperature lifts by a degree or two.

The nocturnal frenzies and scooter races of the local delinquents would have been audible to Tony Blair, who lived yards away in Richmond Crescent. The houses in Richmond Avenue curiously have sphinxes and obelisks either side of the steps up to the front door. Some of the sphinxes have their eyeballs painted in white, which gives them an unsettling look. It's said they reflect the Victorian fascination with all things Egyptian when the houses were built. Graham Hancock believes that the sphinx in Giza is several thousand years older than previously thought and along with the pyramids represent part of a giant star-map laid out on earth pointing towards the Belt of Orion. I can't work out if these sphinxes are aligned with the Belt of Orion but they do appear to be staring directly along the route to the northern heights.

Sphinxes on Richmond Avenue

Following the sphinxes' gaze takes me across Thornhill Square, the mother of the Barnsbury squares. Barnsbury, like other parts of the borough, was depopulated after the war, houses were bomb-damaged, others neglected. It's incredible now to think that some of the most sought-after property in London could barely be given away fifty years ago. The Luftwaffe could be said to have played a significant role in the gentrification of Islington through this process of war-time blight. As the city started to be rebuilt, one side of Caledonian Road was adopted by the property-savvy middle classes, the other spawned new council estates on the bomb-sites. Two Londons sit side by side.

Coming through the Barnsbury streets of towering, white Victorian piles on a No. 153 bus from Hornsey as a student was like being on safari. We gawped out through the moving window at a curious habitat belonging to a different species. What was this secluded world where the houses were marked with Blue Plaques, we wondered? What were its customs and values? It felt like a world that we couldn't access, visible only from the bus for a few stops before it had gone. It still retains that air of distance, even on foot. Chalk to the cheese of the pebbledash civilization of Sudbury.

I'm tempted to stop for a pint in the Hemingford Arms. The inside looks like a bric-a-brac shop turned inside out. I sat one evening nervously sipping a pint under a huge antique pram dangling from the ceiling. There was an accordion and a tuba hanging over the table in front. I picked a book randomly off the shelf; it was *Pilgrim's Progress*, this memory a message from the past urging me forward.

Roman Way is within the sphinxes' gaze and leads behind Pentonville Prison where Pete Doherty did his stir. He wrote a song about it for the Babyshambles album *Albion*. However 'wicked and rough' Doherty found his time, Pentonville had softened since it was built in the 1840s along the lines of a US 'separate system'. All prisoners were held in solitary confinement in cells that were individually plumbed to prevent the convicts communicating by tapping the pipes. Five wings join in an all-seeing eye at the centre of a panopticon. The regime was so harsh it even upset the Victorians. How many men from these tough estates have ended up being incarcerated on the other side of the road in the 'Ville'? Harper points out the irony that the prison is, in fact, in Barnsbury rather than Pentonville. Barnsbury Prison sounds a lot nicer but wouldn't be good for the property prices or the dinner-party conversation.

These are the kind of backstreets it's easy to by-pass unless you have a functional reason to seek them out, an address sent by text inviting you to a party, an unusually cheap flat listed as 'must-see' in *Loot*, or you're on a short-cut taken by a cabbie whose Knowledge extends beyond the tested 'runs'. It's a place between postcodes, N1 crunching against N7, with few people sure what to call it.

I'm looking forward to a mooch among the oddities of Holloway Road. The 'hollow-ways' were sunken tracks leading between raised banks – here cutting a path straight up into the northern heights and out beyond London. Holloway Road was a place you could escape to and lose time. With no other plan, find your way to Holloway Road then follow your senses. It's a place where things always seem to be occurring; you need your wits about you round here. A woman was randomly attacked with a samurai sword in the early hours of Christmas Eve. The No. 43 bus that travels up to Archway and 'suicide bridge' has its own crime statistics.

There's a shop with a window full of magic talismans, round metal pendants labelled 'Circle of Life', 'Earth Star Flower', 'Dharma Wheel', 'Aphrodite's Flower'. Inside are shelves of

Protection Water, Money Sprays, potions to break jinxes. A woman casually calls a friend to ask if she would like her to pick anything up, a bit like if you were at the corner shop calling home to see if you needed any milk or bread. After a long pause she asks the lady behind the counter, 'Have you got anything to ward off evil spirits?' Then back on the phone to her friend: 'Yep, they've got that but it's fifteen quid. Do you still want it?' The friend is clearly sensing psychic disturbance and is prepared to pay the price. Maybe she lives near Barnard Park. 'Thanks, I'll have that and might as well take a couple of housework potions as well.'

The vintage-clothes shop has a rack of velvet jackets sorted into shades from red to blue. This leads to an assortment of 1970s tracksuit tops then leather jackets. I buy a half-price check shirt for my next trip to Walthamstow Village. Blood Brothers Tattoo Studio is boarded up – perhaps it was the name. These are the kinds of shops occultist writer Arthur Machen wrote that 'stir the blood of the adventurer' when he was passing through Holloway on his way to investigate a poltergeist case 'in a certain northern quarter of London'. I'm on my way to the setting of the classic zombie romp *Shaun of the Dead*, so I sense a certain parallel across the 90-year divide between our journeys.

I duck into the Coronet to use the toilet. It's a cinema mutated into a cavernous Wetherspoon's. Voices echo beneath the central dome, which outdoes the cupola of San Pietro in Little Italy. Old folk elegantly probe their fish and chips and peas, with a pint on the side to wash it down. Wetherspoon's pubs are almost like an extension of the welfare state with the way they feed and shelter the elderly and the hard-up. A gallery of old-time movie stars stands over the door as you return to Holloway Road.

The mansion blocks above the shops hold the luminous glow of the sun. The northern heights glimmer in the distance. There is a large campus of my alma mater, City Poly, now merged with North London Polytechnic to form London Metropolitan University. City Poly never had a new annexe built by an award-winning architect. Daniel Libeskind's crumpled tin-foil graduate centre is called the Orion Building. Pulling out my *Geographia Atlas*, it's too much to hope that it forms an alignment with the sphinxes on Richmond Avenue. I place a sheet of A4 across the pages following the line; Holloway Road runs at an angle pointing north-west, slicing across the sphinxes' gaze. My finger follows the road to the point where the lines cross and I correlate that with the site of Libeskind's building. The Orion Building sits directly in line with the sphinxes in Richmond Avenue, just as Graham Hancock believes the Great Sphinx in Egypt is aligned with the Belt of Orion. A beautifully serendipitous accident emerges from the maze of houses, busy thoroughfares and a bestselling book about the mysteries of the ancient world.

Into Hornsey Road and the ascent of the northern heights begins. Machen believed this was the territory to which you should bring the person who thinks they know London. Writing in *Wonderful London* in the 1920s he said, 'Take him to the Hornsey Road and he will discover that his London is but a tiny island in the midst of an unknown, unnavigated sea.' I spy a group of football fans with carrier bags from the Arsenal gift shop who seem to have just come to this realization. They could be refugees from the Gunners' mauling by Bayern Munich the night before. The Emirates Stadium mushrooms out of the end of the road.

Hornsey Road has that feel of a mysterious byway not recorded on any map, a glitch in the Matrix. Its original name was Devil's Lane. 'To the right and left strike off the long roads to worlds undreamed of,' writes Machen of the streets that lead away to Stroud Green, Tollington and Finsbury Park.

Hornsey Road's judgemental windows

Stucco around the windows above the eclectic mix of shop fronts belongs to the time of Machen's visit. The arched detail next to dead square trimmings appears like a sequence of facial expressions – judgemental Victorian eyes gazing down on the people in the street below.

Machen trundled up here by omnibus from King's Cross. The neon lights on the side of the Hornsey Road Baths would have looked new-fangled in the 1920s. It was a fulcrum of community life where aside from a scrub-down in one of the slipper baths you could catch a concert or watch a boxing match. The bricks are burnished lust red by the late-afternoon sun. There is a tedious inevitability about its conversion into the entrance of a complex of 'contemporary' apartments. Machen's omnibus terminated at the Hanley Arms with its polished granite pillars and elaborate, curled, golden ironwork. It lives on as a mosque and the buses rattle all the way up Hornsey Rise and on to Crouch End Broadway. A long cable dangles down from the satellite dishes on the roof above the launderette like a noose. It's tempting to think that Hornsey Road has seen better days but I'm not sure it has.

Through the quiet streets of Stroud Green, my feet starting to get sore, the sun descending behind the western hills of earlier walks. The temperature drops a degree or two. I'm grateful for the new scarf my mother-in-law recently sent from Italy for my birthday.

I turn into another Mount Pleasant, once again in close proximity to a covered reservoir. There are no grand mythologies here that I'm aware of, although the pinched-nose Victorian villas lean back from the steep ascent of the pavement in an unnerving manner. Eyes are naturally drawn up to attic windows half expecting to catch a glimpse of a ghostly spectre. Was this the northern suburb Machen was heading to on his poltergeist hunt?

The Parkland Walk built on the tracks of the railway line to Alexandra Palace passes overhead on a viaduct. Prince of horror Stephen King was inspired to write a short story, 'Crouch End', after taking a walk along there.

Seams of occult history run through these dark hills and valleys. It was the home of revered 15th-century astrologist and necromancer Roger Bolingbroke, arrested for using his powers of communicating with the dead in a plot against Henry VI.

Somewhere in these streets further north on Devil's Lane was where the Highgate Vampire was said to reside. The British Psychic and Occult Society conducted vigils and investigations into claims that a 'black apparition' or 'King Vampire' was at work in the area of Highgate Cemetery on a western spur of the northern heights. For a brief period in 1970 London was gripped in a vampire frenzy that led large mobs of people to converge on the cemetery tooled up with stakes, crucifixes and holy water. This wasn't a pale, sexy, *Twilight* Hollywood vampire but a proper red-eyed, demonic, blood-sucking, fox-mutilating one in the Count Dracula tradition. A rivalry sparked off between the two principal vampire slayers, Sean Manchester and David Farrant, which from a distance seems to have taken on an air of pantomime about it.

Manchester claims to have finally 'staked' the vampire's corpse in a Hornsey back garden in 1973. Now that vampires are all the rage surely it can't be long till the Highgate Vampire lurches out of his coffin again, and gets an agent and a publicist.

I arrive at the junction of Weston Park and Nelson Road in the last ten minutes of twilight, just enough time to carry out the final planned act of this walk. I try not to look as if I'm loitering outside the house that I'm certain was used as the exterior location for Shaun's house in *Shaun of the Dead*. I watch the scene I'm about to re-enact on a YouTube clip on my phone. The same scene is repeated twice in a smooth single tracking shot.

The first time Shaun, played by Simon Pegg, leaves the house on his way to work, a kid is playing football in the street outside (Nelson Road). He crosses Nelson Road and a homeless man with a dog asks him for change. Crossing Weston Park Shaun is nearly hit by a car, a man on the opposite kerb is washing his car. Shaun trips on the kerb, or it could be the bucket. A lady leaves the house next to the shop. A jogger runs past, an old man is sweeping the street. The camera tracks Shaun through the open door of the corner shop, he glances at the biscuits but goes straight to the fridge, picks up a can of Diet Coke, puts it back in favour of a can of proper Coke. There are newspapers on the counter, including a copy of the *Hornsey Journal*. Nelson the shopkeeper says to Shaun, 'No beer today? 'No, it's a bit early for me,' Shaun replies.

The next time Shaun goes to the shop, the morning after a long session in the Winchester Arms with his slacker sidekick Ed, the homeless man is wandering around in the middle of Nelson Road, a shopping trolley is abandoned on the pavement where Shaun was nearly run over, a bollard has been knocked on its side, the windscreen of the car is smashed, a man sprints in panic down the street where there was a jogger, bags of rubbish are spilled over the pavement by the street cleaner's cart. Shaun's glance at the biscuits means he doesn't notice the bloody hand-prints on the fridge door, he picks up the can of Coke but this time puts it back in favour of Diet (he has a note to himself to sort his life out), he nearly slips over on what we can safely assume is blood. He grabs Ed a Cornetto from the freezer by the counter, there are no newspapers. He leaves the change on the counter and ambles back to his house in Nelson Road oblivious to the zombies roaming the streets of Hornsey. After verifying these details standing outside the house in Nelson Road there is just enough light for me to film myself retracing Shaun's footsteps with my pocket camera.

There's no homeless person in Nelson Road. There are no people at all. No car outside the house next to the shops that emit a homely orange glow. No jogger, no street cleaner, no bags of rubbish or passing cars, not even a single zombie outside the shop. The aisle to the fridge is exactly as it is in the film down to the tempting biscuits stacked on the shelves. The fridge is the same, minus the bloody hand-prints. I confess that I paused and looked for a can of Stella for medicinal purposes but couldn't see one. 'No beer today' for me either. There's also no Diet Coke, only bottles of Coke, no cans.

As I approached the counter I quickly glanced at the freezer but suddenly felt self-conscious. It was far too cold for a Cornetto. But the shopkeeper had seen me and had a big smile across his face. 'Don't suppose you have any Cornettos?' I asked. He let out a big laugh. He gets a fairly regular stream of *Shaun* tourists, 'even from the US'. He opens the freezer for me and I get the last 'Classic' Cornetto, just like Shaun. I test his tolerance for *Shaun* trivia: 'No papers, Nelson' – I repeat the line from the film. He looks a bit perplexed. 'It's in the film but also it's a reference to *Sean's Show*, the influential early-90s sitcom on Channel 4.' That baffles him even more. There's an awkward silence till he says, 'Simon Pegg even came back here once,' and he laughs again.

This Hornsey shopkeeper is one of the great unsung heroes of the British tourist industry.

Standing outside the shop trying to open a bottle of Coke and unwrap a Cornetto wearing gloves I feel a deep sense of satisfaction. The timing of my jerky tracking shot is only a couple of seconds longer than Shaun's – and it's a fairly good shot-for-shot match; the kids will be suitably impressed.

Moving through the dark streets towards the Broadway you notice that there's something curious about Crouch End. Hippies were drawn here in the 1960s by the tales that it was a place where two ley lines crossed, marking it out as a location of great psychic energy. Bob Dylan famously came here to record at Dave Stewart's studio and accidentally went for tea with the mother of another bloke called Dave. Trapped in the valley between Hornsey and Highgate it is out of time, a lost village accessible only by bus and the Gospel Oak line at the top of Crouch Hill. It's the place Will Self used as the setting for his short story *The North London Book of the Dead* – Crouch End, the place where people go to live after they die. This area is continuously linked with tales of the undead.

I keep an eye out for Sean Hughes. It's entirely possible that *Sean's Show* has continued running in real time in the parallel Crouch End universe. Anywhere else a clock tower represents a moment in history of civic pride, the way that the opening of Costa Coffee in Leytonstone was celebrated. In Crouch End the glowing clock face could be the mark point for the junction of the ley lines, lit up by the power of the earth grid.

There's that rarest of oddities on the Broadway – a record shop selling vinyl. I buy the Mission's first EP, the cover illustrated with an esoteric symbol. A sign in the window invites you to take purchased records over the road to the Harringay Arms where you can spin them on a turntable and claim a discounted pint. The Harringay Arms is a further throwback, a hush as I enter before the quiet chatter resumes, dart flights and stems for sale behind the bar. Looking around the room the drinkers could either be cast as ghosts, zombies or vampire hunters in the various gloomy tales of Crouch End. It would still be a brave man to break the muffled hubbub by spinning goth rock on the record deck. You could end up in a Wicker Man. I'm not prepared to take any risks at this stage of the day. I settle down in a corner with a pint of ale and start to plot the next expedition.

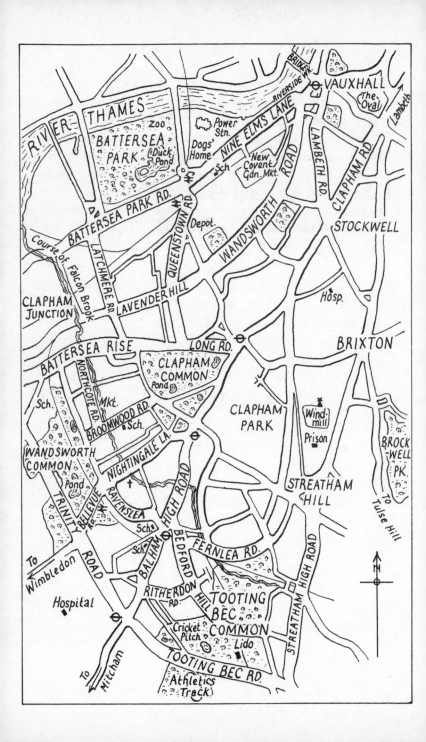

CHAPTER 9

LIFE ON MARS
Vauxhall to Tooting Bec

When the Central Line goes down Leytonstone is stranded like an island hemmed in by forest and marshland. The scramble of commuters piling on to rail replacement bus services is like the Fall of Saigon. The fact that the engineering works are 'scheduled' makes it no less annoying. I'd 'scheduled' a walk in south-west London.

Weeks of school runs had limited my excursions. There had been further forays across the parish border into Upper Walthamstow and the E17 Bohemian Grove. A wander to the southern tip of Leytonstone, where West Ham Cemetery sits behind the back gardens of Cann Hall Road and bare trees form a long ceremonial arch to the war memorial. But I hadn't crossed the River Lea since the yomp up to Hornsey.

The way had finally opened for adventures further afield. The One-Inch map on the box-room wall had a gaping void south of Hounslow and west of Tulse Hill – I had no chance of obtaining the Knowledge but I could at least have a go at adding a slither of the London Borough of Wandsworth to my evolving impression of the city.

Tooting had been on my mind for a while. It crops up in three principal sources – Walter Bell's *Where London Sleeps*, Maxwell's *The Fringe of London* and, notably, in the 1970s sitcom *Citizen Smith*. But most intriguing of all, the name of Tooting is written across the face of Mars. Just west of Olympus Mons on Mars is a 27-km-diameter crater called Tooting, named by planetary scientist Peter Mouginis-Mark in honour of the place of his birth. He couldn't just arbitrarily scribble Tooting on to the Martian map; the naming had to be approved by the International Astronomical Union. Surely there must have been a temptation to come up with something a bit more cosmic than Tooting when submitting an entry for *The Gazetteer of Planetary Nomenclature*. After all the crater sits in the region of Amazonis Planitia. However, Tooting was clearly cosmic enough for the International Astronomical Union. Mouginis-Mark's website not only points out the scientific and geological characteristics of the Tooting crater, with graphics and images from the Martian surface, but also has some nice pictures of Tooting Bec tube station and the No. 155 bus on the Broadway.

It took the *Curiosity* rover 253 days to reach Mars; I'd quite like to get to the Earth Tooting in slightly less time, even with the never-ending tinkering with the 150-year-old tube network. The quickest way was not by rocket but north-east to south-west on the Victoria Line from Blackhorse Road. The first stop south of the river is Vauxhall – that would be as good a place to start as any, my equivalent of Gale Crater where *Curiosity* touched down.

I woke up to a blizzard – the week before Easter and spring feels as likely as the Second Coming. The boys invite me to join them building Lego figures for a zombie-survival scenario. It's a tempting proposition but so is the sight of Battersea Power Station in a snow flurry.

Breakfast is a crispy-bacon roll munched at Leyton Midland Road Station, biting through layers of greaseproof paper to reach the edible content. The cappuccino froth filled to the brim splatters on the platform as I remove the lid and promptly burn my tongue. The shelter acts more as a wind tunnel than providing protection from the elements. This had been my alternative commute to work, a scenic phantom ride above the rooftops of North London – Walthamstow Queens Road, Blackhorse Road, South Tottenham, Harringay Green Lanes, Upper Holloway, Crouch Hill to Gospel Oak – each stop an invitation to get off the train and explore. Today the departure point is Blackhorse Road to start the descent south – scuttling down the Victoria Line to Vauxhall.

My use of the tube today could be recast as a clumsy tribute to Harry Beck, born in a street adjacent to Leyton Midland Road and just honoured with a Blue Plaque at the place of his birth. It's Beck's revolutionary 'topological' map, designed in 1933, that we still use to navigate our way around the London Underground. His great innovation was to separate the geographical reality of the network from the representational map, untangling the matted wad of lines and stations into a fluid diagram. An out-of-hours project that was initially greeted with scepticism eventually became the default model for metro maps around the world, from Moscow to New York and Tokyo. The Victoria Line, however, was added in 1960 without Beck's knowledge, an act that apparently deeply saddened him. It was like someone working for the king of France daubing a moustache on the *Mona Lisa* without asking Leonardo da Vinci.

Vauxhall is a good place to leave – the Vauxhall Cross interchange spits you out of its whirlygig of underground tunnels to be battered by traffic noise and riverine winds. According to *Time Out* it's become 'London's Gay Village', home to the infamous Vauxhall Tavern. There are even attempts to rebrand it 'Voho'.

It's commemorated in the title of one of Morrissey's finest albums, *Vauxhall and I* – a likely merging of film references – *Withnail*, and the Free Cinema Movement documentary *We Are the Lambeth Boys*, shot nearby at Alford House Boys Club in 1959. The track 'Spring-Heeled Jim' plays out with snatches of audio from the film.

The album was released in 1994, the same year as Patrick Keiller's seminal film, *London*. The unseen enigmatic central character, Robinson, lives in a council flat in Vauxhall, 'in the way that people were said to live in the cities of the Soviet Union'. Keiller's film is shot over the course of 1992 against the backdrop of IRA bombings, an improbable Conservative Party general election victory and the economic meltdown of Black Wednesday. This is the atmosphere in which Robinson undertakes a series of journeys on foot from Vauxhall researching an academic project – 'The problem of London'.

The film somehow manages to be elegiac whilst portraying a city in a downward slump, head in hands gazing into a pint of flat beer. It was the year I left polytechnic and was living on the dole in a squat in Hackney – a year that my love for London became fully consummated, on a second-hand mattress on the bare concrete floor. We lived on a dish called 'Tuna Surprise' – the surprise being that it often didn't have any tuna in it. Evenings were spent making our own version of Monopoly for the new London we saw around us – Squatopoly was a minor hit on the Frampton Park Estate. The Bishopsgate bomb that Keiller shows in the film knocked me out of bed one morning and shook all our windows, the BOOM bouncing between the estate blocks. The Tesco on Homerton High Street only sold 'Value' own-brand goods that had those plain blue and white striped labels – nothing else, aisles and aisles of blue and white labels. It was like shopping in the Eastern Bloc. Hackney Council were giving away flats in lotteries. You could buy a maisonette in Victoria Park for under thirty grand – where today you'd have to add an extra nought on the end to even open the bidding. *London* is a 16mm postcard from that strange past.

Robinson's expeditions from Vauxhall take him to the haunts of Romantic poets and European exiles. The narrator tells us how he's adopted a local park for experiments in 'psychic landscaping, drifting and free association'. I perform my own free association by wandering into the St George Wharf development past the signs pointing pedestrians away from the construction site of the St George Tower.

When completed, this 150-metre-tall steel and glass Pringles tube will be London's highest solely residential skyscraper. Where once tower blocks were seen as engines of social decay, One St George Wharf is touted as a 'catalyst to regeneration in the surrounding neighbourhood'. After hearing for years that high-rise living is the perfect recipe for dysfunction and mental illness, it's now being sold as the 'epitome of luxury London living'. That should please Nick in his Childs Hill council block.

Lifts bearing workers clank up and down an exterior shaft. A crane sits atop, obscured by mist. At 8 a.m. on 16 January 2013 a helicopter clipped the top of the crane, sending it spiralling into the street below and setting Wandsworth Road ablaze. News reports talked of 'flaming debris' flying through the air. It's a miracle that the accident only claimed two lives, the pilot and a pedestrian on his way to work. This wasn't the kind of PR that the estate agents were after.

Sitting next to the MI6 building, St George Wharf is like a collision of *Brave New World* and *1984*, a sedated future dystopia under the watchful gaze of Big Brother. Attempts to walk directly between the buildings to the riverbank are continually thwarted by locked gates and 'Private' signs – how can you privatize a reclaimed mudbank? Strictly speaking, this land belongs to Old Father Thames.

St George Wharf portico

Joggers shrink-wrapped in lycra pound through the de Chirico porticos, then do laps of the miniature privet mazes till they get giddy and fall over. Gilles Ivain, aka Ivan Chtcheglov, wrote that in his paintings of imagined Italian townscapes, 'Chirico remains one of the most striking precursors of true architecture. What he was dealing with was absence and presence in time.' It would take more than Robinson's 'psychic landscaping' to see this concrete migraine as representing 'true architecture'.

The 'absence' Chtcheglov writes of in this case is of any kind of soul or humanity. Berthold Lubetkin would shake his head in dismay as it reminded him of the Stalinist Russia he'd left behind. St George Wharf would be at home on the outskirts of Bucharest as an asylum for deposed dictators wandering the corridors still plotting world domination. With penthouses apparently selling for several million pounds a pop there could even be a few retired despots looking down wondering why some mad fool is walking around in circles in the snow.

Ignoring another set of signs declaring the path closed, a view of Battersea Power Station opens up on the next bend of the river. Nine Elms Reach takes its name from the line of trees that were a valuable navigation aid to the Thames watermen. I spent a day out on the river one summer with a Freeman of the Thames who was proudly part of a long line of watermen stretching back centuries. He told me how when he was doing his long apprenticeship the river was so busy in these parts you could skip across from one bank to the other between the barges. The river is quiet today, just an orange powerboat skimming around a single moored barge. The seagulls seem unperturbed by the snow as they come in to land where the waves tiredly bellyflop over the shingle shoreline. Nicholas Barton writes in *The Lost Rivers of London* of a tidal loop at Nine Elms that formed an island. Battersea was originally 'Patricsey' or 'Peter's Island', along with Chels-ea and Thorn-ey Island.

View of the Thames at Nine Elms

The land was drained and put to use. At one point Nine Elms was noted for the quality of its honey. Now it's at the heart of what *The Economist* has called the biggest single redevelopment in London since the Great Fire of 1666. It's being labelled 'London's Third City' after the Square Mile and Westminster. 'Stratford City' is already old news with its hand up at the back of the class, vying for attention: 'Please sir, sir, but I thought I was the "Third City".'

Projected images of the finished development show a *Blade Runner* skyline magicked out of the Thameside mud, with Battersea Power Station the sole reminder that the area had any kind of past before this developer's Year Zero. Whereas London's first two cities are characterized by their idiosyncratic street plans and isolated tall buildings, this Third City is a virtual cloud metropolis – a clusterfuck of skyscrapers. Visitors from Houston or Hong Kong will feel curiously at home, which is just as well as the US will have its new embassy here and it's believed that the Chinese will move in next door. No more noisy anti-war demonstrations and annoying displays by Falun Gong devotees.

Mayor Boris Johnson got so excited that he declared it 'represents the final piece of the jigsaw that completes the central area of London' and his old university chum George Osborne came up with £1 billion of public money to pay for two new Northern Line stations, at Battersea and Nine Elms. They must really like the developers of Nine Elms and Battersea Power Station to build them their own tube stations when most of south-east London remains off the network.

The sculpture of Father Thames fighting a posse of angry-looking eels on William Henry Walk will have to go. The US Embassy is boasting about grand new public gardens that will bring back memories of the famous pleasure grounds at Vauxhall and Battersea – they'd better make sure there are prostitutes and drunken brawls to make it properly authentic.

In the middle of a global economic crisis that has prompted austerity measures forcing millions of people into poverty you have to ask where the billions are coming from to build this missing piece of the jigsaw puzzle. *The Economist* reports that investors include an Irish group and 'Malaysia's state-backed investment fund'. In a world of uncertainty, building blocks of flats on a bog apparently represents a sound investment.

Let them build their Third City but you can't help feeling that the river might have the last word. The Thames will eventually call in the loan and the area will be returned to flooded marshland. The river and its tributaries made London, not a conglomeration of foreign property speculators out for a quick buck. The ancient encampments at Horsenden Hill, Brentford, Hounslow Heath, Erith, Leyton and Barking gaze on with the look of an old head watching a young fool staggering drunk in the street.

What would Robinson make of all this? His investigations led him to the conclusion that 'the true identity of London is its absence, as a city it no longer exists ... London was the first metropolis to disappear' – sucked into a sink hole created by the Nine Elms development that he couldn't have imagined in the beleaguered last years of the Thatcher regime.

The snowflakes are getting bigger. It's becoming bleak by the river. This is an area passed through rather than lingered in and studied. The hounds are howling in Battersea Dogs Home. Wilted flowers are tied to the railing by the bus stop under the railway bridge. In the shadow of Battersea Power Station I went by a workman trudging towards the iconic structure weighed down by a tool belt and heavy box. I considered asking him how it was coming along but he had a weary, defeated look in his eyes. It was time to turn away from this future gated community of architectural phalluses frottaging the grey skies like a pervert in a nice suit on the Northern Line at rush hour. I'm bound for the open Commons.

I turn down Queenstown Road munching a Twix, past mournful Victorian houses that look as if they're blackened by soot from the 1950s. It's possible to believe that they still get London's infamous 'pea-soupers' down this way. Just a bridge away from Chelsea high society, it was the setting for Nell Dunn's 1963 short stories of life in the Battersea slums, *Up the Junction*. The TV version, directed two years later by Ken Loach, brings to life the flirty girls with their saucy banter in the pub with the boys downing pints of Brown. Women packing chocolate Santas on a production line be-bop on their tea-break. The tally man spouts casual racism on his debt-collecting rounds. Teenage girls sing Beatles songs pushing prams under the bridge where I'm sheltering from the snow. 'Used to meet him in a back alley off the Latchmere,' says one. 'I was the youngest bride in Battersea, married at fifteen, had Mike when I was fifteen and a half,' recounts another. Blithely talking about one-night-stands and illicit trysts in the cabin of a ten-tonne truck. Sex in a derelict house with the coat on. Middle-aged lady in a sequined frock playing drums in the local. Young Mods talking about the four-minute warning in the greasy spoon whilst juggling the tomato-shaped ketchup bottle. Fighting with the Old Man in the street outside the pub. It was a shot of social realism from the south side of Swinging London.

Things don't look too different this end of Battersea around Queenstown Road Station – except the hairstyles aren't as nice. 'Let's go swimming up the Common,' one of the boys in the film suggests. That's a good idea; it's where I'm heading. Maybe I'll buy some swimmers and a towel along the way to Tooting Bec.

South London band Squeeze took the title of Nell Dunn's book and twisted it into a glorious pop song that charted at No. 2 in 1979. The girl in their song was from Clapham rather than up from Tooting. The jauntiness of the relocation down the road matches the lifting gloom as the Common comes into sight. Tree roots burst through the pavement and I start to make plans to go to the cinema in the evening.

The blizzard intensifies as I cross Clapham Common. It brings up memories of walking in snowy Fairfield, Iowa, turning away from the two-horse town and finding myself in a featureless white world. I had been rattling around the corridors of the Raj Health Spa, one of about three guests who I only saw at breakfast, where they were tied to an ayurvedic diet and I was craving sinking my teeth into something that had once had a heartbeat. Cabin fever drove me out along Jasmine Avenue to Highway No. 1 where I turned in the general direction of Lake Darling across fields a foot deep in snow.

The Common lacks the vastness of the American Midwest, but at 220 acres it's still a sizeable open space. When bought by the Local Board in 1874 it was 'dedicated to the use and recreation of the public for ever'. Although house builders have exploited every available square of land around its borders the Common will forever remain free of their grasp. Various antiquarians describe it as a sort of 'morass' and that is how it appears today. Ducks paddle around in the deep mud, a cruel wind is sweeping in from Siberia, blowing snow horizontally through the bandstand and splattering the pages of my *Geographia Atlas*. The cold weather doesn't seem to bother the toddlers weebling around in balls of warm clothing, scattering the ducks.

As the snow deepened around me in Iowa and settled in a thick layer over my hat and coat I became aware that rambling across fields in winter with the thermometer at minus 15 was probably a bit stupid, and turned back for the Raj. However bad the weather gets in South London I should be OK as long as I don't lie down for a nap. I push on in the general direction of Balham.

A wooded ridge runs across the end of Broomwood Road, which is folded neatly in half by the Falcon Brook running beneath the tarmac. The Falcon Brook is one of the many lost rivers of London that Nicholas Barton records in his book. The map of these rivers, alongside those still flowing above ground, reveal a vision of London as a city of waterways. These streams, rivers and brooks are all still there, gurgling away through sewer pipes and culverts. Like its Leytonstone cousin the Philly Brook, the Falcon occasionally blows out the street irons and pours on to the street just to remind us of its presence.

Falcon Brook valley

The ridge I'd seen is a line of trees running through the centre of Wandsworth Common. Dogs sniff around the boles of denuded oaks with their walkers hopping from foot to foot to keep warm. Robinson's first walk to Strawberry Hill from Vauxhall ended here as the Common was closed after an IRA bomb had exploded near the train tracks. The bombing was part of a sequence of attacks on the rail network in the lead-up to the 1992 election. The Wandsworth bomb had gone off on Budget Day. Nobody was hurt.

Wandsworth Common forms one corner of a triangle of common land with Clapham and Tooting that collectively amounts to 550 acres of publicly owned land. Just to the south of Tooting is Streatham Common with its 66 acres and nearby is Mitcham Common at an expansive 460 acres. To the west on the other side of the River Wandle is the huge Wimbledon Common covering 1,100 acres. From this high point on Wandsworth Common you are standing at the apex of the Free Lands of South London, three times the size of the City of London, populated not by major financial institutions but by joggers, dog-walkers, cruisers, ducks and earthworms. A metropolis governed by the laws of free access and common rights, enforced by gnarly-toothed gardeners and armies of litter pickers and bulb planters. This is London's Third City – and it's ours.

I'm homing in now on the Martian crater. Streets branch off the bottom of the Common that would take me on various routes into Tooting. Ravenslea Road has an appropriately sounding medieval name to traverse to the ancient manor of Bec. The snow is getting bad, big, wet, blobby snowflakes that give you a slap on the face as they land. A woman struggles along the pavement with five heavy bags of shopping and audibly groans as she bends her head into the blizzard. I momentarily consider offering to give her a hand but then wonder how rude it would be to first enquire how far she has to go. If my act of kindness led too far in the opposite direction I might just lose the will to plough on. In the end my dedication to the quest outweighs my social conscience.

Ravenslea Road sweeps into Balham via a DVD-rental shop with a life-sized stormtrooper in the window. I send a photo to the kids at home. My father shared his love of cricket with me and taught me how to bowl his leg-breaks; I have passed on my love of the original *Star Wars* movies to my sons and given them my Han Solo and Boba Fett action figures.

Oliver instantly rings me, 'Dad, where are you?'

I resist the urge to say, 'On the Death Star,' and instead tell him the truth: 'Balham.'

'Where's that?' he reasonably asks, his world not yet extending south of the river.

'Gateway to the South,' I reply. 'Look it up on YouTube.'

The Balham Stormtrooper

'Bal-ham, gateway to the south,' intones the voice of the American newsreader played by ex-Goon Peter Sellers in a mock radio travelogue recorded in the 1960s. A place of 'happy and contented people'. Fifty years on, the cafés and gastropubs look convivial and enticing – not to mention warm. The former Monkees star Micky Dolenz paid further tribute to Balham by turning Sellers's monologue into a 20-minute film. Not long after this Dolenz produced and directed the popular sitcom *Metal Mickey*, starring a large, talking robot. In the opening scene of the first episode the grandmother throws darts at a board next to a large Squeeze poster. The grandmother was played by Irene Handl who had starred alongside Peter Sellers in the 1959 film *I'm All Right Jack*. All roads lead to Balham.

Stretched out along the Roman Stane Street that runs through Balham, a beguiling urban legend has it that the Nazis planned to have their HQ in the huge 1930s art deco apartment block, Du Cane Court. The German invasion plans for Britain included penetrating London from the south along the military route built by the Romans for moving their legions between London and Chichester, Panzers and Nazi stormtroopers advancing along a way designed for chariots and legionnaires. The legend was given legs by the fact that Du Cane Court was spared from German bombs despite the area being pounded by the Luftwaffe. There is even the belief that seen from the air it's built in the shape of a swastika. No matter how many times I rotated a swastika I couldn't make it fit onto an aerial photo of Du Cane Court – there was always a spare arm sticking out. However, a Google search did turn up a list of Nazi Party members living in Britain in the lead-up to the Second World War, and one of them lived in Du Cane Court.

The art deco Du Cane Court, Balham

The launderette opposite Du Cane Court has a sign in its window notifying customers of Easter opening hours. The Easter Bunny would freeze to death if he came out of his warren now. The 1,000th jogger of the day goes past but this one has an iPad under his arm with headphones plugged into his skull. Things are getting weird as I home in on Mars.

I performed stand-up in a pub on Bedford Hill, Balham. It was a venue where the Clash and U2 had played early in their careers. A vanload of comedians who went on to become household names had also ventured out onto its stage, which as I remember wasn't a stage but a clearing amongst the tables and chairs with a mic on a stand. Noting the heritage of the venue I paraphrased a line used by stalwart MC Ivor Dembina to introduce me at my first gig, that if the gig went badly they could be the ones to say they saw me when I was shit. My diary records that the gig at the Bedford actually went OK. It was August 2002 and my eight-minute set, given over to sardonic opposition to the impending war with Iraq, with quips about a holy crusade against facial hair and sympathy for David Blunkett's guide dog, seemed to go down well. So well in fact that I quit performing stand-up shortly afterwards – go out at the top is what they say.

I turn away from Stane Street as it seamlessly bleeds into Tooting Broadway. Citizen Smith is nowhere to be seen. I look for revolutionary slogans daubed by the Tooting Popular Front, but there's not so much as a Socialist Workers Party flyer stuck to a lamppost. Wolfie Smith, where are you now? The banking system has collapsed and they're building a millionaires' colony on the edge of Battersea subsidized with public money. No, he's not here. Probably grown up, cut his hair, nurtured a beer gut and got a mortgage. I can chalk off one of those dubious achievements.

Tooting was a favourite of music hall comedians looking for a cheap laugh (along with Wigan, for some reason). They have little in common now. Scanning the surface of Tooting today it's hard to see what the gag would be. Club stand-ups get more laughs out of Luton or Brentwood.

Rivulets of housing, criss-crossing like Barton's map of the city's watercourses, run off into Tooting Bec Common – a whole sea of separate lives piled up one on top of the other. Traipses to the supermarket to stock up on ready meals. Early-evening meet-ups at the Wheatsheaf by Tooting tube, hunched over a shared bottle of red wine, swapping confessions. Lads getting the pints in talking *Championship Manager*. Thousands of individual narratives unfolding behind illuminated windows.

You step away from this urban soup once you walk on to Tooting Bec Common. The concerns of nesting rooks are the most pressing issues here. I slosh through deep, cold mud, the London Clay refusing to absorb the water from a long, slushy winter seemingly without end. Oak and hornbeam stand in a lake of flood-water, and brave daffodils that foolishly thought it was time to bloom cling to their roots. William Morden's 1897 description of Tooting's 'swampy fields' in *The History of Tooting Graveney* remains true in 2013. Morden writes that the name comes from the tribe of Totiagas. Another theory combines the name of the Celtic god Teut with 'ing' meaning 'meadow', to make it Teut's Meadow.

Bell's 1926 chapter on Tooting focuses on its manorial records that stretch back to the early 1200s. These document the intimate transactions between the local people and the lord of the manor – a land-holding that came complete with its own 'serfs'. You can imagine little Baldrick-like blokes in hoods and jerkins with warty noses scrambling around on Tooting Common, picking up firewood and nuts, poking around for mushrooms. The 'Bec' in Tooting comes from the Abbey of Bec in Normandy, which owned the land after the Conquest. Now it's controlled by Wandsworth Council.

Tooting Bec Common

I spot a hawthorn in flower – a sign that spring isn't a figment of my imagination. It brings back memories of the walk last May through Wyke Green and the hawthorn bushes in the sunshine.

More wet snow slaps me in the face, bringing me back to reality. I start to question the whole purpose of coming out here today. There's a woman in pink wellies walking her dog – at least she's got an excuse. What's mine? I remember. It wasn't just to join together three of the South London commons or visit Robinson's Vauxhall or look across the busy A24 at Du Cane Court. It was to visit Tooting Bec Lido – but where the hell is it?

I'd walked the length of the common. Freezing mud had found its way through my Gore-Tex boots, the bacon roll and the Twix had worn off, and I couldn't find the biggest open-air swimming pool in London. Maxwell writes of how wild elk roamed over this land in the distant past – if one managed to slip through a fold in time I'd make a jacket from its hide like Han Solo does with a Tauntaun on the ice planet of Hoth in *The Empire Strikes Back*. It could be worse, though – the average temperature of Tooting on Mars is around minus 60 and there are no Tauntauns or elks to keep you warm.

I take heart from the hawthorn flowers and look at my map. The lido is over one hundred years old so is marked on my out-of-date atlas. It takes about twenty minutes to reach the Lido on the far side of the common. The gates are unsurprising padlocked shut at 6 p.m. in cold late March. Through the railings I can see plastic chairs laid out around the gushing fountain. The buildings are all painted an enticing baby blue with the exception of the brightly coloured changing-room doors. There's a real air of art deco glamour hidden amongst the trees. It's so inviting that I'd happily take a dip, even in this weather.

That's exactly what members of the South London Swimming Club do every day, all year round, and have been doing since the Lido opened in 1906. When the water is frozen over the lifeguards break it up and float the ice down to the deep end to thaw. The Sunday-morning races attract up to fifty hardy souls despite the water temperature hovering just above freezing. The Club's Mandy Worsley told me it was an exhilarating experience, the pool full of smiling faces doing laps and widths in the icy blue water.

It was worth walking through the blizzard from Vauxhall to find this vision of summer. *Lido* is the Italian word for 'shoreline' or 'beach'. Just the sight of Tooting Bec Lido stimulates a mental leap forward into a glorious summer of sunburn, BBQs, cold beer, insect bites and moaning about the heat. The Nine Elms development was a psychological Siberian gulag – Tooting Bec Lido is a sun-drenched Venice without the over-priced gondolas.

The snow has finally stopped, and in the bare treetops the birds are optimistically singing in the spring as I make my way back up Bedford Hill.

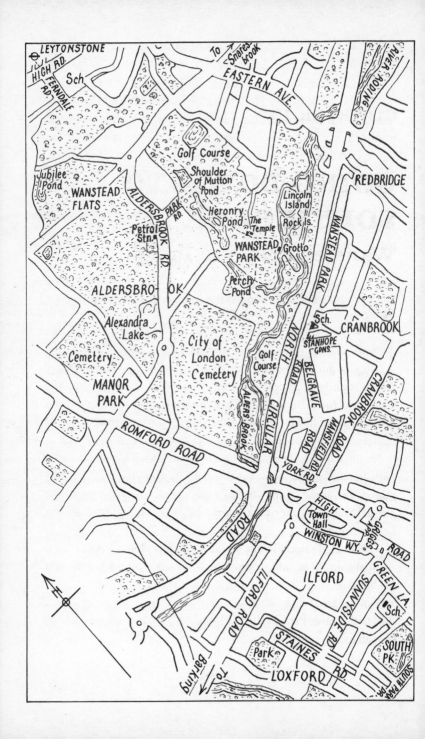

CHAPTER 10

GOING DOWN TO SOUTH PARK
Wanstead Flats to Ilford

It was in the Heathcote Arms after the Orient match that I finally got the boys to agree to come on a walk with me. Ollie's standard response whenever I asked them to join me was, 'You must be joking.' This time Joe gave it some careful thought as he tucked into his BBQ chicken baguette and sipped his lemonade through a straw. 'I'll come on a walk with you … to South Park. Take me on a walk to South Park and I'll come with you.' He was well aware that the South Park of the animated TV show is in Colorado and that Colorado is in the United States of America, and that the USA is a flight away from Leytonstone.

'OK, deal,' I said. 'I'll take you for a walk to South Park.'

'Shake on it,' he said, wiping the BBQ sauce off his hands onto his hoodie.

'I'm in,' said Ollie.

'That's South Park in Ilford,' I said, as we made the deal across the table.

They flung their heads back half in laughter, half in outrage, spitting chewed-up chips across the table as they did so.

'Ilford's not in Colorado!' Joe exclaimed.

'No, but it does have a South Park, and that's the nearest you're going to get to Colorado for a while.'

I now had another reason to justify letting my seven- and nine-year-old sons watch what the unenlightened consider one of the most distasteful and controversial shows on TV. Ollie's initial well-made argument was that a nine-year-old boy should be allowed to watch a cartoon about a group of eight-year-olds. It had clearly taught them a healthy sense of humour, and that the idiocy of adults occasionally needs to be indulged for the greater good, not to mention informing them that the cure for AIDS is an injection of shredded cash, that hybrid cars produce dangerous smug clouds, that Barbra Streisand exists and that *World of Warcraft* has an addictive side. We could now add that it had inspired them to embark on a six-mile pilgrimage to a park to the south of Ilford town centre on the spurious basis that it shares the same name.

The usual preparations and research were mostly put to one side – the main task would be getting the two boys to the other end. Would the conceit wear off by the time we reached the other side of Wanstead Flats where the No. 145 bus passed through to Ilford? It was important for me to co-opt them into my quest. They've been watching me depart on adventures alone, sidling into my box room as I pore over old books and maps, making gentle enquiries about why this study of London fascinated me so much, before leaning over to my laptop and bringing up a funny cat video on YouTube. This was a chance to blood them into the practice of urban rambling.

Of course, they had been on minor excursions with me before. In summer we often walk along the old, narrow Forest Road that runs behind the houses from Leyton up to the Hollow Ponds on the edge of Epping Forest. Or we explore the nearest sections of Wanstead Flats till Joe runs himself puce and collapses on the ground. They've walked the Limehouse Cut to Docklands with Joe reciting his times tables the entire way. They've even ventured through the rump of the forest from Loughton to High Beach in our first autumn out east as a family. But this would be the inaugural walk in which there was real intent to reach an objective no matter how much the legs ached or how sore the feet became.

Our initial attempt to make the journey had failed. Looking from BBC weather reports to the sagging sacks of charcoal clouds in the sky I'd wondered aloud to Heidi whether heading out in such weather with the kids was wise.

'When have we ever done what's wise?' she astutely observed.

Most people would have said the wise thing to do would have been to stay holed up in the spacious Bondi flat I'd moved into with Heidi three weeks after our first date. But then, they probably would also have said it wasn't wise to have moved in together three weeks after our first date. That was 18 years ago. Nor was it particularly advisable to head off to teach English in Italy when turning 30 with hardly any money and nowhere to live. We ended up renting the middle floor of a small *palazzo* for the price of a bedsit. You could say it wasn't overly sensible to start a family when living in a short-term rented basement flat on Liverpool Road, Islington, when neither of us had any savings or a full-time job. She was right. The clouds would clear, the sun would burst through and we'd reach South Park under a glorious sunset.

It started raining before we'd even passed the corner shop. We attempted to take shelter under a bare tree on Wanstead Flats but eventually had to turn back with the rain running out of our pockets. But like Stan and Kenny in the *South Park* episode in which they make the thousand-mile journey to Malibu to get a refund from Mel Gibson because they didn't like his *Passion of the Christ*, we were not to be deterred from our quest.

There was a synchronicity in our reach out for the Far Side of Ilford the week after Easter – *South Park* had first entered our family life when Ollie bought toy figures of three of the characters from the show at a church Easter Fayre. The fact that effigies of the characters were deemed appropriate to be sold in a church at Easter was another reason I let them watch *South Park*. Stan, Kenny and Cartman would be coming on the walk with us.

A large jay swooped into the back garden and perched in the sumac tree on the morning of the walk. With its brightly coloured black, blue and white wing-tips it appeared like an extravagant, unexpected guest. It was a fortuitous sighting as the RSPB website says that they are 'shy woodland birds'. This one must have flown over the rooftops from Epping Forest. I took it as a messenger from the forest telling us that the weather would hold out for us this time but didn't share this with the boys as they'd already denounced me as a 'hippy wizard'. They've had a downer on hippies ever since watching the episode of *South Park* in which the school counsellor becomes a homeless, drug-addicted hippy. Protestations that I'm not actually a hippy would not be helped by claims that birds have been sent by the woodland spirits or even Pan himself. I'm waiting to get them into *The Young Ones* to illustrate that I'm far more like the loser student radical Rick than the lentil-munching hippy Neil.

The hoped-for burst of spring didn't arrive but at least the temperature deigned to raise itself tantalizingly close to double figures for the first time in months. I'd bought us all *South Park* T-shirts for the occasion, on sale in the HMV on Piccadilly Circus. They only had medium and small sizes, meaning that while Heidi and Ollie had T-shirts that fitted, Joe's came down to his knees and mine looked like it had been sprayed on. The merchandise was one part of a range of tactics to get the boys to complete the walk. Another was straightforward bribery with the offer of chocolate and fizzy drinks at various stages. Distraction would also play an important role. As we set off Joe was sharing his latest thoughts with Ollie on the best way to kill zombies – this got us past the Heathcote and the corner shop, and over the dreaded link road to Leytonstone Overground Station.

The railway arches have been grandiosely called the 'Hitchcock Business Centre'. Leytonstone clearly doesn't know how to celebrate the link to its famous son. The town of Predappio in Italy has turned its status as the birthplace of Benito Mussolini into a minor industry, even though it's been run by communists since the war. If Hitchcock had been born in small-town

America there'd be a two hundred-foot-tall fibreglass statue of the great director straddling the High Road, spooky music would be piped through speakers in the pavement, and there'd be a hotel in which shower curtains would be an optional extra.

In Leytonstone there's a sequence of mosaics in the tube station underpass representing scenes from Hitchcock's most famous films in small, ceramic, square tiles and a row of railway arches where you can buy a second-hand fridge. There's a pub with rooms above that's taken his name, but last time I checked it was a South African-themed barbecue restaurant. You can walk the length and breadth of Leytonstone and see not so much as a tea towel on sale bearing Hitch's great jowly face, or even an ironic stuffed bird. A sign with raised silver lettering announcing that you are entering the 'Business Improvement District' has far more Hollywood glamour than the plaque on the forecourt of the petrol station marking the site of Hitchcock's childhood home. It's almost as if Leytonstone doesn't give a shit that one of the world's most famous film directors was born and raised above a grocer's shop on the High Road. He even used to catch the train to work at Gainsborough Studios from this very station.

It's no surprise then that there's nothing left of the Royal Lodge near the station. There's a legend that Charles II used an underground tunnel linking it to Nell Gwynn's country retreat in Ferndale Road. The boys are unimpressed by this trivia, and that Jonathan Ross lived in Ferndale Road as a kid. They're more intent on moving the conversation from zombies to *Minecraft*. I attempt to enlist them in a game of trying to crack the code of the house names carved above the front doors of some of the houses in Ferndale Road. Oak Villa is fairly obvious, as the forest starts at the end of the street. Carlton, Clyde, Percy and Stanley would appear to be references to prominent Victorians. Ollie has already lost interest and has returned to the subject of zombies. It's partly my fault because I'd been telling them about the shop from *Shaun of the Dead* in Hornsey. Ollie is now insisting that I list the weapons I'd use in a zombie-survival scenario and not bother writing down any more house names. I relent – I go for a shotgun, with the classic Shaun cricket bat as my secondary weapon.

Joe is asking why I wouldn't opt for a chainsaw when I point out the long, straight avenue of trees leading diagonally across the corner of Wanstead Flats. These were planted in the mid-1700s as part of the three hundred-yard-long entrance to Wanstead House – once regarded as one of the great palaces of Europe, superior even to Blenheim. We are usually powerless to resist being sucked along the path formed by the trees that now merge into Bush Wood. I ask the boys which route they want to take – across the Flats in a straight line for Ilford or up the avenue towards the grounds of the old house. They opt for the wide open spaces across the football pitches, which today are vacant with litter buffeted around from goalmouth to goalmouth. Wanstead Flats forms the southern edge of Epping Forest and was long regarded as a boggy 'waste' to be used for grazing cattle. Its value has increased as suburban housing has grown up around it on all sides. Regular attempts to build on the Flats have been thwarted. Prefabs encroached after the Second World War but were thankfully only a temporary measure.

Ollie scans the horizon with a pair of binoculars and pans up to the sky. The army placed missiles on the roofs of the tower blocks backing on to the Flats during the Olympics. The residents of Fred Wigg Tower challenged the re-zoning of their home as a military installation in the High Court and predictably lost. That summer there was something more ominous on the skyline aside from birds and recklessly piloted model aircraft.

Fred Wigg and John Walsh towers, Leytonstone

Joe runs up to Ollie. 'Remember that day we came picking blackberries and made blackberry cake? It was just so delicious.' You can see that he's mentally eating the cake again.

The summer before last we each filled an ice-cream tub with sweet, ripe blackberries that flourished beneath the oak trees at the end of the avenue and on the far side of the football pitches. On the way home Joe concocted a recipe for chocolate blackberry cake, 'and it had Smarties on,' he reminds us. After such a bitter, long winter we deserve another good crop of blackberries this summer, and another of Joe's cakes.

We brought my mum and dad over here on a walk last summer, the old fella as sprightly in his late seventies as when he carried me home on his shoulders through Cut Throat Wood in Buckinghamshire when I was a kid. There he was pointing out plants to my sons as he had done to me. Broom in bright-yellow flower that

I'd mistaken for gorse, before Dad pointed out broom isn't prickly and has pea pods with black seeds. He shows us vetch, Canterbury Bells 'or campanula', not normally a wild flower but here growing in bunches near the road, their large, violet blooms rocking in the wind. Also purple loosestrife with its long spikes of cerise petals and the mauve flowers of mallow, which he says grows on marshland, as the Flats become with the slightest rainfall.

'The only things that grow under oak and beech are holly and perhaps a bit of yew because the drippings when it rains off the beech make the soil sour. Hardly any light gets through the canopy when the oak and beech are in leaf,' he told the boys as we passed through Bush Wood.

He found a large field mushroom in the hedgerow near the roadside. 'Here you are, boy. Nice bit of bacon with that and you'll be able to walk for miles,' he says to Ollie. He thinks it's a bit big and could be 'what we used to call Hedge Mogs' or hedge mushrooms, 'which are a little bit sweeter than ordinary field mushrooms. Cut 'em, don't just pick 'em, or they won't come back next year.' Dad never leaves home without a penknife, which always makes me nervous of the legalities of that in East London. He bends down, cuts the mushroom and holds it up. 'Look at that. Is that not a perfect mushroom?' he says, turning it over to reveal the fleshy gills under the cap where the spores lie, running the curved blade of his knife around the gills. 'You'd have found them on old sheep paths years ago,' he says.

Ollie takes a big sniff, 'Oh, yum. Can we eat it?'

Dad breaks it in half so we can see the cross-section, admiring the pungent, sweet aroma. At seventy-seven years old he's as enamoured with the fruits of the fields as he was as a kid wiling away his days wandering the South Chilterns with his ferret.

'We could live on Wanstead Flats. There's nice shelter and we could live on mushrooms,' enthuses Ollie.

When we show Heidi the mushroom she demands that we throw it away, the city girl's fear of accidentally eating toadstools reinforced by a vivid memory of a short story by Italo Calvino about a group of impoverished Italians in Milan getting poisoned by toadstools they mistook for truffles.

It was afternoon excursions like this as a child that engrained a love of walking deep into my psyche and my soul. After Sunday roast we would head out with our Jack Russell, across the playing fields behind our council house, past the paper mill, through the long, echoey tunnel that carries the M40 between London and Birmingham, over the A40 and into Cut Throat Wood, where Dick Turpin had a cave, or so they say.

Dad would cut nut stems from a double hedge to make me bows and arrows, swords and spears. He attempted to teach me the names of trees, plants and birds. Occasionally, he would have a shotgun discreetly hidden inside his jacket that he'd bag a rabbit or pigeon with. I'd have to run to reach the game before the dog, as you've as much chance of getting a dead animal off a Jack Russell as you have of convincing my old man that this was actually poaching. 'You can't own the birds in the sky,' he'd say incredulously. When I rang him after reading Roald Dahl's *Danny, the Champion of the World* to the kids, he went through the list of ways Danny's dad poached pheasant, critiquing each one.

Joe darts into a circle of trees in the central section of the Flats where he'd previously found a mysterious rusty-metal box buried in the ground. The top had broken open and grasses were growing through the hole. This area had been used as a prisoner of war camp during the Second World War and we speculated that the box was a remnant from that time. The goalposts erected by Italian POWs remained here until the 1990s. Heidi's Italian grandfather Valentino had been a British prisoner during the war. He was a man who lived a life as romantic as his name deserved. Was he perhaps held here among these trees on Wanstead Flats? He was an excellent cook and would have made good use of the hedge mogs. Valentino passed away in sunny Sydney at the age of ninety-two, denying us the chance to ask him.

During the Olympics the same patch of ground housed not prisoners but a temporary police HQ. Ominous official notices appeared on the trees where dog walkers leave polite messages and Christmas cards for each other. The Anti-social Behaviour Act was invoked in order to permit the police to disperse any large crowds in the area. A gathering of dogs having a sniff of each other's tails could be rounded-up by anti-terrorism officers. Football matches would be suspect as well – who was to say it wasn't a crafty terrorist plot disguised as a five-a-side?

The footprint left on the ground by the temporary police station has made the boggy land even wetter than usual after the recent rainy weather. A lake has formed on the fairground where the Easter Fair should have been but which passed us by this year. Historically, large crowds have thronged to the Flats from all across East London to visit the circuses and fairs. I carried Joe over here on my shoulders to his very first trip to the circus – he loved it; my first experience of the circus scared the living daylights out of me. He couldn't get enough of it – or the candy floss, chips, fizzy drinks and glowing swords.

The boys get excited by the deep drainage ditches, thinking they had something to do with the POW camp. 'Leap of faith,' shouts Joe as he jumps across. Ollie walks over via a log bridge.

The acid grasses provide a habitat for rare ground-nesting skylarks. 'Help Save Our Skylarks' signs are posted on gateposts. We hear birdsong. Ollie scans the skyline once more with the binoculars.

We make our way to the H-shaped metal frames that tethered barrage balloons to the ground. Joe called them 'suicidal balloons' when I told him some were designed to explode when they tagged low-flying aircraft. There were also anti-aircraft gun emplacements hidden in the wooded fringes. On a previous walk we stumbled on the concrete foundations buried beneath the undergrowth. Joe stops to inspect a ditch and calls Ollie over to him. They emerge carrying a large lump of rusting iron snapped into a jagged triangle. A real archaeological discovery – a possible chunk of Second World War infrastructure. Joe insists that we bring it on the walk with us but it weighs a tonne. 'I'll carry it all the way,' says Joe, but only makes it to the next circle of trees where we leave it hidden in the roots of a fallen tree.

There's a howling wind that makes Heidi and Ollie want to get to shelter. I'd promised them a slap-up lunch at the petrol station on Aldersbrook Road in true Alan Partridge style. It has tables and chairs, a hot-food counter and Costa Coffee. I made the boys watch two episodes of *Partridge* in return for watching a *South Park* video – they were not overly impressed. It was a major blow to my parenting.

The petrol station replaced Aldersbrook Farm although cattle were grazed on the Flats until the BSE outbreak in the mid 1990s. Aldersbrook is an area not only between places but stuck in time. An Edwardian development built in a rapid burst between 1900 and 1910, it is wedged in between Wanstead Flats, Wanstead Park and the huge necropolis of the City of London Cemetery. Most shocking of all, there's no pub – just a small row of shops with an off-licence, barber's, chip shop, newsagent and the Hitchcockian Courtney Hotel. You'd have to cross the Flats to the Golden Fleece on Capel Road if you fancied a pint. Consequently, there's a thriving bowls club and a popular amateur dramatics society that puts on performances in the church hall. Kids play unattended. It's the lost suburb where the locals have continued old habits in isolation, free of the influences of modern life like an isolated expat community in a colonial backwater.

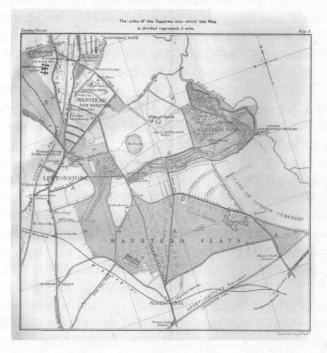

Wanstead Flats in 1908, from *Epping Forest* by Edward North Buxton, 1923

It's held up as being a model Edwardian suburb – part of the expansion of London into the surrounding countryside. Gone are the Italianate and Gothic influences of the Victorian houses. Aldersbrook embraced the 'vernacular revival' with wooden frames around pointed gables and stained glass in the front doors. It always seems like a happy place.

When I have pangs for a quieter life but ones tempered by the terror of leaving the magic spell cast by the red ring of the boundary of Greater London, I come over to Aldersbrook and daydream. When gritty social-realist Mike Leigh shot a film here, *Another Year*, it turned out to be one of his most wistful, light-hearted productions so far. But what kind of life could you have without a local pub? The Courtney Hotel doesn't even have a bar. You'd end up sitting on a bench with cans of beer by the Alexandra Lake throwing crisps for the ducks and the geese.

Fuelled up on pasties, Pepsi and chicken-flavoured crisps we move on down Park Road to the banks of the Heronry Pond in Wanstead Park. William Addison, one of the chroniclers of the history of Epping Forest, mooted the idea that the heronry, which still has actual live herons bingeing on fish, was established in the 16th century by the Heron family who owned the estate. Sir John Heron had been Treasurer to the Household of Henry VIII – a precarious position that caught up with his devout Catholic son, who had his head lopped off for not recognizing the king as head of the Church. The herons are in good health, however.

Heidi is completely disorientated, unable to understand how we've arrived at a point that we usually approach via Bush Wood and the Shoulder of Mutton Pond. The boys wave at the ducks and point out a bench that has been hewn from a fallen tree. The distractions are working.

Water now forms a major part of the landscaping of the park. Shoulder of Mutton, Heronry and Perch ponds act as an aquatic boundary to the edge of what remains of Wanstead House. A neo-classical tea hut shimmers across the long stretch of water, although the food and drink on offer is quintessential park fayre – strong tea, sticky pastries, ice cream, cheese and cucumber sandwiches. We walk along the avenue of limes to the only surviving building of the house – the Temple. Mary Tudor received Princess Elizabeth here on her way to be crowned in London.

A thousand other sycophants who'd opposed her taking the throne rushed out to kiss some royal butt, hoping to save their necks. Liz came back as queen when the Earl of Leicester owned the house and spent a week wandering the grounds not having sex. The estate passed through the hands of various movers and shakers in the post-Elizabethan world, like Alan Sugar flogging an Essex mansion to Simon Cowell who gives it to somebody at ITV who gifts it to a rising star rent-free who is then found dead in a pool. There's something sordid and borderline criminal in the way that the estate was handed around, not so far away from the *Ill Manors* movie made in the area, written and directed by Forest Gate's pop superstar Plan B. The hoodlums didn't haunt the tower blocks of Manor Park but ingratiated themselves into royal circles till the Monarch Mob Boss carted them off to the Tower, Tyburn or exile. The monarchy must be the world's most successful Mafia clan, looking at the changing fortunes of Wanstead Park.

It eventually fell into the hands of Josiah Child. He was Governor of the East India Company, a private corporation that employed a powerful mercenary army and ruled a large chunk of India. One of its primary commodities was opium. Child lavished money on his Wanstead estate in the manner you'd expect of the head of an international drug cartel and laid out the fabulous grounds that we walk over today. The house that one of his descendants planned to be 'a palatial mansion that would be to the east of London what Hampton Court was to the west' was ultimately sold off as building material.

Down in the trees around the lake that surrounds Rook Island Heidi exclaims, 'What's that?' Through the fingers of new growth we can see the Grotto, the other palpable remains of Wanstead House. Film-maker Ian Bourn told me how he'd taken acid over here one day and seen little men at work in its alcoves. Jimi Hendrix is said to have written the LSD hymn 'Purple Haze' in the Upper Cut Club on the other side of the Flats in Forest Gate – had he also dropped a tab and walked this way like Ian?

The Grotto in Wanstead Park

'It's like something from *A Midsummer Night's Dream*,' says the clean-living Heidi. She brilliantly played Puck in a production in Sydney with Greta Scacchi as Titania. We all gang up on her to reprise the role but she claims modesty and offers Joe a chicken sandwich, which he takes.

The sylvan scene inspires me to take out my pruning knife and attempt to make the boys (blunt) swords. I find a suitably straight young branch broken on the ground but I almost slice my thumb off with the first two slashes to shave the bark. Heidi preaches caution and I have to reluctantly concede to my sons that wood-craft clearly isn't a hereditary trait.

Ollie decides to start teasing Joe on the fictional basis that Joe likes One Direction. This is a terrible insult to lay upon a seven-year-old boy, second only to declaring that they are a

'Belieber'. It's just as well I failed to hack out some swords or there'd be a battle royale. Joe hits back with language that defies his tender age, Brian Jones haircut and slight lisp. Suddenly the walk has turned into an episode of *South Park*. I pull the Cartman, Stan and Kenny effigies from my pocket in an attempt to broker a peace. The boys play out their row with the characters – it ends, inevitably, with Kenny dying. 'You killed Kenny, you bastard,' says Stan in the hands of Ollie. They laugh and Ollie compliments Joe on the quality of his Cartman impression.

We cross a bridge partly covered in weeds into a debatable territory of half-growth and fly-tipping. Joe finds moss-covered bricks under the leaves. I show him the 1950s *Geographia Atlas* marked with an isolation hospital nearby where they treated people suffering from diphtheria and scarlet fever. There was also the Redbridge Borough Nuclear Shelter in the vicinity and a sewage farm. Lots of reasons to leave the rubble undisturbed.

Olly has flopped down on the grass beside the River Roding. Distant towers are visible through the trees. 'There's Ilford, Ollie,' I say, to inspire him onwards.

A footbridge takes us over the North Circular, at night a modern monster marvel of sodium lights and tail beams. The first walk of these journeys started by crossing the North Circular in the west at Gunnersbury and by chance the ending is reached by crossing it in the east.

The boys are tiring now, their dedication to the mission of delivering the totem figures of Kenny, Cartman and Stan to our parallel South Park the only thing keeping them going. That and the promise of more sugary treats along the way, followed by pizza and ice cream at home.

We make our way through Cranbrook Park, classic outer-London suburbia of bow-fronted houses interspersed with

Edwardian villas and post-war semis. Where the more affluent commuters snapped up the large houses of Aldersbrook, Ilford and its outliers became home to people on more modest incomes. In both cases the very idea of suburban living was seen at the time as an imitation of the habits of the wealthy city merchants of the past, with their mansions in the peripheral countryside. Enclaves such as Cranbrook Park would have been respectable, optimistic places when they were built.

The community noticeboard in Belgrave Road is simply titled 'Area Committee 7', which has an Orwellian tone in its administrative bluntness. A police notice hints at how the optimism of Cranbrook Park hasn't made it into the 21st century. Ollie reads it out. 'Operation Hawk. Preying on Drug Dealers.'

'What does that mean?' they both ask.

I explain how the hawk is a bird of prey and a deadly predator with excellent vision that swoops out of the sky onto its 'prey'.

'But they're not hawks, they're police,' says Ollie.

'Why don't they just arrest them? Why do they have to pretend to be hawks?' asks Joe.

This is one of many occasions when I'm at a loss to explain the nonsense of the adult world.

A murder in Belgrave Road in 1922 became one of the most notorious crimes of the era. It opened up a debate about the changing morality of youth and the nature of this new aspirant commuter class. It was also a case that forever stayed in the mind of Alfred Hitchcock and might have influenced the sinister tone of his movies and fixation with women in peril.

Late in the evening on 3 October 1922 Edith Thompson and her husband Percy were coming home from seeing a play in the West End when a man jumped out from behind a bush and attacked Percy, ultimately fatally stabbing him. The man turned out to be twenty-year-old Frederick Bywaters, a merchant seaman who'd previously had an affair with Edith. After police found a stash of detailed love letters exchanged by the couple Edith was arrested and charged with the murder, along with Bywaters.

The story of murder, adultery and the fact that Bywaters was much younger than Mrs Thompson meant it was ripe for the tabloids, who had a field day. When they were both found guilty of murder and sentenced to death a popular campaign was launched to have Thompson pardoned. Her conviction had been built largely on a series of moral judgements and assumptions. She had been condemned by her lurid love letters to her passionate younger man, who had wooed her with tales of adventures overseas and his good looks. Bywaters constantly denied Edith had any knowledge of his plans to attack Percy Thompson. Her appeal was unsuccessful, however, and they were hanged at Holloway and Pentonville prisons on the same day at the same time.

Hitchcock had a direct link to the case. He had been taught to dance by Edith Thompson's father, and knew both Edith and her sister when they lived in Leytonstone. He had allegedly planned to make a documentary about the affair. His link to Thompson was one of two amendments that he asked be made to his authorized biography, to avoid embarrassing Edith's sister, who still lived in Leytonstone.

I tried to imagine Belgrave Road as the source of Hitchcock's filmic universe – from these sedate houses you get *Rear Window*, *Vertigo*, *Dial M for Murder*, *The Lodger* and *Psycho*. I don't think this is the kind of image make-over Redbridge Council have in mind for Area Committee 7. These gloomy resonances are dissipated as the boys burst into fits of giggles and it takes me a while to get any sense out of them. They have noticed Fat Joe's Burgers & Grills over the road. It has distracted them from their sore legs, which I reinforce with ice creams from the corner shop – ready for the last push through Ilford to South Park.

Cranbrook Road and the High Street have maintained the 'rush and turmoil' from when Thomas Burke visited Ilford in 1921 on his 'Outer Circle Rambles'. He hated Ilford. He described the 'assaulting and undelightful noise of Ilford Broadway'. 'It is uncouth, leggy; plagued with the humours of the gawk.' He compared it unfavourably with Walthamstow, Peckham, Eltham, Brixton and Upton Park. Since first coming out here a few years ago I have staunchly defended Ilford, even irrationally against people who actually live here and who look astounded when I declare my enthusiasm for the place.

One night in the Heathcote Arms I was sitting in my usual slouched position, beer dripping down my beard, belly covered in crisps, maps on the table, when a vampish woman sat down next to me and asked if I'd like to come back to her dungeon in Ilford. I'm not sure what marked me out as a potential masochist but I was keen to get some inside info on the area, and diverted comments about whips and handcuffs to topographical features and local folklore. Eventually, my enthusiasm for Ilford dampened her passion for tying up random forty-somethings and so I told her about my research. I asked if she'd mind annotating my map, even though I didn't fancy any extra-marital sexual deviancy in her cellar. 'You're an odd one,' she said as she left without so much as looking at my map. That was a bit rich coming from a woman with eccentric ideas about the correct use of clothes pegs.

It's fair to say Ilford has a poor self-image. It ranked fourth in a national survey of 'Unhappiest places to live in Britain'. Burke did say that he 'never saw people so half-happy'. The High Street looks to be suffering from the effect of the Westfield mega mall opening a few miles down the Romford Road in Stratford. Ilford's 'expression of unfulfilled desire' that Burke described now hangs heavily. The Benetton store has been taken over by a pop-up fruit and veg shop. The elegant art deco department stores of the 1920s now house the Money Shop, Premier Work Support, Superdrug and Lidl.

Ilford High Street

You sense a stoicism among the 'half-happy' faces on the Broadway, though. When a V-2 rocket fell on the Ilford Hippodrome in 1945 the orchestra continued their performance of *Robinson Crusoe* drenched to the skin by a burst water tank above the stage and covered in dust and rubble. The coat of arms for the old Borough of Ilford bears the slogan 'In Unity Progress'. In his *Potted History* of the Borough Norman Gunby wrote, 'To anyone who may wonder or ask what history Ilford has, I would answer that there is history in every stone, in every particle of earth, and in every grain of sand.' You can add every late-night shop, park bench and bus stop. Daniel Defoe and Samuel Pepys wrote of Ilford. Even Burke conceded that it has one of the finest parks in

London, not South but Valentine's Park on the border of Gants Hill. Morrissey played a storming gig at Ilford Island in 1995 that I'd heard him mention in a radio interview and fans still rave about on forums. The Dr. Seuss musical, *Seussical the Musical*, is coming to the Kenneth More Theatre. Bollywood Bowling looks to be doing a good trade. Ilford will survive its current travails and reclaim the title of the 'Eastern Queen' that it had once claimed.

Despite a rest in the High Street the boys are done in. Ollie is echoing words similar to those used by Burke when he wrote, 'To go to Ilford is a fool's act.' A final chocolate stop lifts the spirits, further heightened when they see the sign for South Park Road. We place the Kenny, Cartman and Stan figures on top of the sign for a photo. Joe and Heidi undo their jackets to expose their *South Park* T-shirts.

The park gates shimmer like an oasis over the road. The boys collapse on a grassy bank inside. We've successfully delivered the *South Park* effigies to their London home. Ollie has blisters; Joe seems relatively unscathed and is making for the ornamental lake. Heidi gets out the remains of the chicken sandwiches that have been squashed flat at the bottom of her rucksack and the boys feed the bread to the ducks. The Canada geese soon get in on the act, muscling the mallards out of the way; they gobble up the bread then march straight towards the source. The boys run off laughing across the football pitch pursued by two particularly greedy geese.

Running around with the wildfowl has put them in a good mood. I break the news that from here we might as well walk on to Barking as it's the nearest station. I'm keen to finish my series of excursions at the ancient settlement of Uphall Camp, a huge, fortified Iron Age settlement, one of the prehistoric sites that gave birth to the city.

It's golden hour, the time that walks should end, as the first of these expeditions did on Hounslow Heath a year ago. Then I was alone, slurping down a can of Stella on the western fringe of London. Since then I'd ambled through the hill towns of the southern highlands, the Arcadian western fields, revisited myths and legends around the northern heights, and sung Saxon songs in Clapton. But as I'd found when I struck out for Asia as a youth thinking I'd see the world, the more you see the more you realize what lies undiscovered. That couldn't be more true than in the exploration of London, as any black-cab driver stumped by a destination will tell you.

We now arrived at the eastern edge of the city as a family, the boys having completed a six-and-a-half-mile pilgrimage to a park that shares its name with a place in Colorado that they heard about via a cartoon on a VHS cassette bought in a charity shop. Joe suddenly remembers that this was all his idea and laughs.

'I like this walking, I'll do more of this,' says Ollie as we head for the park gates. We pass a bus stop for the No. 145 to Leytonstone. 'Dad, can we just jump on the bus here and go home?' Ollie asks. Joe is already sprawled across the bench. I check the 1950s

Geographia Atlas to see how far we are from the site of Uphall Camp and notice that the area we're in is called Loxford. I'd never even heard of Loxford before, a final unexpected discovery hidden beneath the fields of bricks.

Heidi checks the timetable. The 145 bus is only eight minutes away. The boys look at us imploringly, their minds already turned to pizza and ice cream. It's time to go home. Barking and the beginnings of London at Uphall Camp will have to wait for another adventure.

SELECT BIBLIOGRAPHY

William Addison, *Wanstead Park*, Corporation of London, n.d.

Rose Baillie, 'Prehistoric Islington', in Irene Schwab, *The Archaeology of Islington*, Inner London Archaeological Unit, 1978

Margaret Baker, *Folklore and Customs of Rural England*, David & Charles, 1974

Nicholas Barton, *The Lost Rivers of London*, Historical Publications, 1992 (first published 1962)

Mrs Arthur G. Bell, *The Skirts of the Great City*, Methuen, 1908

Walter George Bell, *Where London Sleeps: Historical Journeys into the Suburbs*, The Bodley Head, 1926

Walter Benjamin, *The Arcades Project*, Belknap Press, 2002

Walter Besant, *The History of London*, London, 1893

Christopher Board, 'The Secret Map of the County of London, 1926, and Its Sequels', *London Topographical Record* 27, 1995

John Allen Brown,*The Chronicles of Greenford Parva or Perivale, Past and Present*, J. S. Virtue & Co., 1891

Samuel and Nathaniel Buck, *Twenty-four views of abbeys and castles in Kent*, London, 1736

Thomas Burke, *The Outer Circle: Rambles in Remote London*, Allen & Unwin, 1921

Edward North Buxton, *Epping Forest*, Stanford, 1923

Humphrey Carpenter, *Spike Milligan: The Biography*, Coronet, 2004

Bob Carr, 'Notes', *Greater London Industrial Archaeology Society*, February 1995, http://www.glias.org.uk/news/156news.html

Carlos Castaneda, *The Teachings of Don Juan: A Yaqui Way of Knowledge*, Penguin, 1972

George Tomkyns Chesney, *The Battle of Dorking: Being an Account of the German Invasion of England: Capture of London & Woolwich*, Toronto, 1871

Gillian Clegg, *The Archaeology of Hounslow*, West London Archaeological Field Group, 1991

Harold P. Clunn, *The Face of London*, Spring, 1970

Robert Colville, *London: The Northern Reaches*, London, 1951

Robert Cope, *Legendary Lore of the Holy Wells of England*, London, 1893

J. T. Coppock and Hugh C. Prince (eds), *Greater London*, Faber and Faber, 1964

John Coulter, *Lewisham*, Sutton, 1994

Terry Courtney, 'Excavations at the Royal Dockyard, Woolwich, 1973', *Transactions of the Greenwich and Lewisham Antiquarian Society*, 1974

Archer Philip Crouch, *Silvertown and Neighbourhood (including East and West Ham) – A Retrospect*, Bradbury, Agnew & Co., 1900

Dartford, Crayford and Erith Marshes, Heritage Review, 2006

Grace Derwent, *Roman London*, Macdonald & Co., 1968

Nell Dunn, *Up the Junction*, Virago, 1988 (first published 1963)

David Farrant, *Beyond the Highgate Vampire*, British Psychic and Occult Society, 1997

P. R. Ferris, *The Flora of Southern Epping Forest. Part 2: Wanstead Flats and Bush Wood*, London Naturalist, 1981

R. S. R. Fitter, *London's Natural History*, Collins, 1945

Geoffrey Fletcher, *The London Nobody Knows*, Hutchinson, 1962

SELECT BIBLIOGRAPHY

J. H. Forshaw and Patrick Abercrombie, *County of London Plan 1943*, Macmillan, 1944

'*Geographia' Greater London Atlas*, revised 10th edition produced under the direction of P. H. Thorpe, Geographia Ltd., 1955

Chris Gerrard, *Medieval Archaeology: Understanding Traditions and Contemporary Approaches*, Routledge, 2002

E. O. Gordon, *Prehistoric London: Its Mounds and Circles*, London, 1914

Christopher Gray, *Leaving the 20th Century: The Incomplete Work of the Situationist International*, Rebel Press, 1998

David Green, 'Little Italy in Victorian London: Holborn's Italian community', *Camden History Review* 15, 1988

Miranda J. Green, *The Gods of Roman Britain*, Shire Publications, 1983

Pamela Greenwood, 'Prehistoric and Roman Leyton: some comments', http://ads.ahds.ac.uk/catalogue/adsdata/arch-457-1/.../07_16_435.pdf

Norman Gunby, *A Potted History of Ilford*, 1991

Greg Hallett & Spymaster, *How to Take Over the World – A Right Royal Con*, FNZ, 2007

Michael Hammerson, '"Our Lost Elysium" – Rural Middlesex: a pictorial essay', *Transactions of the London and Middlesex Archaeological Society* 55, 2004

W. G. Hammock, *Leytonstone and Its History*, London, 1904

Charles G. Harper, *A Londoner's Own London*, Cecil Palmer, 1927

Edward Hasted, *The History and Topographical Survey of the County of Kent: Volume 1*, 1797

David Hayes, 'A parish divided: the Liberties of St Andrew Holborn', *Camden History Review* 26, 2002

Michael Herr, *Kubrick*, Picador, 2000

Geoffrey Hewlett, *A History of Wembley*, Brent Library Service, 1979

W. G. Hoskins, *The Making of the English Landscape*, Penguin, 1955

William Howitt, *The Northern Heights of London*, London, 1869

Alan Ivimey, 'Some Lost Rivers of London', *Wonderful London Vol. 2*, Fleetway House, 1926

Walter Jerrold, *Highways and Byways in Middlesex*, Macmillan, 1909

A. L. Leach, *Eocene Tertiaries: A Survey and Records of Woolwich and West Kent*, Woolwich, 1909

Jim Lewis, *London's Lea Valley: Britain's Best Kept Secret*, Phillimore, 1999

Jim Lewis, *London's Lea Valley: More Secrets Revealed*, Phillimore, 2001

A. G. Linney, *Lure and Lore of London's River*, London, 1932

London Archaeologist 11, Supplement 2, 2005

Donald McDougall (ed.), *Fifty Years a Borough, 1886–1936 – The Story of West Ham*, County Borough Council West Ham, 1936

Kate McEwan, *Ealing Walkabout: Journeys into the History of a London Borough*, Nick Wheatley Associates, 1983

Patrick McGilligan, *Alfred Hitchcock: A Life in Darkness and Light*, It Books, 2004

Arthur Machen, 'Tottenham Hale', *Wonderful London Vol. 1*, Fleetway House, 1926

S. P. B. Mais, *England's Character*, Hutchinson, 1937

Guy Mannes-Abbott, 'Forting', *AA Files* 42, Architectural Association, 2000

Master Atlas of Greater London, Edition 3A, Geographer's A-Z Company, 1975

Gordon S. Maxwell, *Highwayman's Heath*, Middlesex Chronicle, 1935

Gordon S. Maxwell, *Just Beyond London*, Methuen, 1927

Gordon S. Maxwell, *The Fringe of London*, Cecil Palmer, 1925

Arthur Mee, *The King's England: London North of the Thames except the City and Westminster*, Hodder and Stoughton, 1972

SELECT BIBLIOGRAPHY

Ralph Merrifield, *The Archaeology of London*, Heinemann, 1975

Nick Merriman, *Prehistoric London,* Museum of London, 1990

Douglas Monroe, *The 21 Lessons of Merlin: A Study in Druid Magic & Lore*, Llewellyn Publications, 1993

William Edward Morden, *The History of Tooting Graveney: Surrey*, 1897

William Morris, *News from Nowhere and Other Writings*, Penguin, 2004

Kathryn Morrison and Ann Robey, *100 Years of Suburbia: The Aldersbrook Estate in Wanstead 1899–1999*, The Royal Commission on the Historical Monuments of England and London Borough of Redbridge Libraries Service, 1999

H. V. Morton, *H. V. Morton's London*, Methuen, 1942

Newham Council, *The Newham Story*, http://www.newhamstory.com/

Dr Pagenstecher, *The History of East and West Ham*, Wilson & Whitworth, 1908

Nick Papadimitriou, *Scarp*, Sceptre, 2012

Nikolaus Pevsner, *The Buildings of England: London except the Cities of London and Westminster*, Penguin, 1952

Nikolaus Pevsner, *Pioneers of Modern Design*, Penguin, 1960

Chesca Potter, *The River of Wells*, 2000, http://people.bath.ac.uk/liskmj/living-spring/sourcearchive/fs1/fs1cp1.htm

W. R. Powell (ed.), *A History of the County of Essex: Volume 6*, Victoria County History, 1973

C. W. Radcliffe, *Middlesex, The Jubilee of the County Council 1889–1939*, Evans Brothers, 1939

Michael Robbins, *Middlesex*, Phillimore, 1953

John Rogers, *Remapping High Wycombe: Journeys Beyond the Western Sector*, Lulu, 2006

Irene Schwab, *The Archaeology of Islington*, Inner London Archaeological Unit, 1978

Will Self, *The Quantity Theory of Insanity*, Bloomsbury, 1991

Will Self, *Walking to Hollywood*, Bloomsbury, 2010

Montagu Sharpe, *Middlesex in British, Roman, and Saxon Times*, London, 1919

R. L. Sherlock, *British Regional Geology: London and the Thames Valley*, HMSO, 1947

Iain Sinclair, *London Orbital*, Penguin, 2003

Janet Smith, *Tooting Bec Lido*, South London Swimming Club, 1996

Roy Smith, *The Secret Architecture of London*, http://www.geocities.ws/foxeye121/curzon.htm

Luca Matteo Stanca, *St Peter's Italian Church in London*, Rome, 2001

The Family Memoirs of the Rev. William Stukeley, M.D. Vol. III, Surtees Society, 1887

Septimus Sunderland, *Old London's Spas, Baths, and Wells*, London, 1915

Frank Swinnerton, 'The Soul of Suburbia', *Wonderful London Vol. 1*, Fleetway House, 1926

Henry David Thoreau, *Walden; or, Life in the Woods*, Penguin, 1938 (first published 1854)

William Thornbury, *Old and New London,* London, 1878

Understone, newsletter of the Leyton & Leytonstone Historical Society

Cliff Wadsworth, *Dollis Hill Research Station and the Secret Wartime Bunker*, Willesden Local History Society, 2002

Edward Walford, *Greater London*, Cassell, 1883–4

Julian Watson, *Woolwich Revealed*, London Borough of Greenwich, 1986

John Weever, *Antient Funeral Monuments, of Great-Britain, Ireland, and the Islands adjacent*, 1767

Ben Weinreb and Christopher Hibbert, *The London Encyclopedia*, Book Club Associates, 1983

W. H. Weston, *The Story of Leyton and Leytonstone*, Exeter, 1921

SELECT BIBLIOGRAPHY

Alex Wheatle, *East of Acre Lane*, Fourth Estate, 2001
Harry Williams, *South London*, Robert Hale Ltd, 1949
S. E. Winbolt, *Britain B.C.*, Pelican, 1945

ACKNOWLEDGEMENTS AND THANKS

I would like to thank the Borough Archives of Waltham Forest, Greenwich and Ealing for helping with various odd enquiries. Also the Museum of London Archaeological Service, in my quest to find out if Horsa was indeed buried in Horsenden Hill. They all dealt with my naive enquiries with great diligence and professionalism. I greatly appreciated the time and input of Jan at Herne Hill Velodrome, Mandy Worsley of the South London Swimming Club, and the Hackney Tree Musketeers.

Thanks to Nick Papadimitriou who was, as ever, a great person to share the journey with, albeit over the phone with the exception of the one walk we did together, and the previous excursions mentioned. Bob and Roberta Smith for his cover painting and companionship to the Orient, and also for granting permission to reproduce the text of his William Morris painting. Ian Bourn for his endless knowledge of the untold stories of Leytonstone and permission to reproduce his poster for House-watch. Anna Valentine and Carole Tonkinson at HarperCollins for their unwavering support and encouragement. My father, Alan Rogers, is the source not only of my love of walking but of nearly all the plant references in this book – he also gave me his nice waterproof jacket that I wore through a cold, wet winter. My mother, Barbara, is a constant source of reassurance and patience – I'm really sorry for dragging her over to Wanstead Flats in a howling gale that irritated her neuralgia. It was June. How was I to know?

My sister Cathy Rogers, aside from enduring the horrors of my student houses and early years in London, was put through hours of telephone monologues as I processed the meaning of my journey. Her dog Jimmy, however, is a pain in the arse no matter how cute he is. A huge thank you, too, to my dear friend and ally Russell Brand for his frankly flattering foreword.

The biggest thanks has to be to my wife Heidi and my two brilliant sons Oliver and Joseph – Heidi for her Buddha-like serenity and ocean of tolerance, listening to me endlessly waffle on about my most recent walk and the one I was about to embark upon. Ollie and Joe for providing not only the meaning to it all, but unquestionably the best lines in the book and teaching me how to appreciate *South Park*.

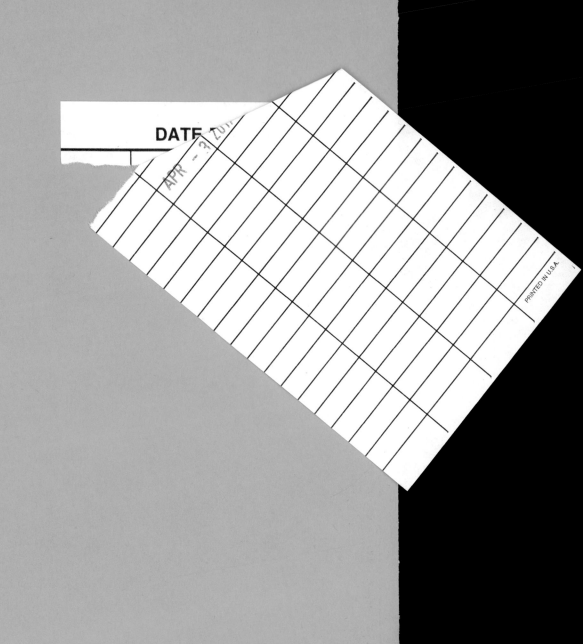

DATE

APR - 3 20~

PRINTED IN U.S.A.